T5-CWL-999

essentials

WORD
2000
basic

KEITH MULBERY
UTAH VALLEY STATE COLLEGE

**Prentice
Hall**

A division of Pearson Education
Upper Saddle River, NJ 07458

Word 2000 Essentials Basic

Copyright © 2000 by Prentice Hall

All rights reserved. Printed in the United States of America. No part of this book may be used or reproduced in any form or by any means, or stored in a database or retrieval system, without prior written permission of the publisher except in the case of brief quotations embodied in critical articles and reviews. For further information, address Prentice Hall, One Lake Street, Upper Saddle River, NJ 07458.

International Standard Book Number: 1-58076-092-9

Library of Congress Catalog Card Number: 98-88896

Printed in the United States of America

First Printing: June 1999

This book is sold *as is*, without warranty of any kind, either express or implied, respecting the contents of this book, including but not limited to implied warranties for the book's quality, performance, merchantability, or fitness for any particular purpose. Neither Prentice Hall nor its dealers or distributors shall be liable to the purchaser or any other person or entity with respect to any liability, loss, or damage caused or alleged to be caused directly or indirectly by this book.

03 02   10 9 8 7

Interpretation of the printing code: the rightmost double-digit number is the year of the book's printing: the rightmost single-digit number, the number of the book's printing. For example, a printing code of 00-1 shows that the first printing of the book occurred in 2000.

Trademark Acknowledgments

All terms mentioned in this book that are known to be trademarks or service marks have been appropriately capitalized. Prentice Hall cannot attest to the accuracy of this information. Use of a term in this book should not be regarded as affecting the validity of any trademark or service mark.

Microsoft is a registered trademark of Microsoft Corporation in the United States and in other countries. Some of the product names and company names used in this book have been used for identification purposes only and may be trademarks or registered trademarks of their respective manufacturers and sellers.

Screens reproduced in the book were created using Collage Plus from Inner Media, Inc., Hollis, NH.

Word 2000 Essentials Basic is based on **Microsoft Word 2000**.

Publisher:
Robert Linsky

Executive Editor:
Sunthar Visuvalingam

Series Editors:
Marianne Fox and
Larry Metzelaar

Annotated Instructor's Manual (AIM) Series Editor:
Linda Bird

Operations Manager:
Christine Moos

Director of Product Marketing:
Susan Kindel

Acquisitions Editor:
Chuck Stewart

Development Editor:
Susan Hobbs

Technical Editor:
Asit Patel

Software Coordinator:
Angela Denny

Senior Editor:
Karen A. Walsh

Book Designer:
Louisa Klucznik

Design Usability Consultant:
Elizabeth Keyes

Project Editor:
Tim Tate

Copy Editor:
Melody Layne

Proofreader:
Debbie Williams

Indexer:
Tonya Heard

Layout Technician:
Liz Johnston

Team Coordinator:
Melody Layne

Usability Testers:
Priscilla Cobb: Butler University
Andy Cromwell: Utah Valley State
College
Lynda Fields: Fox Consulting
Sarah Ann Margulies: B.A. University
of Michigan

About the Author

Keith Mulbery, who previously taught at Bowling Green State University, is currently an Assistant Professor in the School of Business at Utah Valley State College. He teaches a variety of computer applications courses using Word, Excel, PowerPoint, Access, Windows 98, Internet Explorer, WordPerfect, and Quattro Pro. In addition, Keith has written several word processing textbooks and served as the developmental editor for the *Word 2000 Essentials Intermediate* and *Word 2000 Essentials Advanced* books. Keith also conducts hands-on computer applications workshops at the local, state, and national level, including the National Business Education Association Convention. He is a Microsoft Office User Specialist in Word 97 and Excel 97 and received his B.S. and M.Ed. (majoring in Business Education) from Southwestern Oklahoma State University.

Dedication

This book is dedicated to my parents, Kenneth and Mary Lu, and my grandparents who developed my appreciation of education, my interest in books, and my passion for providing quality education to my students.

Acknowledgments

Although the author is solely responsible for its content, this book and the *Essentials* series as a whole have been shaped by the combined experience, perspectives, and input of the entire authoring, editorial, and design team. I am grateful to the Series Editors, **Larry Metzelaar** and **Marianne Fox**, and to the College of Business Administration at Butler University for hosting the listserv on which the implications and value of every series element were thoroughly discussed and finalized even as this book was being written. They also coordinated much of the usability testing at the Butler campus. I acknowledge **Robb Linsky** (Publisher, Que Education and Training) for having provided the initial direction and for having allowed the Essentials 2000 team to shape this edition as they saw fit. You, the reader, are the greatest beneficiary of this ongoing online collaborative effort.

Chuck Stewart adapted the original Que E&T *Essentials* series for corporate training. In early 1998, however, he began revamping the *Office 2000 Essentials* pedagogy to better serve academic needs exclusively. He enlisted the services of Series Editors Metzelaar and Fox because of their extensive background in courseware development, many years of classroom teaching, and innovative pedagogy. Early discussion with the Series Editors revealed the need for the three new types of end-of-chapter exercises you find in the *Office 2000 Essentials*. Chuck continued to provide ideas and feedback on the listserv long after handing over the executive editorship to Sunthar. Together, they completely overhauled the *Essentials* series, paying particular attention to pedagogy, content, and design issues.

Sunthar Visuvalingam took over as Executive Editor for the *Essentials* series in October 1998. He stepped into a process already in full swing and moved quickly to ensure "a level of collaboration rarely seen in academic publishing." He performed admirably the daunting task of coordinating an army of widely dispersed authors, editors, designers, and usability testers. Among the keywords that characterize his crucial role in forging a well-knit "learning team" are decisive leadership, effective communication, shared vision, continuous pedagogical and procedural innovation, infectious enthusiasm, dogged project and quality management, active solicitation of feedback, collective problem-solving, transparent decision making, developmental mentoring, reliability, flexibility, and dedication. Having made his indelible mark on the *Essentials* series, he stayed on to shepherd the transition of the series to Alex von Rosenberg.

Linda Bird (AIM Series Editor and author of both *PowerPoint Essentials* books) and **Robert Ferrett** (co-author of *Office Essentials*, all three *Access Essentials* books, and of the related *Learn* series) made significant contributions to enhancing the concept and details of the new series. A newcomer to the series but not to educational publishing, **Keith Mulbery** seized increasing ownership of *Essentials* and undertook the initiative of presenting the series at the April 1999 National Business Education Association Convention.

Alex von Rosenberg, Executive Editor, manages the Computer Applications publishing program at Prentice Hall (PH). The PH team has been instrumental in ensuring a smooth transition of the *Essentials* series. Alex has been ably assisted in this transition by **Susan Rifkin**, Managing Editor; **Leanne Nieglos**, Assistant Editor; **Jennifer Surich**, Editorial Assistant; **Nancy Evans**, Director of Strategic Marketing; **Kris King**, Senior Marketing Manager; and **Nancy Welcher**, Media Project Manager.

Operations Manager **Christine Moos** and Senior Editor **Karen Walsh** worked hard with Sunthar and Alex to allow authors maximum flexibility to produce a quality product, while trying to maintain a tight editorial and production schedule. They had the unenviable task of keeping the book processes rolling while managing the complex process of transitioning the series to Prentice Hall. Book Designer **Louisa Klucznik** and Consultant **Elizabeth Keyes** spared no efforts in making every detail of the new design attractive, usable, consistent and appropriate to the *Essentials* pedagogy. **Joyce Nielsen**, **Jan Snyder**, **Asit Patel**, **Nancy Sixsmith**, and **Susan Hobbs**—freelancers who had worked on earlier editions of the *Essentials* and the related *Learn* series in various editorial capacities—helped ensure continuity in procedures and conventions. **Tim Tate**, **Sherri Fugit**, **Melody Layne**, and **Cindy Fields** also asked sharp questions along the way and thereby helped us refine and crystallize the editorial conventions for the *Essentials*.

Cynthia Krebs, a colleague of mine at Utah Valley State College, contributed about half of the end-of-project exercises for this book. She provided creative ideas for meaningful exercises for students.

I would like to thank **Susan Hobbs**, my Development Editor, for her excellent ideas in strengthening the content of this book and spending endless hours assisting me through the many changes the series has gone through during the past several months. In addition, I appreciate **Asit Patel**, my technical editor, for helping to ensure consistency and accuracy of the information and instructions. A special thanks to **Tim Tate** for ensuring accuracy and professionalism in a timely manner during the production stage. I also appreciate **Melody Layne's** copy edits. In addition, I truly benefited from the constructive feedback provided by the usability testers: **Priscilla Cobb**, **Andy Cromwell**, **Lynda Fields**, and **Sarah Ann Margulies**. A special thanks goes to **Marianne Fox** and **Larry Metzelaar** for their assistance as series editors.

I am grateful to **Robb Linsky** and **Chuck Stewart** for getting me involved in this project initially. **Alex von Rosenberg**, thanks for your assistance in the transition to Prentice Hall. I look forward to working with you in the future. Finally, I extend my deepest appreciation to **Sunthar Visuvalingam**, Executive Editor, for his support at the NBEA Convention, and especially his vision and direction for dramatically improving the *Essentials* series by making it one of the best, most pedagogically sound series on the market.

Contents at a Glance

Table of Contents

Introduction

Project 3   Editing a Document   55

Project 6   Using Tables   153

Introduction

Essentials courseware from Prentice Hall is anchored in the practical and professional needs of all types of students. This edition of the *Office 2000 Essentials* has been completely revamped as the result of painstaking usability research by the publisher, authors, editors, and students. Practically every detail—by way of pedagogy, content, presentation, and design—was the object of continuous online (and offline) discussion among the entire team.

The *Essentials* series has been conceived around a "learning-by-doing" approach that encourages you to grasp application-related concepts as you expand your skills through hands-on tutorials. As such, it consists of modular lessons that are built around a series of numbered, step-by-step procedures that are clear, concise, and easy to review. Explicatory material is interwoven before each lesson and between the steps. Additional features, tips, pitfalls, and other related information are provided at exactly the place where you would most expect them. They are easily recognizable elements that stand out from the main flow of the tutorial. We have even designed our icons to match the Microsoft Office theme. The end-of-chapter exercises have likewise been carefully graded from the routine Checking Concepts and Terms to tasks in the Discovery Zone that gently prod you into extending what you've learned into areas beyond the explicit scope of the lessons proper. Following, you'll find out more about the rationale behind each book element and how to use each to your maximum benefit.

How to Use This Book

Typically, each *Essentials* book is divided into seven or eight projects, concerning topics such as formatting documents, inserting a table, inserting graphics, and integrating data. A project covers one area (or a few closely related areas) of application functionality. Each project is then divided into seven to nine lessons that are related to that topic. For example, a project on inserting graphics is divided into lessons explaining how to move and size an image, wrap text around an image, create a text box, select a fill and border, and use WordArt. Each lesson presents a specific task or closely related set of tasks in a manageable chunk that is easy to assimilate and retain.

Each element in *Word 2000 Essentials Basic* is designed to maximize your learning experience. Following is a list of the *Essentials* project elements and a description of how each element can help you:

- **Project Objectives.** Starting with an objective gives you short-term, attainable goals. Using project objectives that closely match the titles of the step-by-step tutorials breaks down the possibly overwhelming prospect of learning several new features of Microsoft Word 2000 into small, attainable, bite-sized tasks. Look over the objectives on the opening page of the project before you begin, and review them after completing the project to identify the main goals for each project.

- **Key Terms.** This book includes a limited number of useful vocabulary words and definitions, such as ***nonbreaking space***, ***section break***, ***sizing handles***, and ***background***. Key terms introduced in each project are listed in alphabetical order immediately after the objectives on the opening page of the project. These key terms are shown in bold italic and are defined during their first use within the text. Definitions of key terms are also included in the Glossary.

- **Why Would I Do This?** You are studying Microsoft Word 2000 so that you can accomplish useful tasks in the real world. This brief section tells you why these tasks or procedures are important. What can you do with the knowledge? How can these application features be applied to everyday tasks?

- **Visual Summary.** This opening section graphically illustrates the concepts and features that you will learn in the project. One or more figures, with ample callouts, show the final result of completing the project. This road map to your destination keeps you motivated as you work through the individual steps of each task.

- **Lessons.** Each lesson contains one or more tasks that correspond to an objective on the opening page of the project. A lesson consists of step-by-step tutorials, their associated data files, screen shots, and the special notes described as follows. Although each lesson often builds on the previous one, the lessons (and the exercises) have been made as modular as possible. For example, you can skip tasks that you have already mastered, and begin a later lesson using a data file provided specifically for its task(s).

- **Step-by-Step Tutorial.** The lessons consist of numbered, bold, step-by-step instructions that show you how to perform the procedures in a clear, concise, and direct manner. These hands-on tutorials, which are the "essentials" of each project, let you "learn by doing." Regular paragraphs between the steps clarify the results of each step. Also, screen shots are introduced after key steps for you to check against the results on your monitor. To review the lesson, you can easily scan the bold numbered steps. Quick (or impatient!) learners may likewise ignore the intervening paragraphs.

- **Need to Know.** These sidebars provide essential tips for performing the task and using the application more effectively. You can easily recognize them by their distinctive icon and bold headings. It is well worth the effort to review these crucial notes again after completing the project.

- **Nice to Know.** Nice to Know comments provide extra tips, shortcuts, alternative ways to complete a process, and special hints about using the software. You may safely ignore these for the moment to focus on the main task at hand, or you may pause to learn and appreciate these tidbits. Here, you find neat tricks and special insights to impress your friends and coworkers!

- **If You Have Problems...** These short troubleshooting notes help you anticipate or solve common problems quickly and effectively. Even if you do not encounter the problem at this time, make a mental note of it so that you know where to look when you find yourself (or others) in difficulty.

- **Summary.** This section provides a brief recap of the tasks learned in the project. The summary guides you to places where you can expand your knowledge, which may include references to specific Help topics or the Prentice Hall *Essentials* Web site (http://www.prenhall.com/essentials).

- **Checking Concepts and Terms.** This section offers optional True/False, Multiple Choice, Screen ID, and Discussion questions that are designed to check your comprehension and assess retention. If you need to refresh your memory, the relevant lesson number is provided after each True/False and Multiple Choice question. For example, [L5] directs you to review Lesson 5 for the answer. Lesson numbers may be provided—where relevant—for other types of exercises as well.

- **Skill Drill Exercises.** This section enables you to check your comprehension, evaluate your progress, and practice what you learn. The exercises in this section build on and reinforce what was learned in each project. Generally, the Skill Drill exercises include step-by-step instructions.

- **Challenge Exercises.** This section provides exercises that expand on or relate to the skills practiced in the project. Each exercise provides a brief narrative introduction followed by instructions. Although the instructions are often written in a step-by-step format, the steps are not as detailed as those in the Skill Drill section. Providing less-specific steps helps you learn to think on your own. These exercises foster the "near transfer" of learning.

- **Discovery Zone Exercises.** These exercises require advanced knowledge of project topics or the application of skills from multiple lessons. Additionally, these exercises may require you to research topics in Help or on the Web to complete them. This self-directed method of learning new skills emulates real-world experience. We provide the cues, and you do the exploring!

- **Learning to Learn.** Throughout this book, you will find lessons, exercises, and other elements highlighted by this icon. For the most part, they involve using or exploring the built-in Help system or Web-based Help, which is also accessible from the application. However, their significance is much greater. Microsoft Office has become so rich in features that cater to so many diverse needs that it is no longer possible to anticipate and teach you everything that you might need to know. It is becoming increasingly important that, as you learn from this book, you also "learn to learn" on your own. These elements help you identify related—perhaps more specialized—tasks or questions, and show you how to discover the right procedures or answers by exploiting the many resources that are already within the application.

- **Task Guide.** The Task Guide that follows the last project lists all the procedures and shortcuts you have learned in this book. It can be used in two complementary ways to enhance your learning experience. You can refer to it, while progressing through the book, to refresh your memory on procedures learned in a previous lesson. Or, you can keep it as a handy real-world reference while using the application for your daily work.

- **Glossary.** Here, you find the definitions—collected in one place—of all the key terms defined throughout the book and listed in the opening page of each project. Use it to refresh your memory.

Typeface Conventions Used in This Book

We have used the following conventions throughout this book to make it easier for you to understand the material:

- Key terms appear in ***italic and bold*** the first time that they are defined in a project.

- Text that you type, as well as text that appears on your computer screen as warning, confirmation, or general information, appears in a special `monospace` typeface.

- Hotkeys, the underlined keys onscreen that activate commands and options, are also underlined in this book. Hotkeys offer a quick way to bring up frequently used commands.

How to Use the CD-ROM

The CD-ROM that accompanies this book contains all the data files for you to use as you work through the step-by-step tutorials, Skill Drill, Challenge, and Discovery Zone exercises provided at the end of each project. The CD contains separate parallel folders for each project. The filenames correspond to the filenames called for in this book. The files are named in the following manner: The first three characters represent the software and the book level (such as WD1 for *Word 2000 Essentials Basic*). The last four digits indicate the project number and the file number within the project. For example, the first file used in project 3 would be 0301. Therefore, the complete name for the first file in Project 3 in the Word Basic book is WD1-0301.

Files on a CD-ROM are read-only; they cannot be modified in any way. To use the provided data files while working through this book, you must first transfer the files to a read-write medium, where you can modify them. Because classroom and lab rules governing the use of storage media vary from school to school, this book assumes the standard procedure of working with the file(s) on a 3.5-inch floppy disk.

A word of caution about using floppy disks: As you use a data file, it increases in size or automatically generates temporary work files. Ensure that your disk remains at least one-third empty to provide the needed extra space. Moreover, using a floppy for your work disk is slower than working from a hard drive. You will also need several floppy disks to hold all the files on the CD.

- **Saving to a 3.5-inch floppy disk.** For security or space reasons, many labs do not allow you to save to the hard drive at all. The fourth lesson in Project 1 in this book on the Save As command shows you how to save a file to a 3.5-inch floppy disk. The first lesson in Project 2 shows you how to open a file you've saved to the 3.5-inch floppy disk. For other files, you can open the data file you need from the CD-ROM by selecting the drive letter that contains the CD-ROM, such as E:, from the Look in list in the Open dialog box; then immediately save it with a new file-name to a floppy disk with the Save As command. This is the most portable solution because you can easily take your files with you from the classroom to the lab and back home to complete your exercises.

- **Copying to a 3.5-inch floppy disk.** First, select the files on the CD that you want to copy and ensure that their combined size (shown on the status bar of the Explorer window) will fit on a 1.44MB floppy disk. Right-click on the selection with your mouse, choose Send To on the context menu that appears, and then choose 3 1/2 Floppy on the submenu. After copying, select the copied files on the floppy disk and right-click the selection with the mouse again. This time, choose Properties, choose the General tab on the Properties dialog box that appears, and then uncheck the read-only attribute at the bottom of this page. Because the original files on the CD-ROM were read-only, the files were copied with this attribute turned on. You can rename files copied in this manner after you have turned off the read-only attribute.

  Although you can use the same method to copy the entire CD contents to a large-capacity drive, it is much simpler to use the installation routine in the CD-ROM for this purpose. This automatically removes the read-only attribute while transferring the files.

- **Installing to a hard drive or Zip drive.** The CD-ROM contains an installation routine that automatically copies all the contents to a local or networked hard drive, or to a removable large-capacity drive (for example, an Iomega Zip drive). If you are working in the classroom, your instructor has probably already installed the files to the hard drive and can tell you where the files are located. You will be asked to save or copy the file(s) you need to your personal work area on the hard drive, or to a floppy work disk.

Otherwise, run the installation routine yourself to transfer all the files to the hard drive (for example, if you are working at home) or to your personal Zip drive. You may then work directly and more efficiently from these high-capacity drives.

CD-ROM Installation Routine

If you were instructed to install the files on a lab computer or if you are installing them on your home computer, simply insert the CD-ROM into the CD-ROM drive. When the installation screen appears, follow these steps:

1. From the installation screen, click the Install button.

2. The Welcome dialog box displays. Click the Next button.

3. The Readme.txt appears. The Readme.txt gives you important information regarding the installation. Make sure that you use the scrollbar to view the entire Readme.txt file. When you finish reading the Readme.txt, click the Next button.

4. The Select Destination Directory displays. Unless you are told otherwise by your instructor, the default location is recommended. Click Next.

5. The Ready to Install screen appears. Click Next to begin the installation.

   A directory is created on your hard drive where the student files will be installed.

6. A dialog box appears, confirming that the installation is complete.

The installation of the student data files enables you to access the data files from the Start menu programs. To access the student data files from the Start menu, click Start, click Programs, and then click the *Essentials* title you installed from the list of programs. The student data files are in subfolders, arranged by project.

Uninstalling the Student Data Files

After you complete the course, you may decide that you do not need the student data files any more. If that is the case, you have the capability to uninstall them. The following steps walk you through the process:

1. Click the Start menu, and then click Programs.

2. Click the *Essentials* title that you installed.

3. Click Uninstall.

4. Click one of the Uninstall methods listed:

   - Automatic—This method deletes all files in the directory and all shortcuts created.

   - Custom—This method enables you to select the files that you want to delete.

5. Click Next.

6. The Perform Uninstall dialog box appears. Click Finish. The Student data files and their folders are deleted.

The *Annotated Instructor's Manual*

The *Annotated Instructor's Manual* (AIM) is a printed copy of the student book—complete with marginal annotations and detailed guidelines, including a curriculum guide—that helps the instructor use this book and teach the software more effectively. The *AIM* also includes a Resource CD-ROM with additional support files for the instructor; suggested solution files that show how the students' files should look at the end of a tutorial; answers to test questions; PowerPoint presentations to augment your instruction; additional test questions and answers; and additional Skill Drill, Challenge, and Discovery Zone exercises. Instructors should contact Prentice Hall for their complimentary *AIM*. Prentice Hall can be reached via phone at 1-800-333-7945, or via the Internet at http://www.prenhall.com.

Getting Started with Word

Objectives

In this project, you learn how to

> ➤ **Start Word and Explore the Word Screen**
> ➤ **Use Menu Bars and Toolbars**
> ➤ **Enter Text in a Document**
> ➤ **Save a Document**
> ➤ **Print a Document**
> ➤ **Get Help**
> ➤ **Close a File and Exit Word**

Key terms in this project include

- buttons
- close
- Control menu box
- default
- drop-down list
- ellipsis
- end-of-document marker
- exit
- Formatting toolbar
- full menu
- Help
- Help Topic pane
- horizontal scrollbar
- hypertext link
- insertion point
- maximize
- menu bar
- minimize
- Navigation pane
- Office Assistant
- restore
- ruler
- save
- ScreenTip
- scroll buttons
- short menu
- shortcut
- Standard toolbar
- status bar
- submenu
- title bar
- vertical scrollbar
- view buttons
- word-wrap feature

Why Would I Do This?

Word processing is possibly the most commonly used type of software. People around the world, from students to business professionals, use word processing programs such as Microsoft Word, also known as Word, for a variety of simple to complex tasks. You can create letters, research papers, newsletters, brochures, and other documents with Word. You can even create and send email and produce Web pages with Word.

And after you create your documents, you need to edit and format them. These tasks are a snap with Word. But first, you need to learn your way around the Word window and understand how to create, save, and print your documents. In this project, you learn all of that, plus how to use the built-in Help feature. Let's get started!

Visual Summary

Figure 1.1 shows the process of creating and saving a document you can use later.

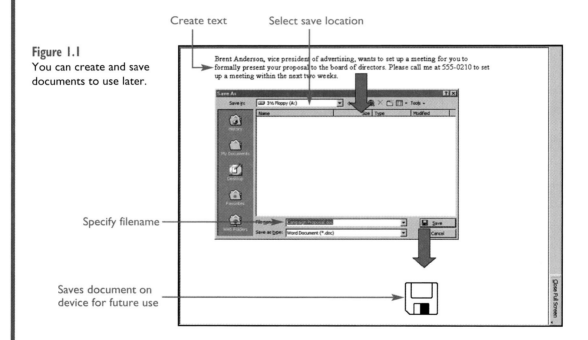

Figure 1.1
You can create and save documents to use later.

Create text

Select save location

Specify filename

Saves document on device for future use

Figure 1.2 shows different ways of obtaining assistance from the built-in Help feature.

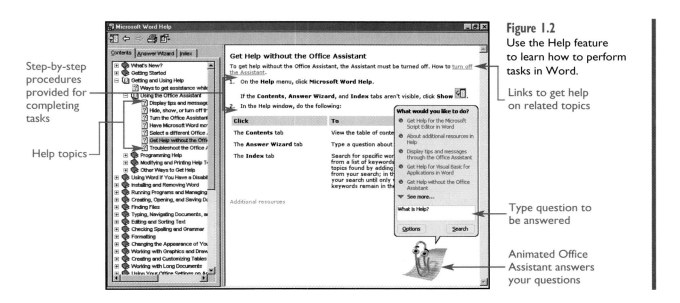

Figure 1.2
Use the Help feature to learn how to perform tasks in Word.

Step-by-step procedures provided for completing tasks

Help topics

Links to get help on related topics

Type question to be answered

Animated Office Assistant answers your questions

Lesson 1: Starting Word and Exploring the Word Screen

Starting Word is the first step to learning and using the software. Your exciting experience with Word all begins with the Start button on the taskbar. After you start Word, you learn your way around the Word screen.

To Start Word and Explore the Word Screen

1 **Click the Start button on the left side of the Windows taskbar.**
The Start menu appears. Use this menu to start programs, get help, choose computer settings, and shut down your computer.

2 **Move the mouse pointer to the Programs menu item.**
The Programs menu appears to the right of the Start menu, as shown in Figure 1.3.

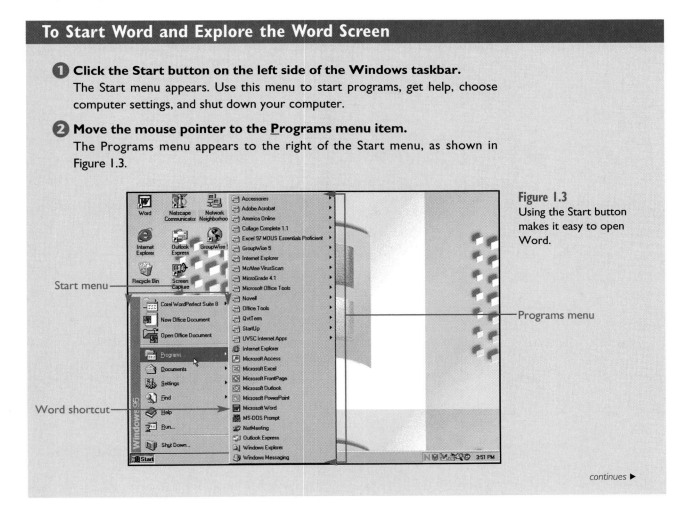

Figure 1.3
Using the Start button makes it easy to open Word.

Start menu

Word shortcut

Programs menu

continues ▶

To Start Word and Explore the Word Screen   (continued)

❸ Find Microsoft Word in the Programs menu and click it once.

 If you don't see `Microsoft Word` on the Programs menu, ask your instructor for further assistance.

ⓘ Using the Word Shortcut Icon
 If you see the Word shortcut icon on the Windows desktop, you can double-click it to immediately start Word, instead of using the Start menu.

Word opens and a blank document appears, as you can see in Figure 1.4. The Word window is made up of a large area on which you place your text and graphics and many different buttons, icons, and menus, all designed to help you create the perfect document for any occasion.

Figure 1.4
The Word Screen contains many useful features.

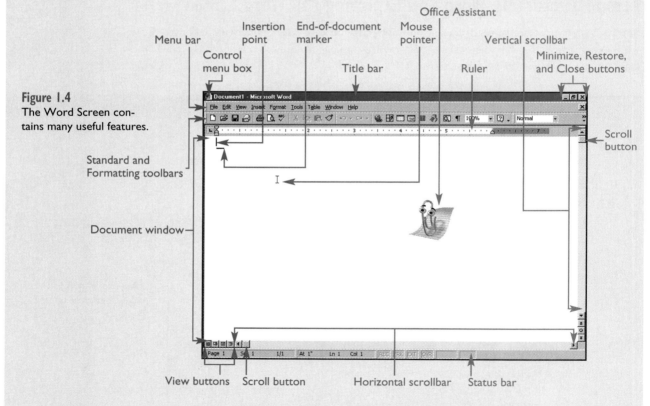

Don't be intimidated by the number of items on the screen. You will continue to learn about these as you work through this textbook.

Table 1.1 lists the default screen elements and gives a brief description of each element. **Default** refers to a standard setting determined by Microsoft and used unless you change it. Figure 1.4 shows the elements listed in Table 1.1 and Table 1.2.

Table 1.1   Icons and Buttons on the Microsoft Word Screen

Icon	Element	Description
	Control menu box	Displays menu that controls the application program. Double-click the box to exit (close) the application program.
	Minimize button	Reduces the current document to an icon on the taskbar. If only one document is open, clicking the Minimize button reduces Word to an icon on the taskbar.
	Restore button	Restores the window to its previous size.
	Maximize button	Restores the window to the full screen size.
	Close button	Closes the document window. If only one document is open, you see another Close button on the same row as the Menu Bar. Click the top Close button to close (exit) Word. Click the bottom Close button to close only the current document window.
	Insertion point	Shows your location in the document.
	End-of-document marker	Indicates the end of the document.

Table 1.2   Parts of the Microsoft Word Screen

Element	Description
Title bar	Shows the name of the file you are currently working on. If you haven't saved the document, Word displays a document number, such as Document2. The title bar also shows the name of the program, such as Microsoft Word.
Menu bar	Lists categories of menus that contain options from which to choose.
Standard toolbar	Contains a row of buttons that perform routine tasks, such as opening, saving, and printing a file. Other toolbars are available for specific types of tasks.
Formatting toolbar	Contains a row of buttons whose functions enhance the appearance of your documents.
Ruler	Shows the location of tabs, indents, and left and right margins.
Document window	Displays text and formats for documents you create.
Vertical scrollbar	Moves up and down in a document.
Scroll buttons	Move quickly through a document. You can scroll up or down one page at a time or scroll to a particular object within the document.
View buttons	Switch between different view modes. These options are also available on the View pull-down menu.
Horizontal scrollbar	Adjusts horizontal view (left to right).
Status bar	Displays the current page number and location of the insertion point.
Office Assistant	Provides help for questions you pose.

You can refer to Figure 1.4, Table 1.1, and Table 1.2 to learn the parts of the Word screen. With a little practice, it won't take long until you know each item on the Word screen and how to use it.

Lesson 2: Using Menu Bars and Toolbars

Menu bars and toolbars make it easy to find and use various features in Word. For example, if you need to insert page numbers or format a document, those commands are literally at your fingertips.

Word's commands are organized in menus. The name of each menu, such as the File menu, is displayed on the **menu bar**. When you click a menu name, a list of commands drops down.

Word's menus appear as short or full menus. The **short menus**, also called adaptive menus, appear first. These menus display a list of commonly used commands (see Figure 1.5). When you first display a menu, it lists the commands that you use most often. As you work with Word, the menus adapt to your use.

Figure 1.5
The short format menu displays the most recently used commands.

The **full menu** includes all commands in that menu category (see Figure 1.6). By default, the short menu appears first; after a moment, the full menu appears. When you select a command from the full menu, Word adapts the short menu by including that command the next time you display the menu.

Figure 1.6
The full format menu displays all format commands.

Additional options appear

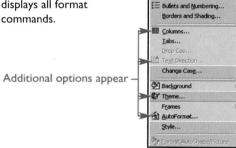

To Use the Menu Bar

1 Click File on the menu bar.
The File menu displays, as shown in Figure 1.7, listing the last four documents used on your computer. Your list might show different document names.

Click to see File menu

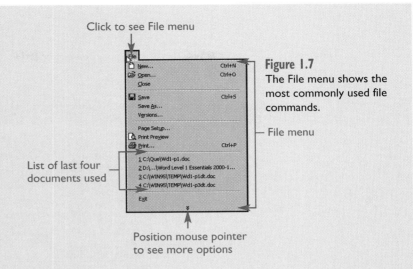

Figure 1.7
The File menu shows the most commonly used file commands.

— File menu

List of last four documents used

Position mouse pointer to see more options

2 **Move the mouse pointer to the bottom of the _F_ile menu, where you see the arrows.**

You now see the full menu, which contains additional options, such as Sen_d_ To and Proper_t_ies.

Selecting Menu Options

If you want to select a menu option, click it. Choosing options with _ellipsis_ (the three dots at the end of a word), such as _P_rint..., displays a dialog box with specific task-related options. Choosing an option with a triangle, such as Sen_d_ To, displays a _submenu_, a menu of more specific options, to the side of the current menu. Choosing options without either symbol immediately performs a task. For example, choosing E_x_it closes Word.

3 **If you decide not to select a menu option, click _F_ile again on the menu bar to close it.**

You can also close a menu by pressing ⒺⓈⒸ twice, or by pressing ⒶⓁⓉ once. Another way is by clicking outside of the menu, such as in the document window.

Selecting Menus from the Keyboard

You can also use the keyboard to select from the menu bar. Notice that one letter (usually the first) of each menu bar option is underlined. For example, "F" is underlined in _F_ile. To choose a particular menu, press ⒶⓁⓉ+the underlined letter. For example, pressing ⒶⓁⓉ+Ⓕ displays the _F_ile menu.

When the menu is displayed, press ⬇ or ⬆ to highlight an option; then press ⏎Enter to select that option. You can also press the underlined letter to immediately select the option of your choice. For example, press Ⓒ for _C_lose on the _F_ile menu.

The menus also display keyboard _shortcuts_, such as ⒸⓉⓇⓁ+Ⓢ for _S_ave (see Figure 1.7). By using keyboard shortcuts, you can keep your hands on the keyboard and maybe save a little time.

The Standard and Formatting toolbars contain **buttons**, or little pictures that represent different tasks. When you click a button, Word performs the action or task associated with that button. Some buttons contain the same commands that you see in menus. For example, click the Save button to save a file. Clicking the Save button might be faster than opening the <u>F</u>ile menu and scrolling down to the <u>S</u>ave command.

To Use Toolbars

 1 Move the mouse pointer to the New Blank Document button on the Standard toolbar. A ScreenTip appears with information about the button.

When you position the mouse pointer on a button, Word displays the name of the button in a little yellow box, called a **ScreenTip**. You should see the ScreenTip New Blank Document (Ctrl+N) now.

Using ScreenTips

Menus and ScreenTips sometimes show shortcut keys, such as Ctrl+N. Learning some of these shortcut keys helps you become more efficient because you can keep your hands on the keyboard instead of moving back and forth from the keyboard to the mouse as often.

If the menus and ScreenTips do not show the shortcut keys, ask your instructor how to display them.

2 Click the right mouse button on the New Blank Document button, or any button on the toolbar.

You see a list of different toolbars, plus the Customize option (see Figure 1.8). The check marks indicate the active toolbars.

Active toolbars indicated by checkmarks   Right-click on any toolbar button

Figure 1.8
The Toolbar menu lets you display, hide, and customize toolbars.

Toolbar menu appears

Choose customize to adjust toolbar settings

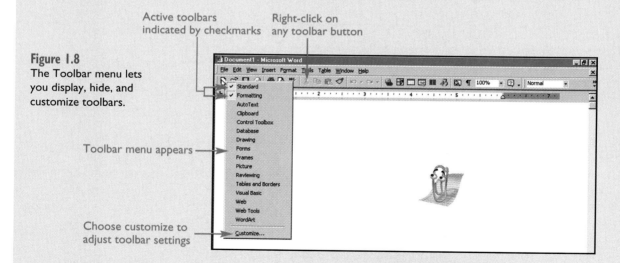

3 Click <u>C</u>ustomize at the bottom of the menu.

The Customize dialog box appears, so you can adjust the way the toolbars appear on your screen (see Figure 1.9).

Make sure the Options
tab is selected

Click to separate Standard
and Formatting toolbars

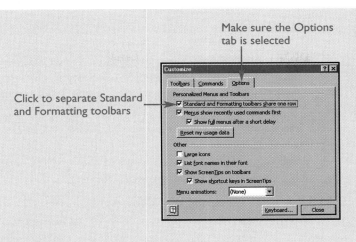

Figure 1.9
The Customize dialog box
lets you adapt the appearance of the toolbars.

4 **Click the Options tab, then click the Standard and Formatting
toolbars share one row check box to uncheck it.**
This option is no longer selected.

5 **Click Close.**
The Standard and Formatting toolbars now appear on separate rows, as
shown in Figure 1.10.

Standard toolbar appears first

Formatting
toolbar
appears
below the
Standard
toolbar

Figure 1.10
The Standard and
Formatting toolbars
appear on separate
rows.

Lesson 3: Entering Text in a Document

You can begin entering text for your document as soon as you start Word. When you
begin a new document, Word provides default settings, such as the margins, tabs, font,
and font size. The document window is where you type and format your documents.
The insertion point should appear below the ruler.

In this lesson, you enter text using the default settings.

To Enter Text in a Document

1 **Type the following text in the document window:**
Your proposal contains some excellent ideas for the new advertising
campaign. We are very impressed with your knowledge of the company
and of our target market.

Don't press ⏎Enter when you reach the end of a line. When you enter more
text than can fit on the current line, the ***word-wrap feature*** continues text
to the next line when it runs out of room on the current line.

continues ▶

To Enter Text in a Document   (continued)

 If the document area is gray instead of white, then the Word document window isn't active and you need to start a new document. Click the New button on the left side of the Standard toolbar.

2 Press ⏎Enter twice when you reach the end of a single-spaced paragraph.

Pressing ⏎Enter tells Word to go to the next line. Pressing ⏎Enter a second time leaves one blank line between paragraphs.

3 Continue by typing the following paragraph:

```
Brent Anderson, vice president of advertising, wants to set up a
meeting for you to formally present your proposal to the board of
directors. Please call me at 555-0201 to set up a meeting within
the next two weeks.
```

Figure 1.11 shows what your document should look like.

Figure 1.11
Your document now contains two paragraphs.

Blank line between paragraphs ——

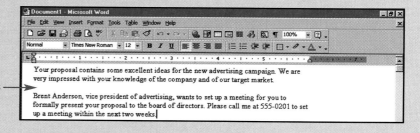

4 Leave your new Word document open onscreen to continue with the next lesson.

 Correcting Mistakes

If you make a mistake as you type the paragraphs, you can press ←Backspace to delete text to the *left* of the insertion point, or you can press Del to delete text to the *right* of the insertion point. After deleting incorrect letters, type the correct letters.

If you see wavy red lines below a word, the word is not in Microsoft's main dictionary. You see these red lines below misspelled words and proper nouns. Simply right-click the word and choose the correct spelling from the menu that displays. You learn more about correcting spelling errors in Project 3, "Editing a Document."

 Seeing Dots and Symbols

You might see dots between words and a paragraph (¶) symbol at the end of the paragraphs. You learn about these marks in Project 2, "Working with a Document." Don't worry about them now; they do not print.

Clicking and Typing
In Print Layout view, you can double-click in a new area of the document (even below the end-of-document marker) and type new text. This new feature is called Click and Type. Depending on where you double-click, you can type text at the left margin, centered between the margins, or flush with the right margin. After completing Lesson 6, you can use Help to learn more about Click and Type.

Lesson 4: Saving a Document

At this point, the document is not saved, or stored for you to use in the future. The document exists only in the computer's random-access memory (RAM) and will be lost if the computer crashes or unexpectedly shuts down. For this reason, you should save your documents frequently. **Save** refers to the process of storing a document for future use. It can be compared to filing a piece of paper in a file folder in a file cabinet. When you save a document for the first time, you designate the location where you're going to store the file, such as on the hard drive or on a floppy disk, and you assign a name to the document.

To Save a Document

1 **Insert a new, formatted floppy disk into the disk drive.**

2 **With your new Word document open, choose File, Save As.**
The Save As dialog box appears (see Figure 1.12). The first step in saving your file is to choose a location where you would like to keep it.

Save in box   Click to see available drives

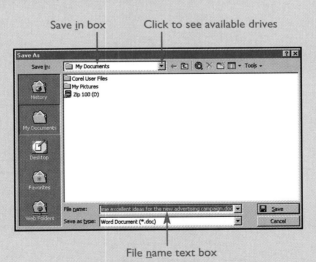

File name text box

Figure 1.12
The Save As dialog box lets you name the document and choose its storage location.

By default, Word saves documents in the My Documents folder on the hard drive.

3 **Click the drop-down arrow on the right side of the Save in text box.**
You see a list of available drives on your computer system (see Figure 1.13). This book assumes you save and open documents on a floppy drive, typically designated as 3 1/2 Floppy (A:). Ask your instructor the correct location for saving files you create during this course.

continues ▶

To Save a Document (continued)

Figure 1.13
The Save in drop-down list shows you the available drives where you can save your documents.

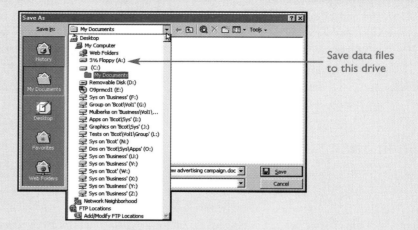

Save data files to this drive

 Choose 3 1/2 Floppy (A:) from the Save in list.

> ✖ If the Save in option displays Desktop and you don't see a list of drives, ask your instructor how to proceed.

❺ **Press** Alt+N **to make the File name text box active. Now you can type over the suggested filename.**

❻ **Type** Campaign Proposal **in the File name text box. You have just named your file.**
When you type a filename, it replaces the default name suggested by Word. You can assign filenames using up to 255 characters, including both uppercase and lowercase letters, numbers, some symbols, and spaces.

❼ **Click Save in the bottom right corner of the dialog box.**
Leave your Word document open onscreen to continue with the next lesson.

> ✖ If you try to save to a floppy disk and get an error message, several reasons are possible. First, make sure you have correctly inserted a disk in the disk drive. Second, make sure you have selected the correct drive; many computers have more than one storage drive. Some network drives may prohibit users from storing files in these locations.
>
> If you are saving to a floppy disk, the disk should be formatted and the write-protect tab should not cover the opening on the disk. Ask your instructor if you need help formatting a disk, or determining if the write-protect tab is on or off.

Using Save vs. Save As

The first time you save a document, you can use either the Save or the Save As command. Either way, you see the Save As dialog box. Once you save a document, however, the Save and Save As options have two different effects.

 If you modify a document and use Save, Word saves the changes under the same filename without displaying the Save As dialog box. This option is useful when you save a document and continue entering text and formatting it. You can periodically save the changes under the same name. In addition to using the Save option in the File menu, you can click the Save button on the Standard toolbar.

Other times, you might want to assign a different name to a modified document so you have your original document as well as another that incorporates changes and modifications. Use the Save As command to save the document with a different filename. The Standard toolbar does not contain a Save As button. In Project 2, you open an existing document, make changes, and save the changes with a different filename.

Lesson 5: Printing a Document

Previewing how your document will look when printed is important. You can see if you need to make margin adjustments or change the size of your font to make your document look better on paper. Previewing saves paper because you correct your document before printing.

To Preview and Print a Document

1 Make sure the printer is turned on, has paper, and is online.

Ask your instructor for help if you need further assistance in using the printer.

2 Click the Print Preview button on the Standard toolbar.

The document appears in the Print Preview window, which lets you see how the printed document will look (see Figure 1.14). You can see the margins, space between paragraphs, formats, page numbering placement, and so on.

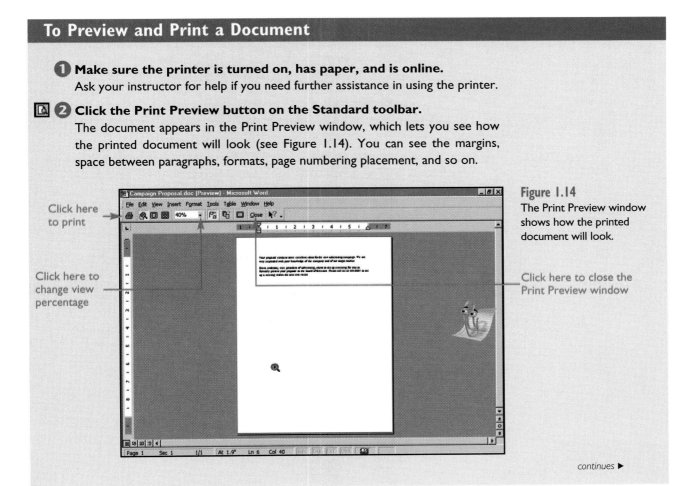

Click here to print

Click here to change view percentage

Figure 1.14
The Print Preview window shows how the printed document will look.

Click here to close the Print Preview window

continues ▶

To Preview and Print a Document (continued)

3 **Click the Close button to close the Print Preview window.**

If the document doesn't need any editing, you can click the Print icon to send the document to the printer. However, if you need more specific print options (e.g., number of copies) or if you need to adjust the document's format, you should return to the document to make your changes.

4 **Click File and then choose Print from the drop-down menu.**

The Print dialog box appears, as shown in Figure 1.15.

Figure 1.15
Choose options in the Print dialog box.

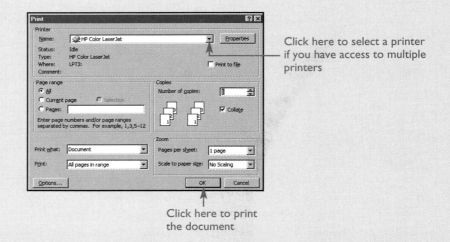

Click here to select a printer if you have access to multiple printers

Click here to print the document

⚠ Clicking the Print Button

Clicking the Print button on the Standard toolbar sends the entire document to the printer without displaying the Print dialog box. Although this is a fast way to print a document, it doesn't give you the opportunity to select print options.

5 **Ask your instructor which printer name is correct for the system you're using. If needed, click the drop-down arrow to the right of the Name option and choose the correct printer name from the list.**

6 **Click OK to print your document.**

Word sends a copy of the document to the printer. Leave your Word document open onscreen to continue with the next lesson.

After you print a document, make sure the text looks good on paper. Check the format. You might need to adjust the formatting and print the document again.

Lesson 6: Getting Help

When you work with Word, you will probably need to know about a specific feature or how to perform a certain task. Although you are learning a lot about Word by completing this book, you might run across a situation in which you need assistance. Word contains an onscreen assistance feature called Help. **Help** provides information about Word features and step-by-step instructions for performing tasks. A quick way to get the help you need is to use the **Office Assistant**, Microsoft's animated Help feature, to find the answer to a specific question.

In this lesson, you use the Office Assistant and the Help Index to learn more about menus.

To Get Help

1 **If the Office Assistant character does not appear on your screen, choose** **H**elp **on the menu bar, then choose Show the** **O**ffice **Assistant from the menu.**
The Office Assistant may appear as one of several different animated characters, such as Clippit the paper clip, Rocky the dog, Nibbles the cat, F1 the robot, and so on. Later, you will learn how to change these characters.

2 **If the text balloon does not already appear on your screen, click the Office Assistant to display it. It should display the message:** What would you like to do?.
The Office Assistant is now ready for you to type a question for it to answer (see Figure 1.16). Your question can be a full sentence or just a word or two. The more specific you are with your questions, however, the better the Office Assistant is able to direct you. After you type a question and click the Search button, the balloon displays a list of topics from which to choose.

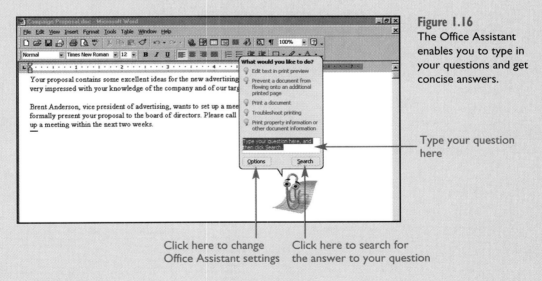

Figure 1.16
The Office Assistant enables you to type in your questions and get concise answers.

Type your question here

Click here to change   Click here to search for
Office Assistant settings   the answer to your question

3 **Type** What are menus?; **then click** **S**earch.
The Office Assistant displays a listing of topics related to menus (see Figure 1.17).

continues ▶

To Get Help   (continued)

Suggested topics
to search through

Figure 1.17
The Office Assistant
provides topics to answer
your question.

Your question
appears here

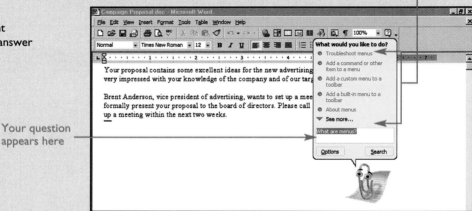

④ **Click the topic titled About menus.**

The Microsoft Word Help window appears, as shown in Figure 1.18. The left side, called the ***Navigation pane***, contains tabs (Contents, Answer Wizard, and Index). The right side, called the ***Help Topic pane***, contains information about the topic you selected. The Help window probably covers part of your document. Don't worry about this; the document window enlarges when you close the Help feature. Underlined keywords and phrases appearing in a different color are called ***hypertext links***. When you click a hypertext link, you see additional information.

Click to hide the Contents,
Answer Wizard, and Index tabs

Help topic pane

Figure 1.18
Identify parts of the Help
window to use it effectively.

More specific Help topics

Navigation pane

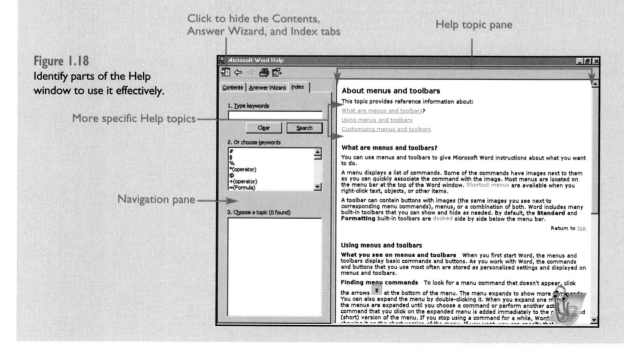

Navigation Pane Not Displayed
If you don't see the Navigation pane, position the mouse pointer on the first icon on the Help toolbar. You should see a ScreenTip that says Show. Click this button to show the Navigation pane.

5 **Click the topic What are menus and toolbars?**
The Help Topic pane displays information about menus and toolbars (see Figure 1.19).

Click to print the Help topic

Hypertext link for additional information

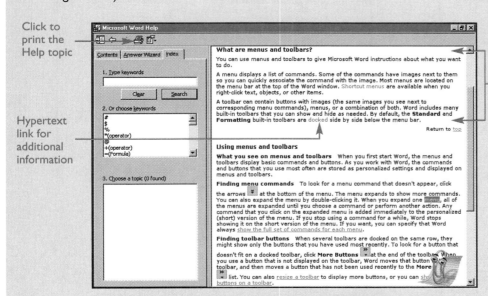

Figure 1.19
Read the information about menus and toolbars.

Explanatory paragraphs

 Printing Help Topics
Although you can see both your document window and the Help topic window, you might want to print the Help topic to have it handy. Printing the Help topic allows you to close the Microsoft Word Help window. You can read your printed copy as you perform the tasks on your document.

6 **Click the Index tab in the Navigation pane, if necessary.**
The Index feature lets you type a topic and search through the alphabetical index of topics. The first step is to enter keywords, or particular words that might be found in the Help topics, and then click the Search button. Alternatively, you can scroll through the list of keywords in the index to find what you're looking for.

7 **Type keyboard and then click Search.**
You see a list of topics in the Choose a topic list box.

8 **Scroll through the list and click Keyboard shortcuts.**
When you click a topic, you see topical information in the right-hand pane (see Figure 1.20).

continues ▶

To Get Help (continued)

Click to search for the keywords you entered

Figure 1.20
Look at the different links for keyboard shortcuts.

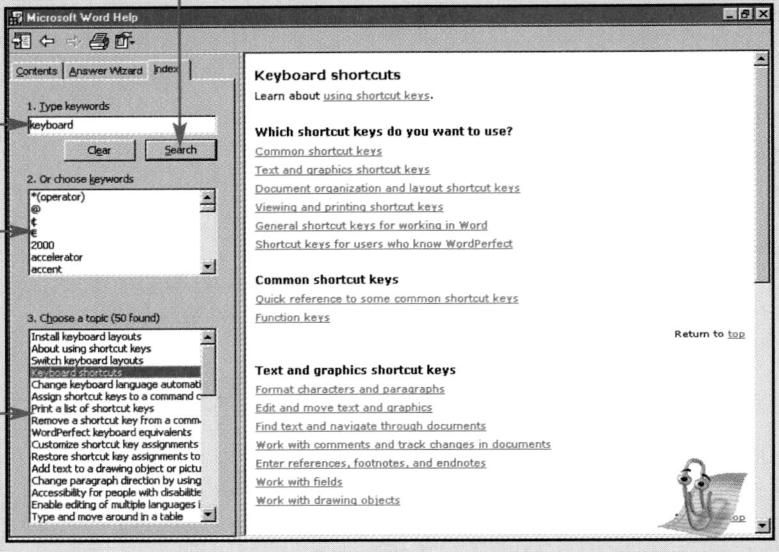

Type keywords here

Scroll through keywords instead of entering them in Step 1, if desired

Select a specific topic from the available choices

9 **Click the using shortcut keys hyperlink.**
The Help window displays information about shortcut keys, showing a list of shortcut keys and other shortcut key information.

X **10** **Click the Close button in the top right corner of the Microsoft Word Help window.**
This closes Help and displays your document on the whole screen again. Leave the document open to continue with the next lesson.

Displaying the Office Assistant
To display the Office Assistant quickly, press F1 at any time or click the Microsoft Word Help button on the Standard toolbar. If the Office Assistant is displayed, click it to open the text balloon where you can type a question.

If Office Assistant can't find topics related to the question you type, a balloon appears telling you so. Make sure your question doesn't contain any misspelled words, or type a more specific question and click Search again.

Changing the Office Assistant
To change the Office Assistant image, right-click the Office Assistant and select Choose Assistant. When you see a gallery, scroll through the available images to select a different one. You can select other Office Assistant settings by right-clicking the Office Assistant and choosing Options.

Some Office Assistant images may not be available. You might be prompted to insert the installation CD to use a particular assistant.

Another useful feature is What's This? to display a ScreenTip about a screen item. To use this feature, choose Help, What's This?, or press ↑Shift+F1. When the pointer resembles a question mark with an arrow, click the mouse pointer on the screen item that you don't understand. Word then provides a ScreenTip that describes that feature. Press ⬆Shift+F1 to turn off the What's This? feature.

If you can't find the information you need within Word, you can access resources available on the World Wide Web. Assuming you have Internet access, you can choose Help, Office on the Web to view information on Microsoft's Web site for Word.

Lesson 7: Closing a File and Exiting Word

Closing and exiting Word are as easy as starting Word. When you are finished working on your documents, you should properly close the files and exit Word. If you simply turn off the computer, you might lose valuable work and create problems within the computer itself. Because you saved the document in Lesson 4 and have not made any changes to it, you can close the document without having to save again.

To Close a File and Exit Word

1 **Choose File, Close from the menu.**
The file closes immediately. If you haven't saved the document after modifying it, Word displays a dialog box asking if you want to save the changes. Click Yes to save the file before closing it, or click No to close the document without saving the changes.

2 **Choose File, Exit from the menu to close Word.**
If other Word files are open, they close immediately if you saved them. If other files have been modified since you last saved them, Word prompts you to save them before the program closes. After Word closes, you see the Windows Desktop if no other programs are running.

 Exiting with the Control Menu Box
You can also exit Word by double-clicking the Control menu box, or by clicking the Close button in the upper-right hand corner.

This concludes Project 1. You can reinforce and expand your knowledge and skills by completing the end-of-project activities that follow the summary.

Summary

You are now familiar with some of the Word screen components. You can also use the menu bar and toolbars to access commands easily. You can enter text, save the document for future use, and print the document. Use the Office Assistant and the Help feature to learn more about the exciting things you can do with Word.

For more information about these and other features, ask the Office Assistant for help or choose Help, Office on the Web. These sources provide a vast array of information to help you become comfortable with and proficient at using Word!

Checking Concepts and Terms ✓

True/False

For each of the following, check *T* or *F* to indicate whether the statement is true or false.

__T __F **1.** The purpose of the Control menu box is to access commonly used commands. [L1]

__T __F **2.** To open a drop-down menu, right-click the menu name on the menu bar. [2]

__T __F **3.** When you use a command from the full menu, Word adapts the short menu to include the command. [L2]

__T __F **4.** Pressing ⏎Enter twice leaves one blank line between single-spaced paragraphs. [L3]

__T __F **5.** The first time you save a document, you can use either Save or Save As. [L4]

__T __F **6.** If you want to assign a new name to a modified document that has been previously saved, choose the Save option. [L4]

__T __F **7.** Clicking the Print Preview button is unnecessary, because the regular screen shows you exactly how your printed document will look. [L5]

__T __F **8.** The Help Index contains an alphabetical list of topics. [L6]

__T __F **9.** The Office Assistant always remains on your screen. [L6]

__T __F **10.** When you are finished with Word, you should simply turn off the computer. [L7]

Multiple Choice

Circle the letter of the correct answer for each of the following.

1. What feature displays an animated graphic that provides onscreen help? [L6]

   a. the standard toolbar

   b. the Office Assistant

   c. the Help Index

   d. the Navigation pane

2. To see a ScreenTip for a toolbar button, what should you do? [L2]

   a. Click the button.

   b. Right-click the button.

   c. Double-click the button.

   d. Position the mouse pointer on the button.

3. What happens when you choose a menu option that displays a triangle? [L2]

   a. You see a submenu.

   b. A dialog box appears.

   c. Word immediately performs the command.

   d. The menu closes.

4. When you use the Save command, all of the following happen except: _____. [L4]

   a. Word saves an existing document with the same filename

   b. the document closes

   c. the Save As dialog box appears if you haven't saved the document before

   d. you are able to use the document in the future

5. If you want to scroll through an alphabetical list of Help topics, which Help feature do you use? [L6]

   a. Index

   b. Contents

   c. Office Assistant

   d. Answer Wizard

6. What is the keyboard shortcut for displaying the Format menu from the menu bar? [L2]

   a. Ctrl+O

   b. Alt+F

   c. Alt+O

   d. ⇧Shift+F

7. Which of the following is not correct? [L3]

   a. Press ⏎Enter at the end of a paragraph.

   b. Double-click in a new area to be able to type there without pressing ⏎Enter.

   c. Press ⏎Enter to leave a blank line between paragraphs.

   d. Press ⏎Enter at the end of each line within a paragraph.

8. You can do all of the following in the Print Preview window, except _____. [L5]

   a. see the amount of space for the margins

   b. look at the space between paragraphs

   c. type and edit text

   d. look at the overall format of the document

9. What should you click if you try to close a file without saving it and decide you want to go back to the document and continue working on it? [L7]

   a. Yes

   b. No

   c. Cancel

   d. any of the above

10. Identify the end-of-document marker. [L1]

   a. ▯

   b.  ▭

   c. ▧

   d. ☒

Screen ID

Label each element of the Word screen shown in Figure 1.21.

Figure 1.21

A. end-of-document marker

B. Formatting toolbar

C. insertion point

D. menu bar

E. mouse pointer

F. Office Assistant

G. sizing buttons

H. Standard toolbar

I. status bar

J. title bar

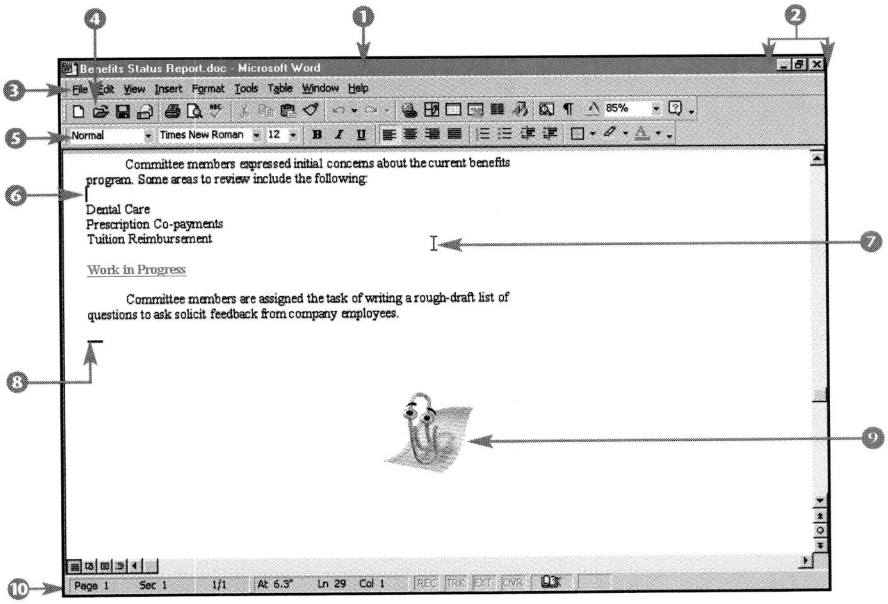

1. _____

2. _____

3. _____

4. _____

5. _____

6. _____

7. _____

8. _____

9. _____

10. _____

Discussion Questions

1. Why do you think Word has multiple ways of performing the same task, such as toolbars, menu bar, and shortcuts? What factors might influence your decision to use one way over another?

2. Describe how the menu bar menus are adaptive. How can this feature be an advantage to the user?

3. Explain the difference between Save and Save As. Provide an example of when you would use each command.

Skill Drill

Skill Drill exercises reinforce project skills. Each skill reinforced is the same, or nearly the same, as a skill presented in the project. Detailed instructions are provided in a step-by-step format.

1. Exploring Menus

You want to review some drop-down menus. The more you study the menus, the more you understand the structure and logic of using Word. [L2]

To explore drop-down menus, follow these steps:

1. Start Word.

2. Click Insert on the menu bar.

3. Choose Picture to display a submenu of additional options.

4. Click Insert on the menu bar to close the Insert menu.

5. Press (Alt)+(O) to display the Format menu.

6. Click the arrows to display the full menu.

7. Press (E) to select Change Case. (You press (E) because e is underlined in Change Case.)

8. Press (Esc) to cancel and close the Change Case dialog box.

9. Click Table on the menu bar.

10. Click the arrows to display the full Table menu.

11. Try choosing Merge Cells. Notice nothing happens because the option is grayed-out. It is available only when you perform a specific task first.

12. Press (Alt) once to close the Table menu without choosing any options.

13. Choose File, Close to close the document. Click No if you are prompted to save the document. Choose File, Exit if you need to end your work session.

2. Using Toolbars

You want to learn more about toolbar buttons and shortcuts, so you plan to study them in more detail. As you point to different buttons, write down the button's name and its shortcut key, if applicable. [L2]

1. Start Word, if it is not already running.

2. Position the mouse pointer on the first toolbar button on the left-hand side.

3. If you don't see the shortcut key combination, (Ctrl)+(N), appear in the ScreenTip, right-click the button and choose Customize. Choose Show shortcut keys in ScreenTips and click Close.

4. Position the mouse pointer on the second button to identify its shortcut key combination.

5. Position the mouse pointer on the button that displays ABC with a blue check mark. What is the name of the button and what is its shortcut key combination?

6. Position the mouse pointer where you see Times New Roman on the Formatting toolbar to see its name and shortcut key combination.

7. Slowly move the mouse pointer over the Formatting toolbar buttons until you find the Italic button. What does it look like?

8. Exit from Word if you need to end your work session.

3. Creating and Saving a Document

You need to compose the main part of a letter to new club members. You decide to use Word to create and save the document. [L4]

1. Start Word if it is not already running.

2. Type the following text:

   On behalf of the members of the Association for Technical Trainers, I want to welcome you to the club. We have many special activities planned to focus on training and technology issues. I am confident you will enjoy them.

3. Choose File, Save As to display the Save As dialog box.

4. In the Save in drop-down list, select where you want to save the file.

5. Type Welcome in the File name text box.

6. Click Save in the bottom right corner of the dialog box.

7. Press ↵Enter twice after the paragraph and type the following paragraph:

   The next club meeting will feature a presentation by Mario Landow, the vice president of Technology Training Innovations. Please call Cammie Nelson at 555-2340 by next Friday to RSVP. I look forward to seeing you soon!

8. Click the Save button on the Standard toolbar to save the modified document using the Welcome filename.

9. Click the Print button on the Standard toolbar to print one copy of the document without displaying the Print dialog box.

10. Click the Document Close button (on the far right side of the menu bar) to close the document.

11. Press Ctrl+N to start a new Word document and continue with the next exercise.

4. Create and Save a Document with a Different Filename

You need to compose a short note to your two primary supervisors telling them that you need to come in later on Friday because you have a special test in the morning. You create the first note, save it, change the supervisor's name, and save the document with a new filename. [L4]

1. Type Dear Ms. Turner: and press ↵Enter twice.

2. Type the following paragraph:

   This Friday I have a special test in my history class at the local community college. This test is scheduled during a specific time, which is controlled by the instructor. I would appreciate being able to come in to work at 11:30 instead of my usual 8:30 time. Thank you for working with my college class schedule.

3. Press ↵Enter twice and type your name.

4. Choose File, Save As.

5. Click the Save in drop-down arrow and choose the appropriate drive in which you have been instructed to save documents.

6. Type Turner Note in the File name text box.

7. Click Save to save the document.

8. Choose File, Print, and then click OK to print the document.

9. Click to the left of Ms. Turner on the first line.

10. Press Del until you have deleted her name.

11. Type Mr. Baxter for your other supervisor's name. Make sure there is still a colon after the name.

12. Choose File, Save As, so you can assign a new name to the modified document.

13. Make sure the correct drive is displayed in the Save in option. Change it if necessary.

14. Type Baxter Note in the File name text box and click Save.

15. Choose File, Print, and then click OK to print the document.

16. Choose File, Close to close the document. Choose File, Exit if you need to exit Word now. Leave Word open if you are continuing with the next exercise.

⟨?⟩ 5. Using the Help Index

You want to continue searching topics in the Help Index and then print a Help topic. [L6]

1. Click the Office Assistant if it's displayed. If it's not displayed, choose Help, Show the Office Assistant and then click it.

2. Click the Options button to display the Office Assistant dialog box.

3. Click the Use the Office Assistant check box to deselect it. Then click OK.

4. Press F1 to display the Microsoft Word Help window.

5. Click the Index tab in the Navigation pane.

6. Type **save** and click the Search button.

7. Read about the first topic.

8. Scroll through the topic to continue reading information about saving documents.

9. Click the Close button in the top right corner of the Microsoft Word Help window to close it.

10. Continue working in Word if you wish to complete the next exercise, or choose File, Exit to close Word.

6. Closing Documents and Exiting Word

You want to see what happens when you choose different options when closing an unsaved document. [L7]

1. Click the New Blank Document button on the Standard toolbar or press Ctrl+N. Then type your name.

2. Choose File, Close.

3. Click No when you are asked if you want to save the changes.

4. Type your name, press Enter, and type your instructor's name.

5. Choose File, Close.

6. Click Cancel to go back to the document without saving or closing it.

7. Double-click the Control menu box in the top left corner of the title bar.

8. Click No when prompted to save the document.

You have exited Word and should be back to the Windows desktop.

Challenge 💡

Challenge exercises expand on or are somewhat related to skills presented in the lessons. Each exercise provides a brief narrative introduction, followed by instructions in a numbered step format that are not as detailed as those in the Skill Drill exercises.

1. Creating, Modifying, Saving, and Printing a Letter

You want to write a short note to your word processing instructor to let him or her know your goals for learning Microsoft Word. Use Figure 1.22 as a guide for the format. [L3–7]

To create your note, follow these steps:

1. Type today's date and press Enter four times.

2. Type your instructor's name and address on separate lines. Press Enter twice after the address.

3. Type the greeting, press Enter twice, and type a first paragraph about yourself.

4. Save the document as **Introduction**.

5. Type a second paragraph that describes why you are learning Word. Then complete the rest of the letter with a complimentary closing and your name.

6. Save the modified document as `Introduction Letter for Instructor`.

7. Print the document and close it.

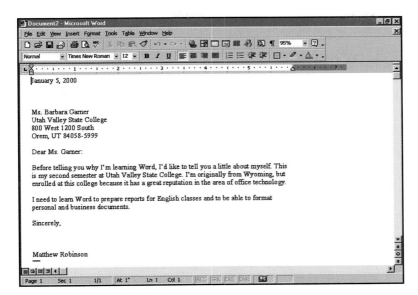

Figure 1.22
Use this sample letter
to format your letter.

2. Creating a Study Guide

You want to create a study guide of some terms introduced in Project 1.

1. Use Figure 1.23 to create and format your name, project reference, and first three definitions. Press Tab‡ between the terms and the definitions to make sure the definitions line up.

2. Save the document as `Project 1 Study Guide`.

3. Type the remaining terms and definitions and save the study guide with the same filename.

4. Print your document and close it.

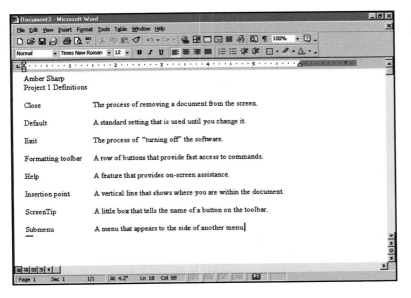

Figure 1.23
Create this study guide.

[?] **3. Using Help Contents**

The Help Contents section provides general topics to get users started with Word. You want to learn about scrolling.

    1. Access onscreen Help.

    2. Scroll through the options and select scrolling topics.

    3. Read about scrolling and click the links to learn about specific options.

    4. Close Help when you're done.

[?] **4. Printing a Help Topic**

As a student, you know that you'll be printing many rough drafts of assignments and research papers. You might want to know how to print more than one page on each sheet of paper. Use onscreen Help to learn about this type of printout.

    1. From a new document window, press `F1`.

    2. Use any of the Help features to find information on how to `print two pages on one page` and then choose the `Print a two-page document on one page` option.

    3. Use the Print button within Microsoft Word Help to print the Help topic.

    4. Exit onscreen Help.

    5. Close the document. Exit Word if you want to end your work session.

Discovery Zone

Discovery Zone exercises require advanced knowledge of topics presented in *Essentials* lessons, application of skills from multiple lessons, or self-directed learning of new skills.

[?] **1. Displaying Other Toolbars**

You read that Word contains more than the Standard and Formatting toolbars. Ask the Answer Wizard in Help how to display other toolbars. After reading the information, display the Reviewing toolbar. Then hide the Reviewing toolbar.

[?] **2. Saving a File with a Password**

You need to create a highly confidential document. You want to save the document so the user must enter a password to open the document. Use the Help Index or Office Assistant to find out how to save a document with a password. Print the specific step-by-step help instructions. Then test the procedure by typing a sentence and saving it with a password.

[?] **3. Learning About Shortcut Keys**

One of your friends firmly believes that using keyboard shortcuts improves her ability to create and format documents faster than using the Menu Bar and the Toolbars. You want to learn some of the keyboard shortcuts. Use the Help Contents to find out about function keys and keyboard shortcuts. Follow the instructions to print a list of the shortcut keys. After you print the document, use the Save shortcut and save the document as `Shortcuts` on your data disk. Then close it. Exit Word.

Working with a Document

Objectives

In this project, you learn how to

➤ **Open an Existing Document**

➤ **Display Formatting Marks**

➤ **Scroll in a Document**

➤ **Select Text**

➤ **Delete and Change Text**

➤ **Insert Text**

➤ **Change View Modes**

➤ **Create an Envelope**

Key terms in this project include

- AutoComplete
- formatting marks
- Full Screen view
- hard return
- Insert mode
- inside address
- Normal view
- opening
- Overtype mode
- Print Layout view
- salutation
- scrolling
- selecting
- WYSIWYG
- zoom

Why Would I Do This?

I n Project 1, "Getting Started with Word", you learned how to create, save, print, and close a document. You will often need to access a previously created document and modify it. This is one of the best features of a word processing program; you can start a document, save what you've written so far, and return to modify it at a later date. No more first, second, or third drafts on a typewriter! For example, you might be working on a business proposal for a client. Because the proposal evolves over time, you can add to and modify the existing document until you complete it.

In this project, you learn how to open the Campaign Letter document you created in Project 1 and modify it to produce a letter. You also learn the different ways you can view your document with Word's viewing options and the advantages of each view.

Visual Summary

Figure 2.1 shows the letter you will create in this project.

Figure 2.1
Your completed letter will look like this.

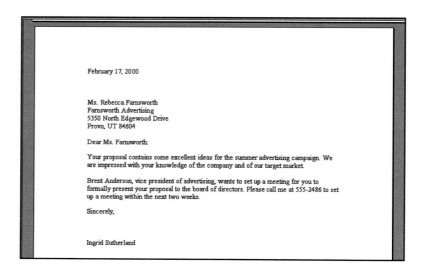

Figure 2.2 shows the envelope you will create in this project.

Figure 2.2
You will also create an envelope for the letter.

Lesson 1: Opening an Existing Document

One of the greatest benefits of using a computer is the ability to save documents and then use them again later. Using documents previously created saves valuable time in retyping and reformatting the document.

Opening is the process of displaying a previously saved document. After you open a document, you can make changes, add new text, format text, save, and print it.

To Open an Existing Document

1 **If Word is not already running on your system, start the program as described in Project 1.**

 2 **Click the Open button on the Standard toolbar.**
The Open dialog box appears, as shown in Figure 2.3. Notice that it looks similar to the Save As dialog box you saw when you saved a document in Project 1.

Click to see list of drives

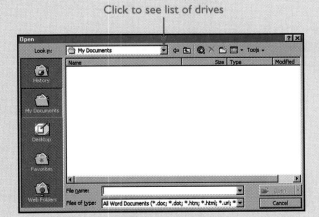

Figure 2.3
Use the Open dialog box to display a previously saved file.

> **Displaying the Open Dialog Box**
> You can also display the Open dialog box by choosing File, Open, or by pressing Ctrl+O.

3 **Click the arrow to the right of the Look in box.**
The Look in list is identical to the Save in list you saw in Project 1. It lists the available storage drives, such as 3 1/2 Floppy (A:).

4 **Choose the drive that contains your data files for this class.**

> If you don't know which drive contains your data files, ask your instructor where the files are located.
>
> If you are trying to access files from a data disk and your screen displays the message The selected drive is not in use. Check to make sure a disk is inserted, make sure your disk is fully inserted into its proper drive.

continues ▶

To Open an Existing Document (continued)

⑤ Double-click the Project I folder, and then click `Campaign Proposal` **in the file list to select it.**

⑥ Click Open.
Word accesses the document from your disk and displays it in a document window. The filename `Campaign Proposal` appears on the title bar (see Figure 2.4).

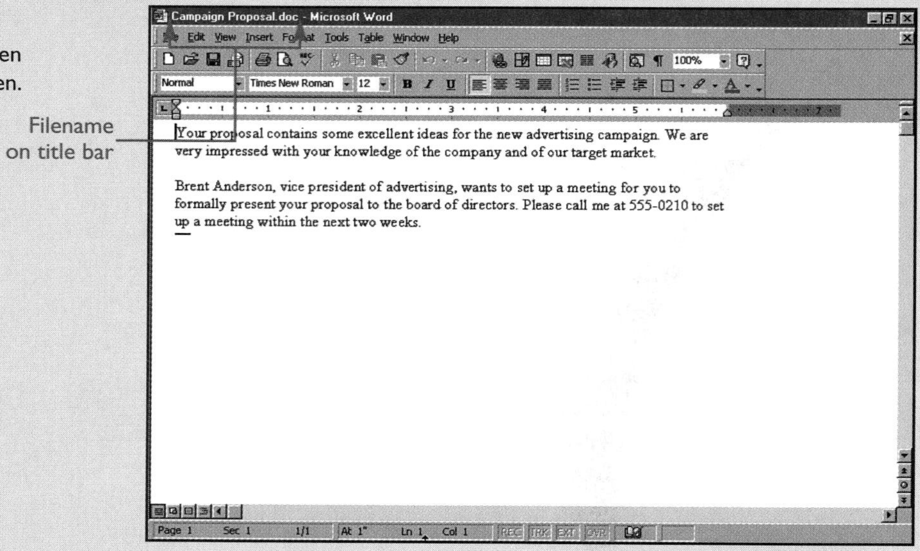

Figure 2.4
Your document is open and displayed onscreen.

Filename
on title bar

⑦ Keep the document onscreen to continue with the next lesson.

ⓘ Opening Recently Used Files
The File menu lists the last four documents that have been used on your computer. If this menu lists the name of the document you want to work with, you can choose it from the menu to open that document. If the current disk does not contain the file, you see an error message.

Lesson 2: Displaying Formatting Marks

The document on your screen looks basically like what its printout looks like. This is known as "what you see is what you get" (**WYSIWYG**). Usually, you see exactly what you've done to format your document. However, this is not always true. For example, you might not know at a glance whether you pressed Tab or Spacebar to indent text. In the short run, either method might not be a problem. However, the spacing might look different if you print your document on a different system.

To help you see how your document is formatted, you can display formatting marks. **Formatting marks** are nonprinting symbols and characters that indicate spaces, tabs, and hard returns. A **hard return** is where you press ↵Enter to start a new line instead of letting Word wrap text to the next line. Table 2.1 shows the main formatting marks and what they indicate.

Table 2.1   Formatting Marks

Symbol	Description
·	space
→	tab
¶	end of paragraph

To Show and Hide Formatting Marks

1 Click the Show/Hide ¶ button on the Standard toolbar.

You now see formatting marks within your document, as shown in Figure 2.5. Although these marks display onscreen, they do not appear in your printed document.

Click to display or hide the formatting marks

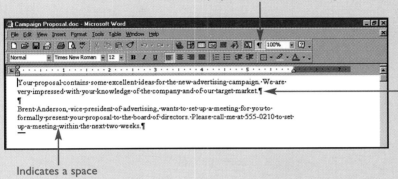

Figure 2.5
Display formatting marks to help you see how a document is formatted.

Indicates the end of a paragraph

Indicates a space

2 Position the insertion point on the blank line between the paragraphs.

3 Press Tab↹. You now see a right arrow, or tab mark, between the paragraphs, as shown in Figure 2.6.

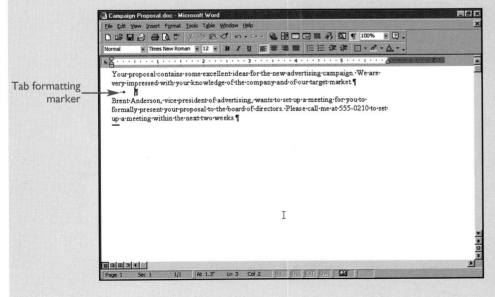

Tab formatting marker

Figure 2.6
The formatting mark for a tab looks like an arrow.

continues ▶

To Show and Hide Formatting Marks   (continued)

4 Press ⊕Backspace to delete the tab marker.

5 Keep the document onscreen to continue with the next lesson.
You don't need to save the document, because you returned it to its original format after deleting the tab marker.

Displaying Formatting Marks
If you don't see all three types of formatting marks, you need to display the Options dialog box to change the default. To view all formatting marks, click Tools on the menu bar and choose Options. When the Options dialog box appears, click the View tab and then click the All check box in the Formatting marks section. Click OK to close the dialog box.

Lesson 3: Scrolling in a Document

To make changes and corrections quickly and easily, you need to know the various ways of **scrolling**, or moving around in a document. For example, you can use either the mouse or the keyboard to move the insertion point in Word. Table 2.2 shows useful keyboard shortcuts for moving around in a document.

Table 2.2   Keyboard Shortcuts for Working in a Document

Key(s)	Moves the Insertion Point
←	one character to the left
→	one character to the right
↑	up one line
↓	down one line
Home	to the beginning of the line
End	to the end of the line
PgUp	up one window or page
PgDn	down one window or page
Ctrl + Home	to the beginning of the document
Ctrl + End	to the end of the document
Ctrl + ←	one word to the left
Ctrl + →	one word to the right
Ctrl + ↑	up one paragraph
Ctrl + ↓	down one paragraph
Ctrl + PgUp	to the top of the previous page
Ctrl + PgDn	to the top of the next page

The Campaign Proposal file should be open on your screen. In the next lesson, you practice scrolling through the letter using both the mouse and the keyboard.

To Scroll Through the Document

1 **Press** Ctrl+End **to move the insertion point to the end of the document.**

2 **Position the mouse pointer between the space marker and the word** proposal **on the first line in the first paragraph; then click the left mouse button.**

When the mouse pointer is shaped like an I-beam, click within the document to place the insertion point at that location. This is a fast way of positioning the insertion point when you want to add new text within an existing paragraph.

3 **Press** Ctrl+↓ **to position the insertion point on the blank line between paragraphs.**

4 **Press** Ctrl+↓ **again to position the insertion point at the beginning of the next paragraph.**

Paragraph Marks and Scrolling

Each paragraph formatting mark indicates the end of a paragraph. Even blank lines caused by hard returns are treated as paragraphs. This is why Word places the insertion point on the blank line between text paragraphs when you press Ctrl+↓.

5 **On the vertical scrollbar, click the down scroll arrow two times.**

Clicking items, such as the down scroll arrow or the up scroll arrow, on the vertical scrollbar does not move the insertion point. Using the vertical scrollbar merely lets you see different parts of the document. The insertion point remains where you last positioned it (see Figure 2.7).

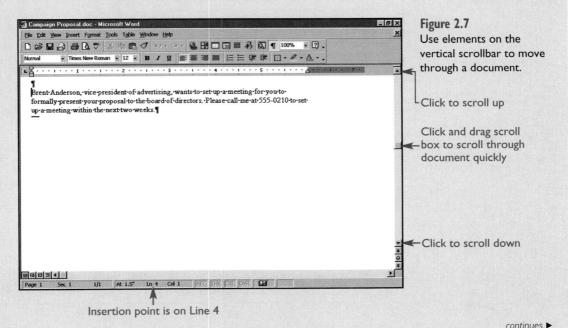

Figure 2.7
Use elements on the vertical scrollbar to move through a document.

Click to scroll up

Click and drag scroll box to scroll through document quickly

Click to scroll down

Insertion point is on Line 4

continues ▶

To Scroll Through the Document   (continued)

6 Click and drag the scroll box to the top of the vertical scrollbar. You can now see the top of your document again.

7 Press Ctrl+Home to move the insertion point to the top of the document. Take a minute now to practice some of the other keyboard shortcuts that are listed in Table 2.2.

In most cases, you save changes to your document before continuing to the next lesson. Because you just practiced scrolling in the document, you don't need to save the document because no changes were made.

8 Keep the document onscreen to continue with the next lesson.

Using the Vertical Scrollbar

You can click the Previous Page button or the Next Page button to move the insertion point to the beginning of the previous page or the beginning of the next page, respectively.

The vertical scrollbar is extremely helpful when scrolling in a multiple-page document. When you click and drag the scroll box, you see a ScreenTip that tells you what page you'll see when you release the mouse button. See Figure 2.8 for an example of a page ScreenTip.

Figure 2.8
Drag the scroll box or use the Previous Page or Next Page buttons to move through your document.

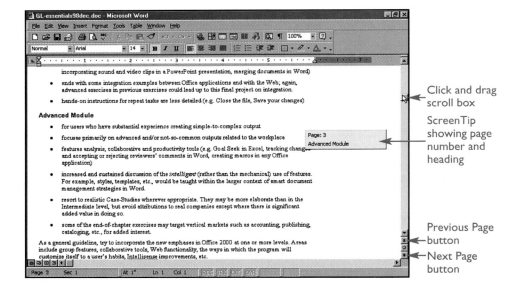

Using the Go To Option

You can move the insertion point to a specific location using the Go To option in the Find and Replace dialog box. Click Edit, Go To, or press Ctrl+G to display the Go To options. See Figure 2.9 for an example of the Go To options.

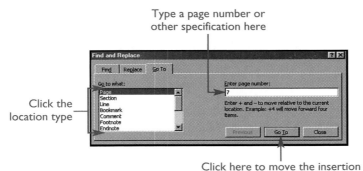

Type a page number or
other specification here

Click the
location type

Click here to move the insertion
point to the new location

Figure 2.9
Use the Go To option to
specify where you want to
quickly position the insertion
point.

Lesson 4: Selecting Text

Making changes to a Word document is a simple process, especially when you can select text to change it. For example, you might want to delete an entire sentence or group of sentences. Instead of deleting characters one by one with (+Backspace) or (Del), you can select and delete text.

Selecting is the action of defining a section of text so you can do something to it, such as delete or format it. When you select text, Word displays it in white with a black background. In this lesson, you learn how to select text.

To Select Text

① Double-click the word proposal in the first paragraph to select it and the space after it.

 Selecting by Clicking in the Left Margin
You can also select text by clicking in the left margin area when you see a right-pointing arrow. Click once to select the current text line. Double-click to select the current paragraph, and triple-click to select the entire document.

② Press and hold down (Ctrl); then click anywhere in the first sentence of the first paragraph.
This action selects the entire sentence, along with any additional blank spaces after the period.

③ Triple-click anywhere inside the first paragraph.
This action selects the entire paragraph, including the hard return at the end of the paragraph (see Figure 2.10).

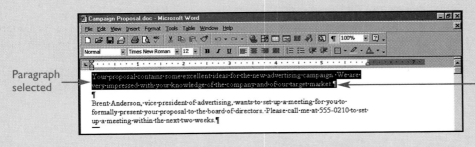

Paragraph
selected

Figure 2.10
Triple-clicking selects the
entire paragraph.

Paragraph formatting
mark selected

continues ▶

To Select Text (continued)

 If the paragraph is not selected, make sure you click three times in quick succession and that you don't move the mouse as you click.

4 **Click anywhere inside the document window to cancel the current selection and return the text to normal.**

5 **Click at the beginning of the document and hold down the mouse button while you drag the mouse down to the middle of the second paragraph. Then release the mouse button.**
Clicking and dragging is a fast way to select a specific block of text, as shown in Figure 2.11.

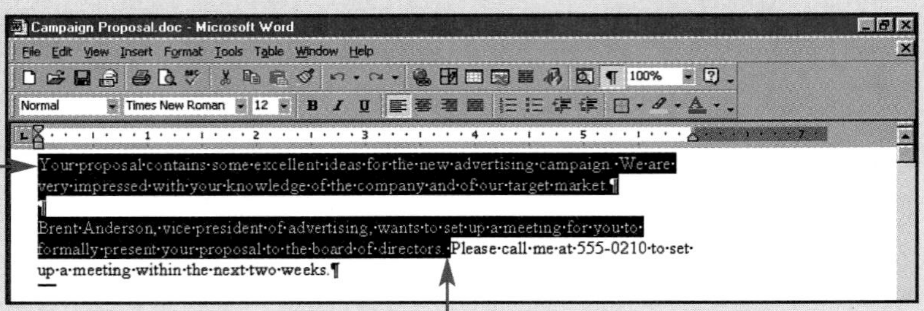

Figure 2.11
Click and drag to select specific blocks of text.

Start clicking and dragging here—

Drag down to here

6 **Click in the document window to deselect the text.**

7 **Keep the document onscreen to continue with the next lesson.**

 If you click and drag too fast, you might end up selecting too much text. If this happens, try this method instead of clicking and dragging: click at the point where you want to start selecting text, press and hold down ⬆Shift), and click at the point where you want to end the selected text. This selects from the insertion point to the place where you ⬆Shift)+click.

Selecting Text with the Keyboard
You can also use the arrow keys on the keyboard to select text. You might find this method more convenient when selecting a small section of text or if you prefer to keep your hands on the keyboard. First, you position the insertion point where you want to start selecting text. Press ⬆Shift) and then use the arrow keys to select text. Release ⬆Shift) to end the selection. Press any arrow key to turn off the selection.

If you want to select the entire document, press Ctrl)+A).

Lesson 5: Deleting and Changing Text

As you read the first draft of your letter, you may decide that you don't like the way a particular sentence sounds, or you may find that you have simply entered the wrong information. Word lets you delete text you don't want, enter new text, and correct existing text. In this lesson, you learn how to make basic corrections to text in a document.

To Delete and Change Text

1 **In Campaign Proposal, double-click the word new on the first line of the first paragraph.**
You want to replace the word new with summer.

2 **Type summer.**
When you select text and type new text, the new text replaces the selected text.

3 **Position the insertion point at the beginning of the word very in the second sentence of the first paragraph.**

4 **Press Ctrl+Del to delete the word to the right of the insertion point.**

> **ⓘ Deleting Text**
> You can delete the word to the left of the insertion point by pressing Ctrl+Backspace. To delete larger sections of text, select the text first; then press Del.

5 **Position the insertion point before the first 0 in the phone number.**
This phone number is incorrect. You need to replace it with the correct phone number.

6 **Double-click the OVR indicator on the status bar (see Figure 2.12).**
The OVR indicator turns darker. You are now in the **Overtype mode**, which overwrites (or replaces) existing text as you type new text.

7 **Type 2486 to insert the correct phone number and replace the old number, as shown in Figure 2.12.**

make sure to get rid of it / OVR

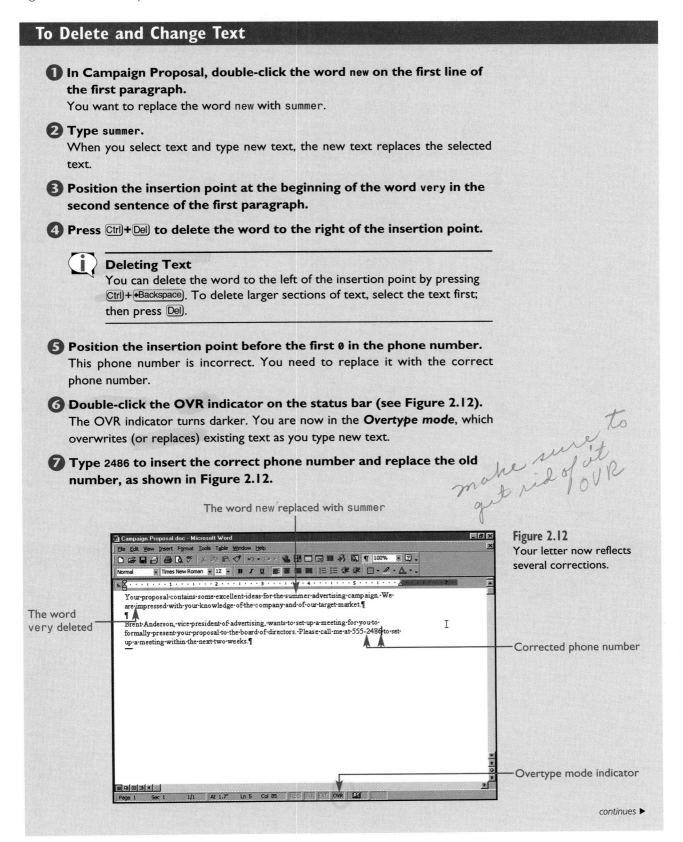

The word new replaced with summer

The word very deleted

Corrected phone number

Overtype mode indicator

Figure 2.12
Your letter now reflects several corrections.

continues ▶

To Delete and Change Text   (continued)

 If you forget to turn off the Overtype mode, you might accidentally delete text and replace it with other text, instead of simply inserting new text. Double-click the OVR indicator or press ⌊Insert⌋ to turn off the Overtype mode.

8 **Double-click the OVR indicator to return to the Insert mode.**

9 **Choose F̲ile, Save A̲s.**

10 **Type** Campaign Proposal Letter **in the File n̲ame text box and click S̲ave.**
You have just saved the changes with a new name, Campaign Proposal Letter. Leave the document onscreen to continue with the next lesson.

 Insert and Overtype Modes
In addition to clicking OVR on the status bar, you can press ⌊Insert⌋ on the keyboard to toggle between the Insert and Overtype modes.

Lesson 6: Inserting Text

In the last lesson you learned to turn on the Overtype mode and type over existing text. The default mode is the **Insert mode**, which lets you insert new text within existing text. Word inserts new text at the insertion point's location and the existing text makes room for the new text as you type it.

Now that you corrected the paragraphs, you need to insert other elements to complete the letter. You need to insert the date at the top of the letter, along with the **inside address**, the address of the person who will receive the letter. You also need to insert the **salutation**, otherwise known as the greeting, and the closing.

To Insert Text

1 **In Campaign Proposal Letter, press** ⌊Ctrl⌋+⌊Home⌋ **to move the insertion point to the beginning of the first paragraph in the document.**

2 **Choose I̲nsert, Date and T̲ime.**
This option displays the Date and Time dialog box (see Figure 2.13). The dialog box shows sample dates and times. Your dates and times are probably different. You can choose from a variety of date and time formats for practically any situation. A check box at the bottom of the dialog box lets you insert a date or time that automatically updates each time you open the document. Use this type of date when creating form documents, such as memos, fax cover sheets, and invoices, so the document reflects the date on which you create it.

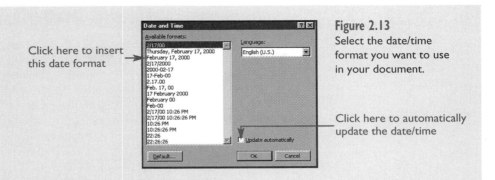

Figure 2.13
Select the date/time format you want to use in your document.

Click here to insert this date format

Click here to automatically update the date/time

For this letter, choose the format that spells out the name of the month, followed by the numeric day, followed by a four-digit year (for example, February 17, 2000).

3 **Double-click the date format to add the date to your letter.**

4 **Press ⏎Enter four times to add blank lines between the date and inside address.**

5 **Type the following text, pressing ⏎Enter once after each line:**

```
Ms. Rebecca Farnsworth
Farnsworth Advertising
5350 North Edgewood Drive
Provo, UT 84604
```

Word moves the existing paragraphs down to make room for the new lines of text you are inserting. Your letter should look like Figure 2.14.

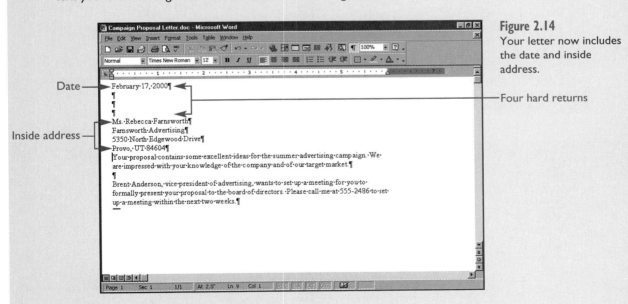

Figure 2.14
Your letter now includes the date and inside address.

Date

Four hard returns

Inside address

6 **Press ⏎Enter again to leave one blank line between the inside address and the salutation.**

7 **Type Dear Ms. Farnsworth: and press ⏎Enter twice.**
You should now have one blank line between the salutation and the first line of the first paragraph.

continues ▶

To Insert Text (continued)

 Using the Letter Wizard
The Office Assistant might appear, asking if you want help to create the letter. If you ask for more help, the Office Assistant starts the Letter Wizard, which helps you create letters and gives you a variety of formats from which to choose. For example, you can choose letter formats, recipient information, and letter design by selecting from the Letter Wizard options. If you don't want to use the Letter Wizard, click Cancel to finish the letter yourself.

8 Press Ctrl+End and press ↵Enter twice to move the insertion point to the end of the letter.

9 Type Sincerely, and then press ↵Enter four times to allow enough room to sign your printed letter.

10 Type your name.
The letter is now complete. Compare your letter with the one in Figure 2.15.

Figure 2.15
The completed letter to Ms. Farnsworth should look like this.

Blank line above and below salutation

Blank line between last paragraph and closing

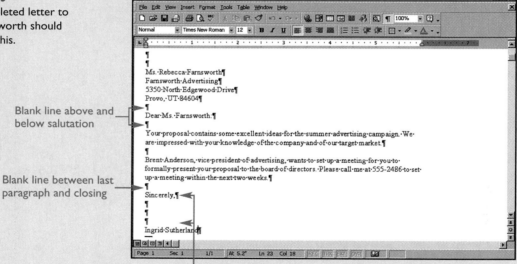

Four hard returns after closing

11 Click the Save button to save the changes. Keep the letter onscreen as you continue with the next lesson.

 Using the AutoComplete Feature
If you start typing the current date, you see a ScreenTip that displays the full date, such as March 15, 2000. When you see this ScreenTip and press ↵Enter, Word automatically completes the date for you. This feature, known as *AutoComplete*, helps complete other text as well.

Use the Help feature to learn how to create your very own AutoComplete entries to save typing time. For example, you can create an AutoText entry that completes your name when you start typing it.

Lesson 7: Changing View Modes

When you work with a document, you might want to adjust how it appears on the screen. For example, you can adjust the document to display the layout with the margins; or you can maximize the amount of screen space devoted to seeing text. In addition, you can adjust how the spacing or size of the characters appears on your screen without changing the size of the printed characters. This lesson teaches you how to use view options to focus on particular elements of your document, such as layout or text.

The default view option is **_Normal_**, which shows text without displaying space for margins, page numbers, or other supplemental text. Normal view is appropriate when you are simply typing and editing text and want to use the screen space for displaying text without seeing the margins.

To Change View Options

1 **Press** Ctrl+Home **to move your insertion point to the top of the document.**

2 **Click the Show/Hide ¶ button on the Standard toolbar to turn off the formatting marks.**

3 **Click the Print Layout View button to the left of the horizontal scrollbar.**
Print Layout view shows you what the document will look like when it's printed. This view shows margin space, graphics locations, headers, footers, and page numbers. Although your document does not contain headers, footers, or page numbers, you can look at the margins (see Figure 2.16). If needed, change the Zoom percentage to 88%.

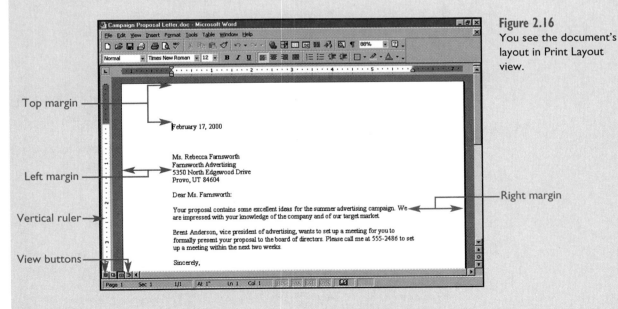

Figure 2.16
You see the document's layout in Print Layout view.

4 **Click the Normal View button to change back to the regular view.**
Although you can see more text in Normal view, you still want to see more text on your screen.

continues ▶

To Change View Options   (continued)

⑤ Choose View and click the down arrows at the bottom of the menu to display the full View menu.

⑥ Choose Full Screen.

Full Screen view uses the entire screen to display the document text, as shown in Figure 2.17. In this view, you don't see the title bar, menu bar, toolbars, or other Word elements.

Figure 2.17
You can see a lot more text with the Full Screen view.

Title bar and other bars not displayed

Click to close Full Screen view and display bars

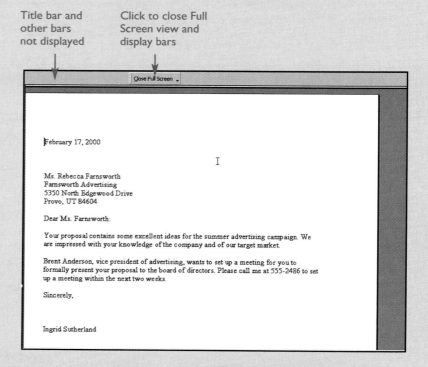

⑦ Click Close Full Screen or press Esc to close the Full Screen view.

ⓘ Working in the Full Screen view
Although you can't see the menu bar, you can still access the menus. Simply press Alt and the hotkey to display the desired menu. For example, press Alt+V to display the View menu.

The keyboard shortcut for closing the Full Screen view is Alt+C.

⑧ Click the arrow to the right of the Zoom box.

You see the *Zoom* menu (see Figure 2.18). This menu lets you choose the magnification percentage of your document on the screen.

Figure 2.18
Select a zoom option for displaying the document on your screen.

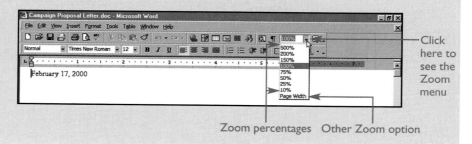

Click here to see the Zoom menu

Zoom percentages   Other Zoom option

9 Choose 150%.

The document is now displayed at 150% of its regular screen size, as shown in Figure 2.19. Changing the zoom does not, however, change the size of the text when it is printed.

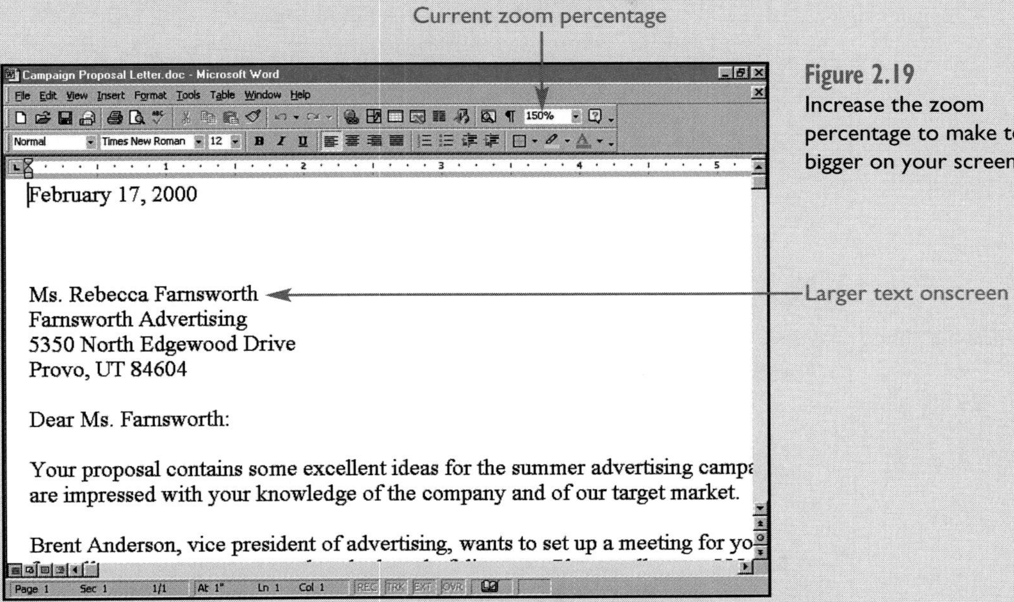

Current zoom percentage
Campaign Proposal Letter.doc - Microsoft Word
File Edit View Insert Format Tools Table Window Help
150%
Normal
Times New Roman
12
February 17, 2000
Ms. Rebecca Farnsworth
Farnsworth Advertising
5350 North Edgewood Drive
Provo, UT 84604
Dear Ms. Farnsworth:
Your proposal contains some excellent ideas for the summer advertising campa
are impressed with your knowledge of the company and of our target market.
Brent Anderson, vice president of advertising, wants to set up a meeting for yo
Page 1 Sec 1 1/1 At 1" Ln 1 Col 1 REC TRK EXT OVR
Larger text onscreen

Figure 2.19
Increase the zoom percentage to make text bigger on your screen.

10 Click the arrow to the right of the Zoom box again and choose 100%.

11 Click the Print button on the Standard toolbar to print the document.

12 Keep the document on the screen to continue with the next lesson.

Using the Zoom Dialog Box

While the Zoom menu gives you several percentages and options to choose from, you might want to magnify your document at a different percentage. To do this, choose View, Zoom. The Zoom dialog box provides preset options and a Percent option that allows you to specify the exact magnification (see Figure 2.20).

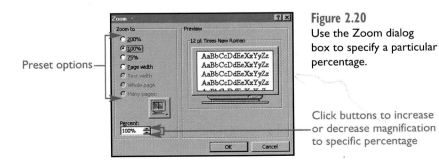

Preset options
Zoom
Zoom to
200%
100%
75%
Page width
Text width
Whole page
Many pages:
Percent:
100%
Preview
12 pt Times New Roman
AaBbCcDdEeXxYyZz
AaBbCcDdEeXxYyZz
AaBbCcDdEeXxYyZz
AaBbCcDdEeXxYyZz
OK
Cancel
Click buttons to increase or decrease magnification to specific percentage

Figure 2.20
Use the Zoom dialog box to specify a particular percentage.

Using Zoom Options
When you select the Print Layout view, you can select Whole Page or Two Pages from the Zoom menu. Viewing the whole page or two pages is nice because it allows you to see the overall layout, such as spacing and margins. These options are not available when you use the Normal view.

Lesson 8: Creating an Envelope

You have a printed copy of your letter, but you still need an envelope to mail it. You can use Word's Envelope feature to quickly create and print an envelope for your letter. The Envelope feature creates the address from the existing letter and lets you select the envelope type and other options. In this lesson, you create and print an envelope for the `Campaign Proposal Letter` that is displayed on your screen.

To Create an Envelope

1 **Choose Tools, Envelopes and Labels.**
The Envelopes and Labels dialog box appears, as shown in Figure 2.21. Word copies the inside address from your letter to the Delivery address section in the dialog box.

Figure 2.21
Select the options you want to create an envelope for your letter.

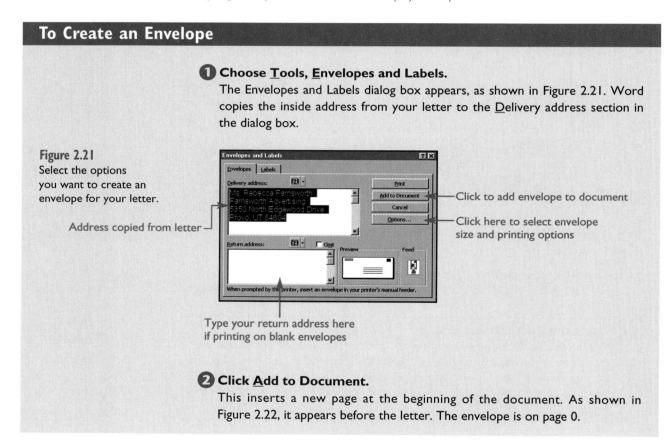

Address copied from letter —

Click to add envelope to document
Click here to select envelope size and printing options

Type your return address here if printing on blank envelopes

2 **Click Add to Document.**
This inserts a new page at the beginning of the document. As shown in Figure 2.22, it appears before the letter. The envelope is on page 0.

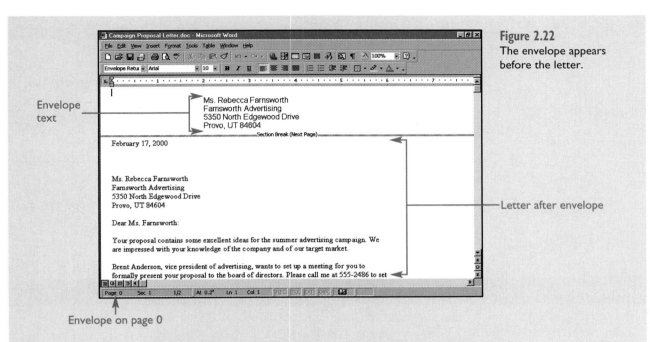

Figure 2.22
The envelope appears before the letter.

Envelope text

Ms. Rebecca Farnsworth
Farnsworth Advertising
5350 North Edgewood Drive
Provo, UT 84604

Letter after envelope

Envelope on page 0

3 **Click the Print Layout View button to the left of the horizontal scrollbar.**

4 **Click the Zoom drop-down arrow and choose 50%.**
The envelope text now looks like it's placed on an envelope onscreen (see Figure 2.23).

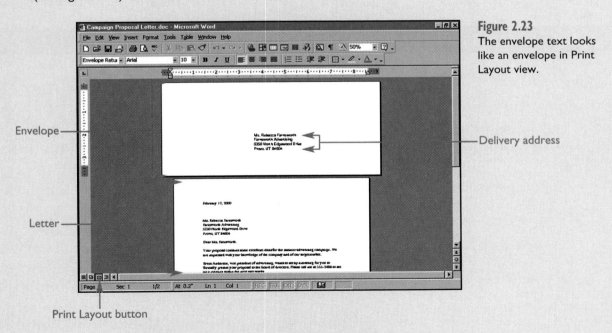

Figure 2.23
The envelope text looks like an envelope in Print Layout view.

Envelope

Delivery address

Letter

Print Layout button

5 **Click the Save button on the Standard toolbar.**
You have now saved the envelope settings as part of the document.

6 **Click File, Print to display the Print dialog box.**

continues ▶

To Create an Envelope (continued)

7 **Click the Current page option button. Then click OK.**
You will probably see a message instructing you to manually insert the envelope into the printer. Ask your instructor for assistance if needed. If you don't have an envelope to print on, simply insert a regular sheet of paper into the printer.

 Creating Envelopes
You can select a variety of envelope options by clicking Options in the Envelopes and Labels dialog box. For example, you can select a different envelope size, add a bar code, and specify how you want to insert the envelope into the printer.

Summary

In this project you learned some very important word processing tasks. You learned how to open a document you previously saved and how to efficiently navigate through it. You also learned how to select, insert, and delete text to edit your document. In addition, you learned how to change the view options to see your document from different perspectives. Finally, you created an envelope in which to mail your letter.

To expand your knowledge and skills, look up these topics in Help. You'll find additional information to make you more proficient in using each of these features.

Checking Concepts and Terms

True/False

For each of the following, check *T* or *F* to indicate whether the statement is true or false.

__T __F **1.** The process of selecting a drive to open a file is about the same as selecting a drive on which to save a file. [L1]

__T __F **2.** If you print a document when the formatting marks are displayed, the formatting marks also print. [L2]

__T __F **3.** Pressing and holding down ⬇ is just as efficient for moving the insertion point to the end of a document as pressing Ctrl+End. [L3]

__T __F **4.** Triple-clicking the mouse selects the current sentence. [L4]

__T __F **5.** To delete the word to the left of the insertion point, press Ctrl+◆Backspace. [L5]

__T __F **6.** The only way to turn on the Overtype mode is to double-click OVR on the status bar. [L5]

__T __F **7.** If you want to add new text in the middle of a paragraph, make sure the Insert mode is active before typing the additional text. [L6]

__T __F **8.** Normal view shows more of your document onscreen than the Print Layout view does. [L7]

__T __F **9.** Even if you display the Envelopes and Labels dialog box when a letter is displayed onscreen, you must type in the delivery address yourself. [L8]

__T __F **10.** Envelope text looks more like it appears on an envelope in Print Layout view than in Normal view. [L8]

Multiple Choice

Circle the letter of the correct answer for each of the following.

1. What feature would you use to adjust the percentage of how much of a document displays onscreen? [L7]
   a. Print Layout
   b. Zoom
   c. Full Screen
   d. Normal view

2. Which menu lists the most recently used documents? [L1]
   a. Edit
   b. Format
   c. Open
   d. File

3. How can you move the insertion point to the beginning of the previous page? [L3]
   a. press Ctrl+PgUp
   b. press PgUp
   c. click the Previous Page button below the vertical scrollbar
   d. either a or c

4. Why would you use the Date and Time dialog box to insert the date or time? [L6]
   a. You can choose from a variety of formats.
   b. You can select an option to update the date the next time you open the file.
   c. Using the dialog box might be faster than typing a full date, such as Saturday, January 29, 2000.
   d. all of the above

5. What option would be the most efficient for moving the insertion point from page 3 of your document to the top of page 12? [L3]
   a. Press Ctrl+PgDn nine times.
   b. Click the Next Page button nine times.
   c. Display the Go To dialog box, type 12, and click the Go To button.
   d. Press ↓ repeatedly until you're on page 12.

6. What method selects the current sentence? [L4]
   a. Double-click the sentence.
   b. Triple-click the sentence.
   c. Press Ctrl while clicking the sentence.
   d. Position the mouse in the left margin and click by the sentence.

7. Which formatting mark indicates a space? [L2]
   a. ¶
   b. →
   c. Δ
   d. ·

8. If you want to delete the word to the right of the insertion point, what should you do? [L5]
   a. Press Ctrl+Del.
   b. Press Ctrl+◆Backspace.
   c. Triple-click and press Del.
   d. all of the above

9. If you are in the Overtype mode, you can double-click _____ onscreen to toggle back to the Insert mode. [L6]
   a. Insert
   b. OVR
   c. Normal View
   d. the Next Page button

10. When you create an envelope from a letter onscreen, what part of the Envelopes and Labels dialog box is filled in automatically from the letter? [L8]
    a. the Return address
    b. Options
    c. the Delivery address
    d. all of the above

Screen ID

Label each element of the Word screen shown in Figure 2.24.

Figure 2.24

A. Next Page button

B. Normal View button

C. Preview Page button

D. Print Layout View button

E. scroll-down arrow

F. scroll-up arrow

G. vertical scroll box

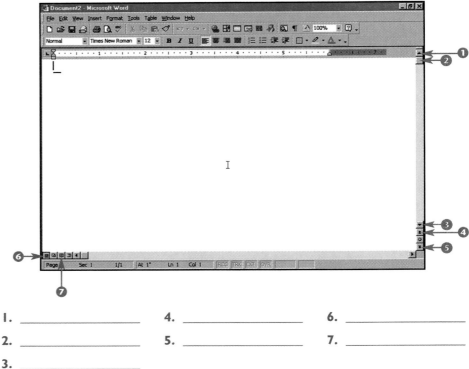

1. _____   4. _____   6. _____

2. _____   5. _____   7. _____

3. _____

Discussion Questions

1. What is the purpose of displaying the formatting marks? Provide an example of when you should have the formatting marks displayed.

2. Explain why a person should know and use both the keyboard and the mouse for scrolling. When would

it be more advantageous to use the keyboard for scrolling?

3. What is the purpose of the Overtype mode? Why should you turn it off when you are finished using it?

Skill Drill

Skill Drill exercises reinforce project skills. Each skill reinforced is the same, or nearly the same, as a skill presented in the project. Detailed instructions are provided in a step-by-step format.

1. Opening a Document

You know you can perform the same tasks with different methods. Because you want to learn the different methods and see which you like best, you decide to practice some of the different ways to open a document. [L1]

1. Press Ctrl+O to display the Open dialog box.

2. Type A: and press ↵Enter to display the contents on your data disk.

3. Double-click the Project 1 folder, and then click WD1-0201 and press ↵Enter to open the document.

4. Choose File, Save As, type Chambers Letter in the File name box. Click OK.

5. Choose File, Close to close the document.

6. Choose File and look at the bottom of the menu.

7. Choose A:\Chambers Letter from the bottom of the menu.

8. Leave the document onscreen as you continue to the next exercise.

2. Displaying Formatting Marks

A relative told you that she learned to insert two spaces between sentences in her typing class back in the early 80s. You know that modern standards say that it's acceptable to have only one space. Because you just learned how to use the formatting marks, you want to see the difference. [L2]

1. With Chambers Letter displayed, click the Show/Hide ¶ button on the Standard toolbar.

2. Click between the first and second sentences in the first paragraph.

3. Press Spacebar to add another space.

4. Press ←Backspace to delete the extra space.

5. Click to the left of the date.

6. Press ↵Enter ten times to insert ten paragraph marks.

7. Turn off the formatting marks.

8. Save the document and keep it on the screen to continue to the next exercise.

3. Scrolling in a Document

Before you start working on longer documents, you decide to review different ways of scrolling in a document. [L3]

1. With Chambers Letter onscreen, press Ctrl+Home to move the insertion point to the beginning of the document.

2. Click and drag the scroll box until the ScreenTip shows Page: 1; then release the mouse button.

3. Click the Previous Page button.

4. Click the Next Page button.

5. Press Ctrl+End to move the insertion point to the end of the document.

6. Press Ctrl+G to display the Go To option.

7. Type 0 in the Enter page number box, click Go To, and then click Close.

8. Click at the beginning of the first paragraph in the letter.

9. Press Ctrl+↓ twice to move the insertion point to the beginning of the second paragraph.

10. Leave the document on the screen to continue to the next exercise.

4. Selecting and Changing Text

You want to use the same letter to send to someone else. Instead of typing a new letter, you decide to select and delete the original envelope and select and replace the inside address and salutation. [L4–5]

1. With Chambers Letter onscreen, select the entire inside address.

2. Type the following new address while the old address is selected.

   Mr. Aaron Chambers
   McClure and Associates
   305 West Main Street
   Toledo, OH 43615

3. Select Ms. Farnsworth in the salutation; then type Mr. Chambers.

4. Click the Normal View button to the left of the horizontal scrollbar.

5. Position the mouse pointer in the left margin. The mouse pointer is an arrow pointing to the right.

6. Click and drag to select the envelope, including the lines that mention the section break. Press [Del] to delete the entire envelope page.

7. Click to the right of the hyphen in the phone number.

8. Double-click the OVR mode on the status bar, type **7356**, and double-click the OVR mode again.

9. Save the document and keep it onscreen to continue to the next exercise.

5. Inserting Text

After reading the letter, you decide to insert additional text using the Insert mode. [L6]

1. With Chambers Letter onscreen, click to the left of `vice president` in the second paragraph.

2. Type **senior** and press [Spacebar].

3. Click at the beginning of the second paragraph.

4. Type the following paragraph.

   `As you are probably aware, we're expecting`
   `sales from the summer campaign to generate`
   `a 25 percent increase over last summer's`
   `campaign. The economy is very favorable,`
   `and we have a lot of new products to hit`
   `the market.`

5. Press [↵Enter] twice after the paragraph to have a blank line between paragraphs.

6. Click to the left of `economy` and type `regional`. Make sure you have a space before and after the new word.

7. Click to the left of the date and press [Ctrl]+[Del] four times to delete the date. Don't delete any hard returns.

8. Choose Insert, Date and Time

9. Click the third format and click OK.

10. Click the Save button on the Standard toolbar and keep the document on the screen to continue to the next exercise.

6. Viewing the Document

You want to review view options to look at the overall format and to adjust the magnification onscreen. [L7]

1. With Chambers Letter onscreen, click the Print Layout View button to the left of the horizontal scrollbar.

2. Choose View, Zoom to display the Zoom dialog box.

3. Click the Percent increment button to 125% and click OK.

4. Click the Normal View button to the left of the horizontal scrollbar.

5. Click the Zoom drop-down arrow and choose 75%.

6. Keep the document onscreen to continue to the next exercise.

7. Creating an Envelope

You are satisfied with the letter. Now you need to create an envelope for it.

1. Choose Tools, Envelopes and Labels.

2. Click the Add to Document button.

3. Save the document with the envelope.

4. Print the envelope and letter.

5. Close the document.

Challenge

Challenge exercises expand on or are somewhat related to skills presented in the lessons. Each exercise provides a brief narrative introduction followed by instructions in a numbered step format that are not as detailed as those in the Skill Drill section.

1. Editing Radio Ad Copy

To publicize a new business, you have created a radio advertisement that will air on a local station. You now need to open that document and improve it by inserting, deleting, and changing the text. [L5–6]

1. Open WD1-0202 and save it as Ad Copy.
2. Insert the title Radio Advertisement at the top of the document. Leave one blank line between the title and the first paragraph.
3. Delete the extra word all in the second sentence of the first paragraph.
4. Change the phone number in the second paragraph to 555-4431.
5. Change East to North in the second paragraph.
6. Add your name and company name below the last paragraph. Leave one blank line between the last paragraph and your name.
7. Save the document and print it.

2. Creating a Personal Envelope

You and a friend at another college like to exchange newspaper clippings from your college papers. To save time addressing envelopes, you decide to create an envelope and print it several times. [L8]

1. Display the Envelopes and Labels dialog box from a blank document window.
2. Type your name and address in the Return Address section.
3. Type your friend's address in the Delivery Address section.
4. Add the envelope to the document. The envelope page should be the only page in the document.
5. Save the envelope as Friend Envelope.
6. Print three copies of the envelope.

3. Editing a Memo

You composed a memo to inform employees about a new parking rule. You need to open it and make a few changes before sending it out. [L1–2, 4–6]

1. Open WD1-0203 and save it as Parking Memo.
2. Use the Date and Time dialog box to insert today's date in the correct location. Use the format that provides the day of the week with the full date.
3. Insert your name on the From line.
4. Display the formatting marks and insert tabs to tab between the date heading and the actual date in the memo heading. Insert tabs for the rest of the items in the heading. Line up the information in the second column by adding additional tabs if needed.

ıst efficient method for changing **8:30** to **8:45**.

ost efficient method, delete the last sentence in the memo.

deleted sentence with this sentence: `Please do your best to follow lines.`

6. Save the document, print it, and close it.

4. Letter Requesting Donations from Retail Store

You belong to a campus organization. Your organization is sponsoring a track meet for underprivileged children in your area. As president of the organization, you are responsible for writing letters to local retail stores to solicit donations for the event. You would like to receive cash and food donations. The money will help defray the cost of sponsoring the event, and the food donations will help your members prepare a cookout after the event. [L6, 8]

1. From a blank document window, insert the date and the following inside address:

```
Mr. John Davis
Fresher Groceries, Inc.
344 NW First
Racine, WI 53402
```

2. Insert and correctly format the salutation.

3. Type a three-paragraph letter that describes what your organization is sponsoring and the type of donations you seek. End with a statement showing appreciation for any donation the retailer might provide.

4. Include an appropriate closing with your name. Type your organization name on the line below your typed name.

5. Save the document as `Donation Letter`.

6. Create an envelope without a return address. Insert the envelope in the document.

7. Save the document and print both the envelope and the letter.

5. Researching Help Topics

The software trainer at your company has asked you to help her answer questions for some of the staff. You decide to use the Help Index to assist you in finding the answers.

1. Display the Help Index and search for `select`. Answer these questions:

- How do I select a sentence with the mouse?
- How do I select a large block of text with the mouse?
- What is the keyboard shortcut for turning on the extend mode for selecting text?
- What is the keyboard shortcut for turning off the extend mode?

2. Print the Help topic about selecting with the keyboard.

3. Close the Help Index when you're done.

[?] 6. Using the Office Assistant to Research View Options

You have used the view options to look at your documents from different perspectives. You want to learn more about these and other view options.

1. Display the Office Assistant and ask it: **What are view options?**

2. Choose the first option, **Different ways to view a Word document**. Follow the prompts to click the topics to learn about each view option. Print the Help topics if necessary.

3. In Word, compose one paragraph about each of the following view options based on what you learned from Help. Do not copy the wording exactly from Help. Paraphrase the information.

   - Print Layout view
   - Web Layout view
   - Normal view
   - Outline view
   - Web Page view
   - Print Preview

4. Save your document as **View Options**, print it, and close it.

Discovery Zone

Discovery Zone exercises require advanced knowledge of topics presented in *Essentials* lessons, application of skills from multiple lessons, or self-directed learning of new skills.

[?] 1. Writing a Letter Using Letter Wizard

You need to write a letter to welcome new members to your campus organization. Choose File, New and click the Letters & Faxes tab. Then double-click the Letter Wizard and tell the Office Assistant that you want to send one letter. Follow the wizard to set the formats. Use the following guidelines:

- Contemporary page design
- Semi-block letter style
- Business Salutation

Insert the name and address of a classmate. When the wizard is finished, compose the letter. Describe the purpose of your organization, the members, and plans for the year.

Save the letter as **Welcome Letter** and print it. Edit your rough-draft letter by noting what you need to delete, change, and insert. Then use the features discussed in this project to edit the letter. Save the letter again and print the final copy.

[?] 2. Creating a Document for the Web

Many students are creating personal Web pages about themselves. Some of your friends even have Web pages that advertise some part-time work they do, such as painting, typing, and so on. You decide you want to have a personal Web page by the end of the month.

Create a short document about yourself. Think of a part-time job you can do to earn extra money. After learning more about Word, you might consider computer training for other students. Save your document as `Personal Web Page`.

Use Help to learn about Web Page Preview and then preview your document in this mode. With the document viewed through Internet Explorer, save the document as a Web page (html extension) under the name `Personal Web Page`. Both versions are saved, each with a different extension.

[?] 3. Creating a Small Envelope with a Bar Code

One of your college professors said he would mail your final grade to you if you provide a self-addressed stamped envelope. You only have 6 1/2" x 3 5/8"-sized envelopes.

Create the envelope in the Envelopes and Labels dialog box. Use your name and address in the Delivery Address section and your professor's name and address in the Return Address section. Use Help to learn how to insert a bar code on the envelope. Also refer to Help about changing the envelope size. Make these adjustments before adding the envelope to your document. Save the document as `College Instructor Envelope` and print the envelope.

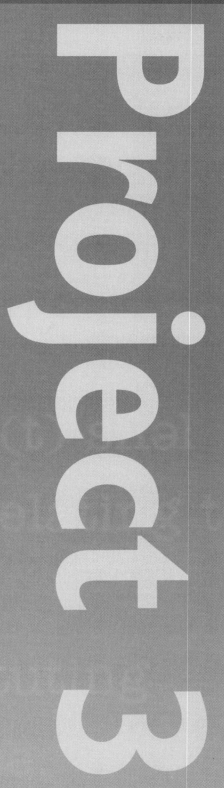

Editing a Document

Objectives

In this project, you learn how to

- ➤ **Enhance Text**
- ➤ **Copy Formats with Format Painter**
- ➤ **Change the Case of Text**
- ➤ **Move and Copy Text**
- ➤ **Use the Undo Feature**
- ➤ **Use AutoCorrect**
- ➤ **Correct Spelling Errors**
- ➤ **Correct Grammatical Errors**
- ➤ **Select Synonyms**

Key terms introduced in this project include

- ■ action
- ■ AutoCorrect
- ■ casing
- ■ copy
- ■ cut
- ■ Format Painter
- ■ heading
- ■ object
- ■ Office Clipboard
- ■ paste
- ■ redo
- ■ synonym
- ■ text enhancements
- ■ Undo feature

Why Would I Do This?

In the last project, you used basic editing techniques such as deleting and inserting text. You are now ready to learn additional editing tasks to improve your document. In this project, you learn how easy it is to change the appearance of your text by adding bold, italic, and underlining. You also learn how to change the color of your text to add emphasis and draw the reader's eye to specific parts of your document. You also learn that it's just as easy to correct errors, move text around in your document, and improve the spelling, grammar, and word choices. Completing these tasks improves your document's appearance and communicates your ideas more clearly. In this project, you improve the appearance and correct errors in a status report.

Visual Summary

Figure 3.1 shows the unformatted document that contains errors.

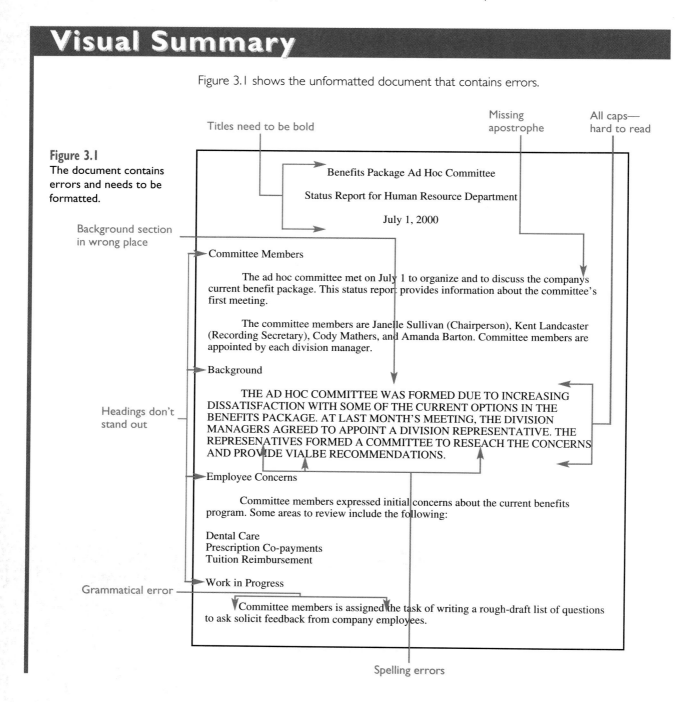

Figure 3.1
The document contains errors and needs to be formatted.

Titles need to be bold

Missing apostrophe

All caps—hard to read

Background section in wrong place

Headings don't stand out

Grammatical error

Spelling errors

Benefits Package Ad Hoc Committee

Status Report for Human Resource Department

July 1, 2000

Committee Members

The ad hoc committee met on July 1 to organize and to discuss the companys current benefit package. This status report provides information about the committee's first meeting.

The committee members are Janelle Sullivan (Chairperson), Kent Landcaster (Recording Secretary), Cody Mathers, and Amanda Barton. Committee members are appointed by each division manager.

Background

THE AD HOC COMMITTEE WAS FORMED DUE TO INCREASING DISSATISFACTION WITH SOME OF THE CURRENT OPTIONS IN THE BENEFITS PACKAGE. AT LAST MONTH'S MEETING, THE DIVISION MANAGERS AGREED TO APPOINT A DIVISION REPRESENTATIVE. THE REPRESENATIVES FORMED A COMMITTEE TO RESEACH THE CONCERNS AND PROVIDE VIALBE RECOMMENDATIONS.

Employee Concerns

Committee members expressed initial concerns about the current benefits program. Some areas to review include the following:

Dental Care
Prescription Co-payments
Tuition Reimbursement

Work in Progress

Committee members is assigned the task of writing a rough-draft list of questions to ask solicit feedback from company employees.

Figure 3.2 shows the same document after you format it and correct errors.

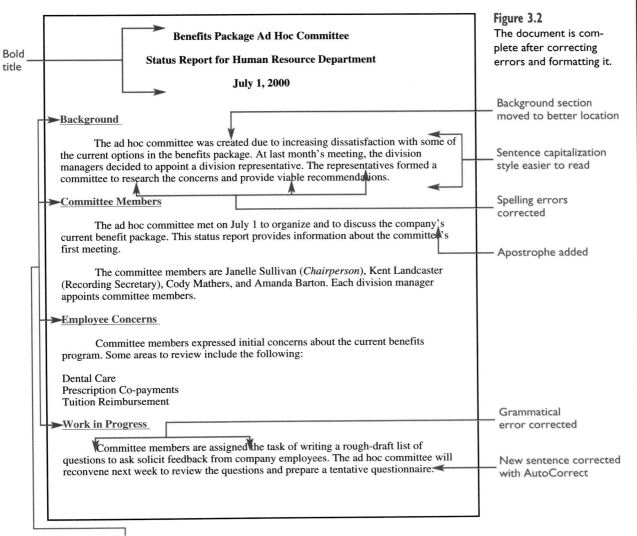

Bold title

Figure 3.2
The document is complete after correcting errors and formatting it.

Benefits Package Ad Hoc Committee

Status Report for Human Resource Department

July 1, 2000

Background section moved to better location

Background

The ad hoc committee was created due to increasing dissatisfaction with some of the current options in the benefits package. At last month's meeting, the division managers decided to appoint a division representative. The representatives formed a committee to research the concerns and provide viable recommendations.

Sentence capitalization style easier to read

Committee Members

Spelling errors corrected

The ad hoc committee met on July 1 to organize and to discuss the company's current benefit package. This status report provides information about the committee's first meeting.

Apostrophe added

The committee members are Janelle Sullivan (*Chairperson*), Kent Landcaster (Recording Secretary), Cody Mathers, and Amanda Barton. Each division manager appoints committee members.

Employee Concerns

Committee members expressed initial concerns about the current benefits program. Some areas to review include the following:

Dental Care
Prescription Co-payments
Tuition Reimbursement

Grammatical error corrected

Work in Progress

Committee members are assigned the task of writing a rough-draft list of questions to ask solicit feedback from company employees. The ad hoc committee will reconvene next week to review the questions and prepare a tentative questionnaire.

New sentence corrected with AutoCorrect

Headings stand out with bold, underline, and color

Lesson 1: Enhancing Text

In the last project, you learned how easy it is to select and delete text. In addition to deleting selected text, you can also enhance the appearance of selected text by adding bold, italic, or underlined formatting.

You use **text enhancements** to emphasize ideas as well as improve readability and clarity. Additionally, some reference manuals specify that you italicize or underline certain items, such as book titles in bibliographic entries.

To Enhance Text

① **Open** WD1-0301 **and save it as** Benefits Status Report. **Click the Show/Hide ¶ button to display the nonprinting symbols.**
Word displays wavy red and green lines below potential spelling and grammatical errors, respectively. Ignore those for now; you correct them later in this project.

② **Click and drag to select the three lines in the title at the top of the document.**
The title is centered between the left and right margins. You learn to center text in Project 4, Formatting Documents.

B **③** **Click the Bold button on the Formatting toolbar.**
The title is now bold, so it stands out from the regular text. After bolding the title, you need to deselect it.

④ **Click outside the title to deselect it.**
Notice how boldface text differs from regular text (see Figure 3.3).

Figure 3.3
Use buttons on the Formatting toolbar to add enhancements to your text.

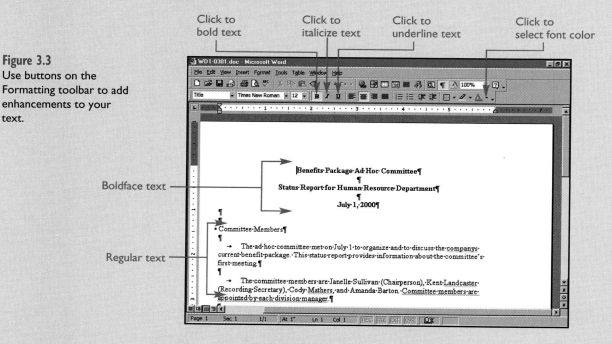

⑤ **Select** Chairperson **in the second paragraph so you can emphasize it by adding italics.**

 ⑥ **Click the Italic button on the Formatting toolbar.**

> **ⓘ** **Using Bold and Italic**
> Although both bold and italic formatting is used to emphasize text, use bold for stronger emphasis and italic for lesser emphasis.

7 **Select the first heading,** `Committee Members`**.**
A *heading* is a descriptive word or phrase placed between sections to help readers understand the organization of your document. Many reference manuals suggest you bold and underline these headings so they stand out.

8 **Click the Bold button.**
The heading is now bold. You can now apply other enhancements, such as underlining, while the text is still selected.

 9 **Click the Underline button.**
You can also use color to enhance text, especially headings.

10 **Click the Font Color drop-down arrow on the Formatting toolbar.**
The Font Color palette appears (see Figure 3.4). It allows you to choose a color for the selected text. As you move your mouse over each color, you see a ScreenTip that tells you the exact color name, such as Blue, Light Blue, and Sky Blue.

> **X** If you click the Font Color button, you immediately apply the default color, which is the last color someone selected. If this happens, select your text and make sure you click the Font Color drop-down arrow to see the palette. The new color you choose replaces the previous color.

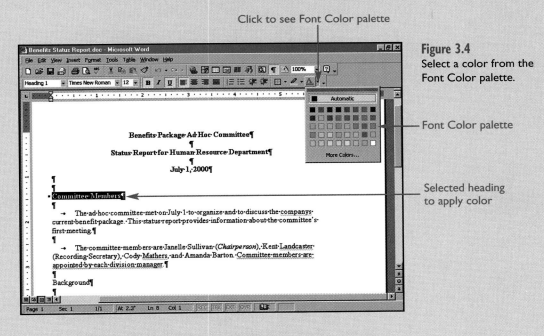

Click to see Font Color palette

Figure 3.4
Select a color from the Font Color palette.

— Font Color palette

— Selected heading to apply color

11 **Click Blue on the color palette to apply blue color to the selected heading; then deselect the text.**
The heading is now bold, underlined, and blue (see Figure 3.5).

continues ▶

To Enhance Text (continued)

Figure 3.5
Adding color to your text draws the reader's eye to specific places.

Text enhancements applied to heading →

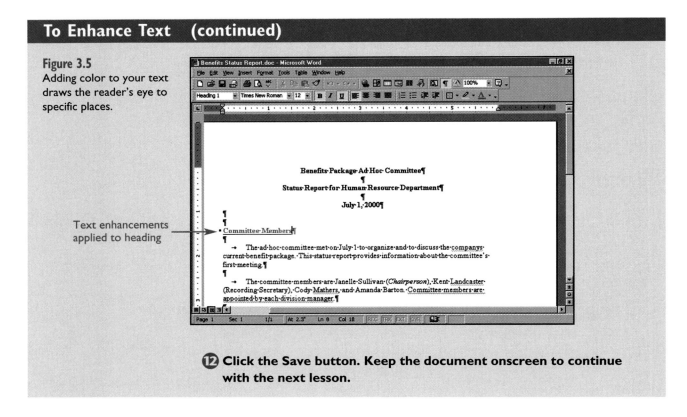

 Click the Save button. Keep the document onscreen to continue with the next lesson.

 Keyboard Shortcuts
The keyboard shortcuts are Ctrl+B for Bold, Ctrl+I for Italic, and Ctrl+U for Underline. You can use these keyboard shortcuts to enhance selected text or to turn these enhancement features on and off.

You can also find other text enhancement options in the Font dialog box, such as double underline, small caps, and engrave. The Font dialog box is covered in Project 4. Refer to Help for more information about the Font dialog box.

Lesson 2: Copying Formats with Format Painter

All similar headings within a document should have the same formatting. However, selecting every heading individually and clicking the desired format buttons (such as bold, underline, and font color) can be time-consuming. You also run the risk of missing a format and only discovering this after you've printed your document.

By using the **Format Painter**, you can copy existing text formats to ensure consistency. As an added bonus, using the Format Painter takes fewer mouse clicks to format text than formatting each instance individually. In this lesson, you use Format Painter to copy formats (bold, underline, and blue color) from the first heading to the other headings. You can also use Format Painter to copy formats within a paragraph.

Single- and Double-clicking the Format Painter Button
If you single-click the Format Painter button, you can copy the formats only one time; then Word turns off Format Painter.

If you double-click the Format Painter button, you can continue formatting additional text. To turn off Format Painter when you're done, click the Format Painter button once.

To Copy Formats Using Format Painter

1 **In the Benefits Status Report document, click anywhere inside the first heading, Committee Members.**
This lets Word know what formats you want to copy.

2 **Double-click the Format Painter button on the Standard toolbar.**
When you double-click the Format Painter button, the mouse pointer turns into a paintbrush next to the I-beam (see Figure 3.6). Be careful where you click and drag with the Format Painter turned on; Word immediately formats any characters you select.

Click inside formatted
text before turning
on Format Painter

Double-click to
turn on Format Painter

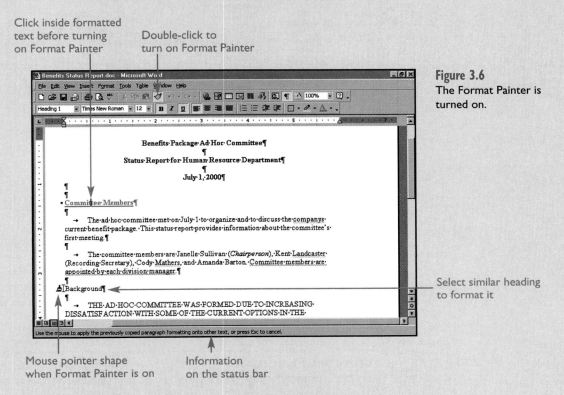

Figure 3.6
The Format Painter is
turned on.

Select similar heading
to format it

Mouse pointer shape
when Format Painter is on

Information
on the status bar

3 **Select the next heading, which is Background.**
The second heading now has the same text enhancements as the first heading. Using Format Painter saves you from having to click three separate buttons (Bold, Underline, and Font Color) to format the heading.

4 **Click the scroll-down arrow on the vertical scrollbar until you see the other two side headings, Employee Concerns and Work in Progress.**
You need to select these two headings to apply the text enhancements.

5 **Select Employee Concerns. Then select Work in Progress to apply the text enhancements to both of these headings.**
After formatting the last heading, turn off the Format Painter.

6 **Click the Format Painter button to turn off this feature.**

7 **Click outside the heading to deselect it.**
Your document headings are now formatted consistently (see Figure 3.7).

continues ▶

To Copy Formats Using Format Painter (continued)

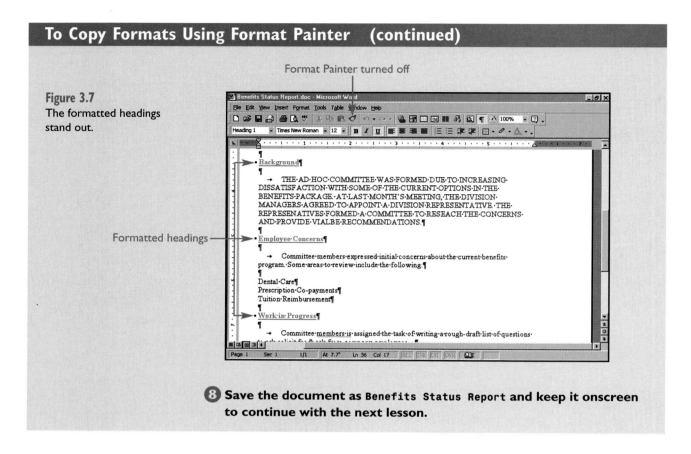

Format Painter turned off

Figure 3.7
The formatted headings
stand out.

Formatted headings

8 **Save the document as** Benefits Status Report **and keep it onscreen to continue with the next lesson.**

 Using Format Painter
Completely format a section of text with the text enhancements that you want. Make sure the insertion point is inside the formatted text before turning on the Format Painter. If the insertion point is elsewhere when you turn on the Format Painter, you might apply the wrong formats to other text.

 Formatting Paragraphs
You can also apply text enhancements within a paragraph, not just a heading.

If you think you might change your mind about text enhancements, create a paragraph style from a formatted heading. When you use styles instead of Format Painter, you can reformat one heading, and Word automatically reformats the other headings. Refer to Help for information about creating styles that update.

Lesson 3: Changing the Case of Text

It's frustrating to discover you've typed an entire paragraph (or more) in all capital letters before realizing you've forgotten to turn off Caps Lock! Instead of deleting and retyping everything you've worked so hard to type, you can select the text and change its *casing*, which is how the text is capitalized.

In this lesson, you realize that a full paragraph is capitalized. You need to change the casing of the text to be consistent with the other paragraphs.

To Change the Case of Text

❶ In the Benefits Status Report document, select the third paragraph. It is currently formatted in all capital letters.
You must select the text that you want to change to a different case.

❷ Choose Format, Change Case.

 If you don't see the Change Case option, position the mouse pointer on the downward pointing arrows at the bottom of the Format menu to see the full menu.

The Change Case dialog box appears (see Figure 3.8). Sentence case capitalizes only the first letter of each sentence. lowercase changes all selected text to lowercase letters. UPPERCASE changes all selected text to all capital letters. Title Case capitalizes the first letter of each word. tOGGLE cASE reverses the capitalization of selected text. For example, it changes uppercase letters to lowercase and lowercase letters to uppercase.

Figure 3.8
The Change Case dialog box contains options for changing the capitalization of selected text.

❸ Click Sentence case, and click OK.
Now only the first letter of each sentence is capitalized. After changing casing, you should read the text and individually capitalize the first letter of proper nouns.

❹ Deselect the paragraph.
Figure 3.9 shows how your paragraph should look after changing the case.

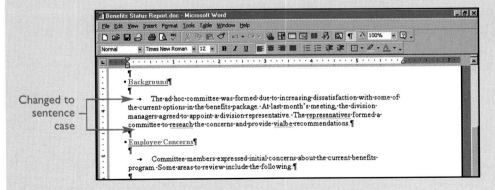

Changed to sentence case

Figure 3.9
The paragraph is no longer in all capital letters.

❺ Save the document and keep it onscreen to continue with the next lesson.

 Using Title Case
After you use the Title Case option from the Change Case dialog box on headings, you should lowercase small words, such as in and the in the middle of the heading.

Using Keyboard Shortcuts

You can press ⟨⬆Shift⟩+⟨F3⟩ to change selected text to uppercase, lowercase, or sentence caps. Keep pressing this shortcut to cycle through the casing options until your text appears in the casing you want.

To quickly change selected text to all capitals, press ⟨Ctrl⟩+⟨⬆Shift⟩+⟨A⟩.

Lesson 4: Moving and Copying Text

After you create a document, you might decide to rearrange sentences and paragraphs to improve the clarity and organization of the content. You might need to move a paragraph to a different location, rearrange the sentences within a paragraph, or move sentences from different paragraphs to form one paragraph.

The three main terms that describe moving and copying text are cut, copy, and paste. When you **cut** text, you remove it from its present location. When you **copy** text, you leave the original text in its current location and make a copy to put elsewhere. When you **paste** text, you insert the cut or copied text in the new location.

The **Office Clipboard** is an area in memory reserved for text and objects you cut and copy. An **object** is a non-text item, such as clip art, bar charts, and so on. When you cut or copy text or an object, the text or object stays on the Clipboard. You can then paste it repeatedly to different locations.

Using the Clipboard with Multiple Applications

The Office Clipboard is particularly helpful in copying items from one application, such as Excel, to another application, such as Word. In Project 8, "Integrating Information and Using Specialized Features," you learn how to copy Excel data into a Word document by using the Clipboard.

In this lesson, you move the `Background` section from its current location so that it's above the `Committee Members` section.

To Move and Copy Text

1 In the Benefits Status Report, make sure that you can see the nonprinting symbols.

2 Select the heading `Background`, the paragraph below it, and the paragraph symbol above `Employee Concerns`, as shown in Figure 3.10.

Click to cut selected text

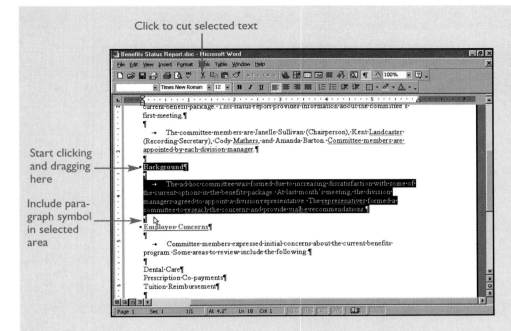

Start clicking and dragging here

Include paragraph symbol in selected area

Figure 3.10
The Background section, including its blanks lines, is selected.

  If you're having problems selecting this text, place the insertion point at the beginning of Background, and press Ctrl+⬆Shift+⬇ four times.

The Background section is selected, so you can move it. You must select text and any blank lines you want to cut or copy. Make sure the paragraph symbol between the paragraph and the next heading is selected.

✂ ❸ Click the Cut button.
The Background section disappears from the document. It is stored in the Office Clipboard.

❹ Position the insertion point to the left of C in the heading Committee Members.
After cutting or copying text, you need to place the insertion point where you want the text to appear. In this case, you want to place the Background section before the Committee Members section.

📋 ❺ Click the Paste button.
When you paste the Background section in its new location, the Committee Members section moves down to accommodate it (see Figure 3.11).

continues ▶

To Move and Copy Text (continued)

Figure 3.11
The section is pasted in its new location.

Background section pasted here

Existing text moves down

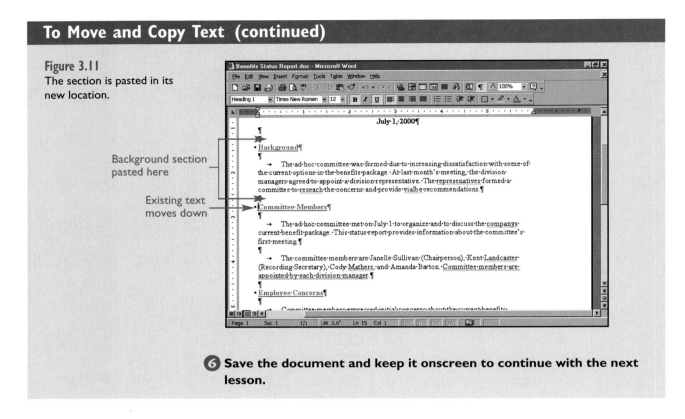

6 **Save the document and keep it onscreen to continue with the next lesson.**

Copying and Pasting Text
The steps for copying text are the same as those for cutting text. The only difference is that you click the Copy button instead of the Cut button. After copying text, position the insertion point where you want the copy to appear and then click the Paste button. The original text remains in place and a copy is created elsewhere.

In addition to using the Cut, Copy, and Paste buttons, you can use the following methods for moving and copying text:

- To move text, point inside the selected text and drag it to a new location. When you release the mouse button, the text is moved from its original location to the new location. If you hold down Ctrl while dragging, you copy the selected text rather than cut it.

- Press Ctrl+X to cut text, Ctrl+C to copy text, and Ctrl+V to paste text.

- Choose Cut, Copy, and Paste from the Edit menu.

- Right-click in the selected area to see a shortcut menu and then select Cut, Copy, or Paste.

You can cut or copy up to 12 items to the Office Clipboard. By default, when you click the Paste button, Word pastes the last item you cut or copied to the Office Clipboard. If you want to select a previous item in the Clipboard, you need to display the Clipboard toolbar by choosing View, Toolbars, Clipboard.

The Clipboard toolbar shows how many items are currently in the Office Clipboard. To see what an item is, position the mouse pointer on it to see the ScreenTip, as shown in Figure 3.12. (Your Clipboard might have different items than the one shown in the figure.)

Click an item to paste it at the insertion point location.

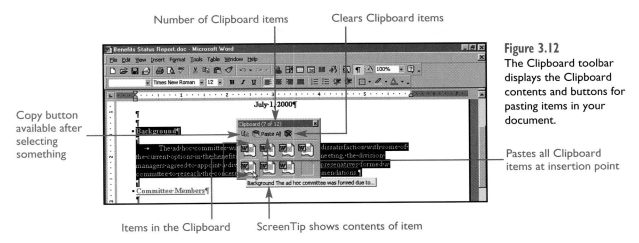

Number of Clipboard items

Clears Clipboard items

Copy button available after selecting something

Items in the Clipboard

ScreenTip shows contents of item

Figure 3.12
The Clipboard toolbar displays the Clipboard contents and buttons for pasting items in your document.

Pastes all Clipboard items at insertion point

Click the Paste All button to paste all of the Office Clipboard items at the insertion point location.

 Click the Clear Clipboard button to clear the items in the Office Clipboard.

Lesson 5: Using the Undo Feature

The **Undo feature** reverses actions you perform in a document. When you use Undo, Word reverses actions in sequential order, starting with the last action you performed. Clicking Undo again reverses the second-to-the-last action, and so on.

For example, assume you paste a paragraph in the wrong location. Using the Undo feature removes the pasted text. If you accidentally click the Underline button, using the Undo feature removes the underline. Undo works for almost every action you perform within a document—formatting, deleting, sorting, placing graphics, and so on. Some actions cannot be reversed with Undo, though. If you click the Save button instead of using Save As, you can't undo the saving process.

In this lesson, you "accidentally" delete a sentence in the first paragraph. You use Undo to restore the deleted text. In addition, you use Undo to remove underlining from a sentence.

To Undo Actions

1 **In the Benefits Status Report, position the insertion point in the first sentence in the first paragraph.**

2 **Press and hold** Ctrl **while clicking the first sentence.**
This is the sentence you "accidentally" delete.

3 **Press** Del**.**
The sentence is not in the Clipboard, because you deleted it instead of cutting it. Figure 3.13 shows the document after deleting the sentence.

continues ▶

To Undo Actions (continued)

Click the Undo button
to reverse actions

Figure 3.13
The sentence is deleted
from the paragraph.

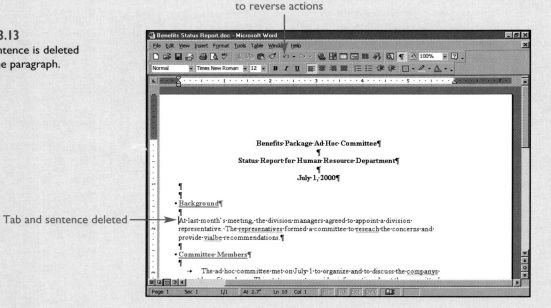

Tab and sentence deleted

 4 Click the Undo button on the Standard toolbar.

> (i) **Undo Keyboard Shortcut**
> The keyboard shortcut for undo is Ctrl+Z.

The Undo feature reserves your last action. In this case, your last action deleted a sentence. Clicking Undo undeletes the text, and it reappears in your document.

5 Select the first sentence, if it is not already selected, and click the Underline button to underline the sentence.

6 Deselect the sentence to see the underlined text.
You realize you accidentally clicked the Underline button.

7 Click the Undo button.
Undo reverses the last action by removing the underline from the selected text.

8 Because no changes were made to your document, you don't need to save it. Keep Benefits Status Report onscreen to continue with the next lesson.

 If Undo doesn't undelete the text or remove the underline, you probably performed another action on the document. Any change you make to the document, such as adding a space, is considered an **action**.

Undo List

Clicking the Undo button reverses the last action. If you need to restore previous actions, click the Undo button again. Each time you click the Undo button, you work backward, reversing actions you have taken.

You can reverse a series of actions by clicking the Undo drop-down arrow. When you select an action from the list, Word reverses the most recent actions including the one you select. Figure 3.14 shows that the last four actions will be undone.

Click to see list of actions

Select how many actions you want to reverse

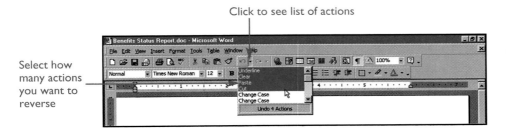

Figure 3.14
The Undo list lets you reverse the last several actions at one time.

If you decide you don't want to reverse an action after clicking the Undo button, click the **Redo** button to reverse the Undo action.

Lesson 6: Using AutoCorrect

AutoCorrect corrects errors "on the fly," which means it corrects errors as you type them. For example, it changes `teh` to `the`. It also corrects other types of errors, such as capitalization at the beginning of a sentence. It even helps you change manually-typed symbols to "real" symbols, such as changing :) to ☺. You can even insert AutoCorrect entries to change abbreviations to fully expanded text, such as changing `uvsc` to `Utah Valley State College`.

In this lesson, you type a sentence at the end of the document. Although you type it with errors, AutoCorrect will correct the errors for you.

To Use AutoCorrect

❶ In the Benefits Status Report, press `Ctrl`+`End` **and move the insertion point after the period and space after the last sentence.**

❷ Type `teh` **and press** `Spacebar`.
AutoCorrect changes `teh` to `The` when you press `Spacebar`. Notice that it also capitalizes the first letter of the sentence.

❸ Type `ad hoc comittee will reconvene next week to reveiw the questons and prepare a tenative questionaire.`
Your sentence should look like the one shown in Figure 3.15.

continues ▶

To Use AutoCorrect (continued)

Capitalized and corrected spelling

Figure 3.15
AutoCorrect corrects some spelling errors as you type them.

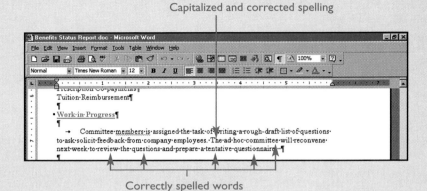

Correctly spelled words

Now let's look at AutoCorrect to see what words are detected and corrected for you.

4 **Choose Tools, AutoCorrect to display the AutoCorrect dialog box.**

 If you don't see AutoCorrect on the Tools menu, click the down-pointing arrows to display the full Tools menu.

5 **Click the scroll-down arrow on the right side of the dialog box to scroll through the list until you see committee in the second column.** The first column shows misspelled words, and the second column shows the correct spellings, as shown in Figure 3.16.

Figure 3.16
You can customize the changes AutoCorrect makes with the AutoCorrect dialog box.

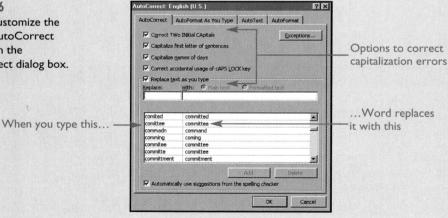

When you type this...

Options to correct capitalization errors

...Word replaces it with this

6 **Click OK to close the dialog box.**

7 **Save the document and keep it onscreen to continue with the next lesson.**

 Adding Entries
You can add words you typically misspell or abbreviations in AutoCorrect. Refer to onscreen Help for information on how to add and delete entries from AutoCorrect.

Lesson 7: Spell-checking a Document

Even the best typists and writers make mistakes. However, Word contains three proofing tools to help you correct errors. These tools are Spelling Checker, Grammar Checker, and Thesaurus. You learn about Spelling Checker in this lesson.

Word's spelling feature identifies potentially misspelled words, duplicate words, and irregular capitalization. You probably notice red wavy lines below words and phrases as you type. The red wavy lines indicate spelling errors and appear so you can correct them "on the fly," meaning that you can correct the errors as you type. If you prefer, you can keep typing and correct the errors later.

In this lesson, you correct spelling errors in the status report.

To Spell-Check a Document

1 In the Benefits Status Report document, right-click the word representatives in the first paragraph.
When you right-click a word that has wavy red underlines, Word displays a menu with possible corrections (see Figure 3.17).

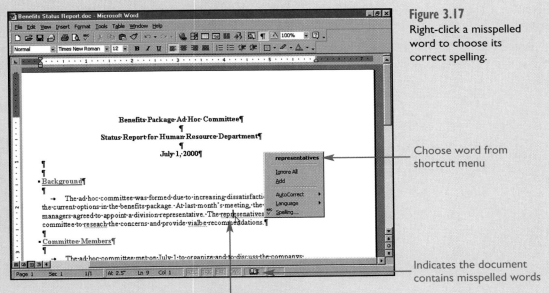

Figure 3.17
Right-click a misspelled word to choose its correct spelling.

Choose word from shortcut menu

Indicates the document contains misspelled words

Right-click on the word with wavy red lines

 The Spelling Icon on the Status Bar
The open book icon on the status bar lets you know if you have any spelling errors in your document. You see a red X if the document contains spelling errors or a red check mark if the document does not contain spelling errors. Double-click the icon to go to the misspelled word.

2 Choose representatives at the top of the shortcut menu.
Word replaces the original word with the replacement word you choose.

continues ▶

To Spell-Check a Document (continued)

3 **Right-click the word** reseach **and choose** research **from the shortcut menu.**

4 **Right-click the word** vialbe **and choose** viable.

5 **Right-click the word** companys.
You have three options (see Figure 3.18). Read the sentence to determine which suggestion is correct.

Figure 3.18
Choose the correct option on the shortcut menu.

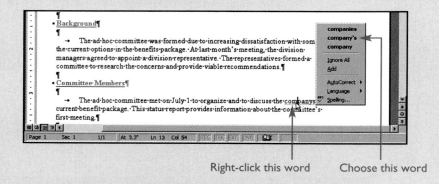

Right-click this word   Choose this word

6 **Choose** company's **from the shortcut menu.**

7 **Right-click** Landcaster **in the next paragraph.**
Landcaster is spelled correctly. However, this name is not listed in Word's dictionary. Either you can ignore the word by choosing Ignore All, or you can add the word to a custom dictionary.

8 **Choose Ignore All.**
Word skips all occurrences, if there are any others, of Landcaster in the current document. However, it marks Landcaster if you type it in other documents.

9 **Right-click** Mathers **and choose Ignore All.**

10 **Save the document and keep it onscreen to continue with the next lesson.**

 Spelling and Grammar Dialog Box
If you want more options than the shortcut menu offers, you can use the full Spelling and Grammar dialog box. To do this, choose Tools, Spelling and Grammar. The Spelling and Grammar dialog box opens and shows the misspelled word and possible replacements (see Figure 3.19). Click the correct replacement word; then click Change.

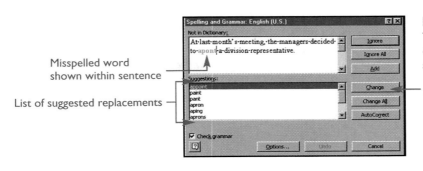

Figure 3.19
The Spelling and Grammar dialog box provides additional options.

Misspelled word shown within sentence

List of suggested replacements

Click to replace word with highlighted suggestion

Refer to Help for more information about the Spelling and Grammar dialog box.

Proofreading Is Essential
Although Word can help detect misspelled words for you and make it easy to correct them, you are still responsible for proofreading your documents. Word can't always determine if you've used words correctly, such as to, too, and two.

Lesson 8: Correcting Grammatical Errors

Word's grammar checker proofs a document for problems with grammar, style, punctuation, and word usage. The green wavy lines indicate possible problems. Like correcting spelling errors "on the fly," you can immediately right-click text marked with green wavy lines and correct it.

In this lesson, you correct two grammatical errors in the status report.

To Correct Grammatical Errors

1 In the Benefits Status Report document, scroll down to the third paragraph.
Green wavy lines mark the second sentence, indicating that you need to correct a grammatical error.

> If you don't see green wavy lines, click Tools, Options to display the Options dialog box. Click the Spelling & Grammar tab. Make sure that both Check grammar as you type and Check grammar with spelling are selected. If not, select them and click OK.

2 Right-click the second sentence.
Word displays one or more possible corrections (see Figure 3.20).

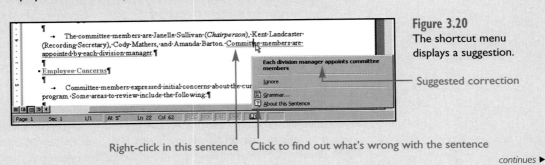

Figure 3.20
The shortcut menu displays a suggestion.

Suggested correction

Right-click in this sentence   Click to find out what's wrong with the sentence

continues ▶

To Correct Grammatical Errors (continued)

❸ Click `Each division manager appoints committee members` **from the shortcut menu.**

You have now changed your text to a grammatically correct sentence.

Learning About the Error

If you don't understand why Word detected an error, right-click the error and choose <u>A</u>bout this Sentence from the shortcut menu. Word displays grammar information and rules, along with samples to help you better understand the error.

❹ Scroll down to the last paragraph.

Notice that the phrase `members is` has green wavy lines.

❺ Right-click the phrase `members is` **and choose** `members are`.

The correct phrase replaces the grammatical error. Figure 3.21 shows the corrected text.

Figure 3.21
The document is grammatically correct.

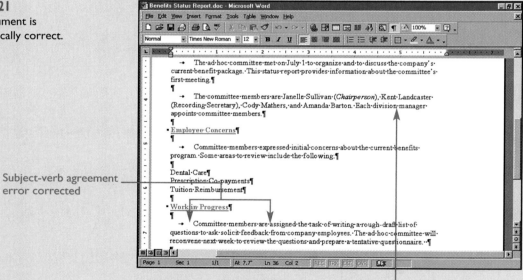

Subject-verb agreement error corrected

Passive voice sentence corrected

Ignoring an Error

If you see wavy green lines below `Committee`, right-click it and choose <u>I</u>gnore.

❻ Save the document and keep it onscreen to continue with the next lesson.

Checking Grammar Through the Dialog Box

If you need more assistance in correcting grammatical errors, choose <u>T</u>ools, <u>S</u>pelling and Grammar to display the Spelling and Grammar dialog box. Word might detect more errors than are indicated by the green wavy lines.

In addition to using Word's grammar-checking feature, you should proofread carefully. Although Word is helpful in finding and correcting errors, it can't determine exactly what you are communicating. Therefore, it might not catch an error, or it might suggest an error as a replacement.

Lesson 9: Selecting Synonyms

Finding the perfect word to communicate your ideas clearly is sometimes difficult. You might type a word but then realize it doesn't quite describe what you're thinking. It might not have the impact for which you were searching. The Thesaurus tool helps you choose words to improve the clarity of your documents. You can select **synonyms**, words with similar meanings, from Word's Thesaurus feature and get your point across with greater ease.

In this lesson, you use the shortcut menu to select synonyms for words.

To Choose Synonyms

1 **In the Benefits Status Report document, right-click the word formed in the first paragraph to display the shortcut menu.**

2 **Choose Synonyms from the shortcut menu.**
A list of synonyms appears (see Figure 3.22). You can choose a word from this list, or you can access the Thesaurus feature by clicking Thesaurus from the shortcut menu.

Right-click on the word

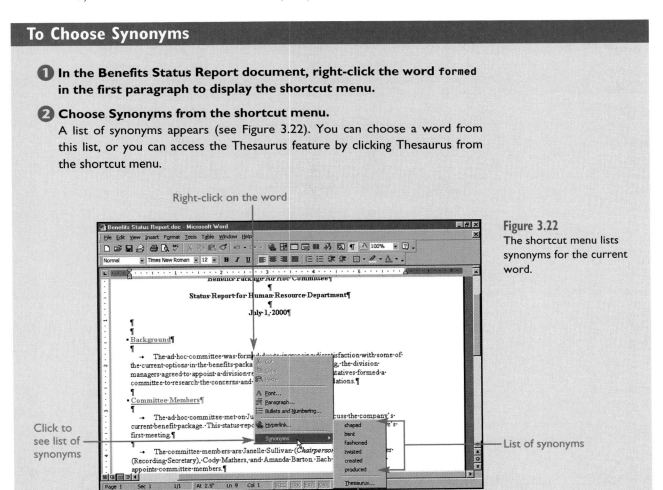

Click to see list of synonyms

List of synonyms

Click to access Thesaurus

Figure 3.22
The shortcut menu lists synonyms for the current word.

You see an error message if Thesaurus is not loaded on your computer. If you have the Microsoft Office 2000 installation CD, insert it and follow the prompts to install Thesaurus.

continues ▶

To Choose Synonyms (continued)

 Choose created.
Word replaces the current word with the synonym you select from the shortcut menu.

4 Right-click agreed in the first paragraph.

5 Choose Synonyms; then choose decided.
Word replaces agreed with decided.

6 Save the document and close it.

 Thesaurus
If you want to use the full Thesaurus feature, you can also choose Tools, Language, Thesaurus or press ◆Shift+F7. The Thesaurus shows you synonyms based on noun, verb, and adjective forms of the current word.

Summary

You now know how to perform several essential tasks to enhance text and improve the clarity of your document. You used Format Painter to copy text enhancements from one heading to another for consistency. In addition, you changed the capitalization of text, moved text to a different location, and used Undo to reverse actions. You also learned how to correct spelling and grammatical errors and to improve word choices by choosing synonyms. You also know that AutoCorrect corrects errors as you type. You can extend your learning by experimenting with the full Grammar Checking, Spelling Checker, and Thesaurus. Review the onscreen Help to explore the full capabilities of these proofing tools.

Checking Concepts and Terms

True/False

For each of the following, check *T* or *F* to indicate whether the statement is true or false.

__T __F **1.** To italicize existing text, you must first select it. [L1]

__T __F **2.** Each heading should have different text enhancements. [L2]

__T __F **3.** Before turning on the Format Painter to format other headings, place the insertion point inside the original formatted heading. [L2]

__T __F **4.** If you accidentally capitalized all words in a paragraph, the most appropriate Change Case option is Title Case. [L3]

__T __F **5.** Before using the Cut command, you must first select text. [L4]

__T __F **6.** When you cut text from a document, it is temporarily stored in the Clipboard. [L4]

__T __F **7.** You can use the Undo feature to reverse the second-to-the-last action without reversing the last action. [L5]

__T __F **8.** Word's AutoCorrect feature corrects some misspelled words as you type. [L6]

__T __F **9.** A red wavy line below a word indicates that the word is possibly misspelled. [L7]

__T __F **10.** To display possible corrections for a grammatical error, double-click the sentence that contains the wavy green lines. [L8]

Multiple Choice

Circle the letter of the correct answer for each of the following.

1. What text enhancement is the most common for a document title? [L1]

   a. underline

   b. italic

   c. bold

   d. bold italic

2. All of the following have keyboard shortcuts except: [L1]

   a. underline

   b. font color

   c. bold

   d. italic

3. Where does the insertion point need to be before turning on the Format Painter? [L2]

   a. within text that you need to format

   b. anywhere in the document

   c. at the top of the page

   d. within formatted text that you want to copy

4. After turning on the Format Painter, you apply the formats to several words (such as headings) at the same time by doing what? [L2]

   a. double-clicking the text to format

   b. clicking and dragging across the text to format

   c. pressing Ctrl and clicking the first word of the text to format

   d. all of the above

5. What Change Case option capitalizes the first letter after a punctuation mark, such as the period, question mark, or exclamation mark? [L3]

   a. Sentence Case

   b. Title Case

   c. tOGGLE cASE

   d. UPPERCASE

6. What is the first step to moving text? [L4]

   a. choosing the Cut command

   b. positioning the insertion point where you want the cut text to appear

   c. using the Paste command

   d. selecting the text you want to move

7. What feature reverses the last action you performed on the document? [L5]

   a. Redo

   b. Paste

   c. Undo

   d. Format Painter

8. AutoCorrect does all of the following except: [L6]

   a. correct some misspelled words as you type

   b. capitalize the first letter of a sentence if you don't

   c. change some keyboard symbols to other symbols, such as a smiley face

   d. place red wavy lines below grammatical errors

9. What is the purpose of right-clicking a sentence that contains green wavy lines, then choosing About this Sentence from the menu? [L8]

   a. You see the number of spelling errors in the sentence.

   b. Word tells you what's grammatically wrong with the sentence.

   c. You can choose a list of synonyms to improve the clarity of the sentence.

   d. Grammar Checker opens with extended options.

10. What is the purpose of using Word's Thesaurus? [L9]

   a. You can choose words that improve the clarity of your document.

   b. Word corrects misspelled words for you automatically.

   c. You can eliminate passive voice.

   d. It corrects mistakes as you type.

Screen ID

Label each element of the Word screen shown in Figure 3.23

Figure 3.23

A. Bold button

B. Clipboard toolbar

C. Copy button

D. Cut button

E. Format Painter button

F. Grammatical error

G. Italic button

H. Paste button

I. Spelling error

J. Synonyms error

K. Underline button

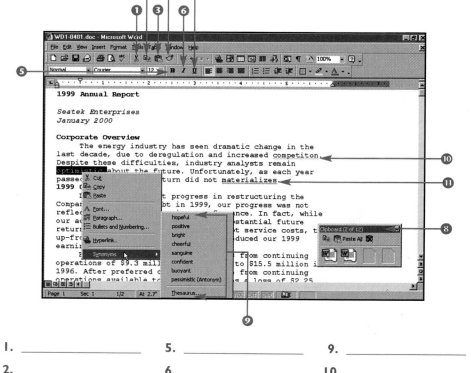

1. _____   5. _____   9. _____

2. _____   6. _____   10. _____

3. _____   7. _____   11. _____

4. _____   8. _____

Discussion Questions

1. When would you want to single-click instead of double-click the Format Painter button?

2. What is the purpose of AutoCorrect? How does it help you improve your efficiency?

3. Practice the drag and drop feature for moving text. Explain how it might be helpful to use this feature. Discuss any disadvantages you experience in using the drag and drop feature compared to using the Cut and Paste commands.

4. In addition to AutoCorrect, what other tools help improve the accuracy of your documents?

5. Find two examples of documents (e.g., the minutes of a meeting, the letter to stockholders in a company's annual report, or a magazine article) that use text enhancements. Identify the types of text enhancements and evaluate their effectiveness. If the enhancements are not effective, provide suggestions for improving the document.

Skill Drill

Skill Drill exercises reinforce project skills. Each skill reinforced is the same, or nearly the same, as a skill presented in the project. Detailed instructions are provided in a step-by-step format.

1. Enhancing an Interoffice Memo

You just finished composing a status report memo to your manager. You want to improve the appearance of the memo. [L1–2]

1. Open **WD1-0302** and save it as **Newsletter Memo**.

2. Change **Andy Barton** to your name in the memo heading.

3. Select the first heading, **News articles**.

4. Click the Bold button, and then click the Underline button.

5. Click the Font Color drop-down arrow and choose Orange from the Font Color palette.

    Your manager's favorite color is orange. Using this color creates a positive first impression for your message.

6. Double-click the Format Painter button on the Standard toolbar.

7. Scroll through the document until you see additional headings.

8. Use the mouse pointer to drag across **Classified advertisements** to add the orange color, bold, and underline to it.

9. Click and drag across **Art work**.

10. Click the Format Painter to turn off this feature.

11. Drag the vertical scroll box to the top of the memo.

12. Click inside **To** and click the Bold button.

13. Click inside each of the remaining memo headings (**From**, **Date**, and **Subject**) and click the Bold button.

14. Save the document and keep it onscreen to continue with the next exercise.

2. Changing the Capitalization of Headings

You want to adjust the capitalization of the words in the headings. [L3]

1. In the Newsletter Memo document, double-click the word **To**.

2. Choose Format, Change Case.

3. Click the UPPERCASE option button, and then click OK.

4. Double-click the word **From**.

5. Press ◆Shift+F3 until you see **FROM** in all capital letters.

6. Use the same process to capitalize **Date** and **Subject**.

7. Click the Show/Hide ¶ button on the Standard toolbar to display the nonprinting symbols.

8. Click after the colon after **FROM:** and press Del to delete one tab symbol (the arrow) and line up your name with Jennifer's name.

9. Click after the colon after **DATE:** and press Del to delete one tab symbol and line up the date with your name.

10. Select the first heading, **News Articles**.

11. Press ◆Shift+F3 to choose the Title Case capitalization style.

12. Use the same process to apply the Title Case capitalization style to the other two headings.

13. Save the document and keep it onscreen to continue with the next exercise.

3. Moving Text and Using Undo

As you read through the memo, you decide to move the `Art Work` section below the `News Articles` section. You make two other changes and then decide to reverse those actions. [L4–5]

1. In the Newsletter Memo document, click at the beginning of the heading `Art Work`.

2. Click the Show/Hide ¶ button to see the nonprinting symbols if they are not already displayed.

3. Select the `Art Work` heading and the paragraph below it. Make sure you include the ¶ symbol below the paragraph.

4. Use any of the Cut methods you learned about in this project to cut the text from its location.

5. Position the insertion point to the left of the heading, `Classified Advertisements`.

6. Paste the text between the `News Articles` and `Classified Advertisement` sections.

7. Select the last sentence in the first paragraph in the `Classified Advertisement` section. The sentence begins with `The residents have expressed`.

8. Cut the sentence.

9. Position the insertion point at the beginning of the sentence that begins with `We are currently accepting` in the same paragraph.

10. Paste the sentence here. It should now be the second sentence in the paragraph.

11. Press (Spacebar), if necessary, to leave a space between sentences.

12. Use the Paste command again to insert another copy of the sentence from the Clipboard.

13. Select the first paragraph and click the Font Color button to apply orange to it.

    Oops! You decide that you don't want the first paragraph to be orange. You also realize that you "accidentally" pasted two copies of the sentence in the `Classified Advertisements` section. Now you need to reverse these last two actions.

14. Click the Undo button to remove the orange color.

15. Click the Undo button again to remove the duplicate pasted sentence.

16. Save the document and keep it onscreen to continue to the next exercise.

4. Using AutoCorrect as You Type

You need to add a sentence to the document. As you quickly type it, you make some mistakes. AutoCorrect will correct them for you. [L6]

1. With Newsletter Memo open, position the insertion point at the end of the first paragraph in the `News Articles` section.

2. Type the following sentence exactly as shown with mistakes:

    `some topiks for artecles include informing residents ofthe new recycling program and` `trafic issues during home football games in september and october.`

3. Check to make sure AutoCorrect corrected the misspelled words as you typed them.

4. Save the document and keep it onscreen to continue with the next exercise.

5. Correcting Spelling Errors

Knowing that spelling errors create a poor impression, you decide to use Word's Spelling Checker feature on the memo to correct five misspelled words. [L7]

1. Right-click `shcedule` in the first paragraph.

2. Choose `schedule` from the shortcut menu.

3. Right-click `dilegently` in the first paragraph; then choose `diligently`.

4. Right-click `severel` in the first paragraph in the `News Articles` section; then choose `several`.

5. Right-click `libary` in the next paragraph and choose `library`.

6. Right-click `businesses` in the first paragraph in the `Classified Advertisements` section; then choose `businesses`.

7. Right-click `Paramore` and choose <u>I</u>gnore All, because that is the correct spelling of his name.

8. Save the document and keep it onscreen to continue with the next exercise.

6. Correcting Grammatical Errors and Choosing Synonyms

Before printing the memo, you notice green wavy lines, indicating potential grammatical errors. These errors must be corrected before sending the memo to your supervisor. In addition, you want to find a synonym for a particular word. [L8–9]

I. In the Newsletter Memo document, right-click the two consecutive commas (,,) in the first paragraph and choose one comma (,) on the shortcut menu.

2. Right-click `deal` in the second paragraph in the `News Articles` section and choose `deals`.

3. Right-click `its` in the same paragraph and choose `it's`.

4. Right-click `currently` and choose S<u>y</u>nonyms.

5. Choose `presently` to replace `currently`.

6. Save the document and close it.

[?] 7. Using Help to Learn About Spelling and Grammar Options

You want to learn more about Spelling and Grammar options. You'll use the Help feature to do this.

I. Press F1 to open the Microsoft Word Help dialog box.

2. If the Show icon appears in the upper-left corner, click it to display the Contents, Answer Wizard and Index tabs.

3. Click the <u>C</u>ontents tab.

4. Scroll down and double-click `Checking Spelling and Grammar`.

5. Click the subtopic named `Set rules for grammar and writing styles`.

6. Read the information on the right side of the Help window and click the `Select a grammar and writing style` link.

7. Close the Help dialog box.

Challenge 💡

Challenge exercises expand on or are somewhat related to skills presented in the lessons. Each exercise provides a brief narrative introduction followed by instructions in a numbered step format that are not as detailed as those in the Skill Drill section.

1. Preparing a Resume

You can make a resume look more appealing by enhancing certain text and rearranging existing text. Use the sample resume, or substitute your personal information in each category. [L1, 4–5, 7–8]

I. Open `WD1-0303` and save it as `Resume`.

2. Emphasize the name and address at the top of the resume with boldface. Make the heading `EXPERIENCE` bold and select blue font color. Add a heading to the section on education. Make sure that it matches the `EXPERIENCE` heading. Leave a blank line before and after the heading.

3. Underline every occurrence of the company name, `CDs and Things, Inc.`, and change every occurrence of the subhead `Duties:` to italic. Include the colon in the italics.

4. Highlight your degrees by using bold, underline, and italic.

5. Move the EDUCATION section above the EXPERIENCE section.

6. Undo the move because it looks better the original way.

7. Check the spelling and grammar in the document and make appropriate changes.

8. Save the changes and print a copy for your instructor.

2. Enhancing a Radio Ad

You need to enhance some radio ad copy for a new business. You'll apply text attributes and edit the document. [L1–2, 4]

1. Open WD1-0304 and save it as **Radio Ad**.

2. Apply red text color and boldface to the title. Change the case to uppercase letters.

3. Rearrange the sentences so that the information about where the store is located precedes the information on what the store sells. Make sure you have one blank line between paragraphs after moving text.

4. Boldface and italicize the name of the store throughout the document. After formatting the first occurrence of the store name, use Format Painter to apply the formats to the other occurrences of the store name.

5. Italicize the name of each type of music.

6. Apply red font color to CD and tape exchange.

7. Replace the text (Student's Name) with your name; then copy the address and the phone number on the line below your name. Put each item on a separate line.

8. Save the document and print it.

3. Creating a Health Benefits Memo

You work in your company's Benefits Office. You need to prepare a memo to inform employees of a few changes and of upcoming seminars that further explain the changes.[L1, 4]

1. From a new window, create the document shown in Figure 3.24.

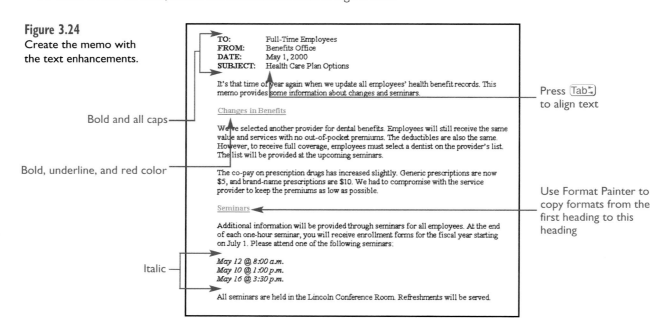

Figure 3.24
Create the memo with
the text enhancements.

Bold and all caps

Bold, underline, and red color

Italic

Press Tab
to align text

Use Format Painter to
copy formats from the
first heading to this
heading

2. Apply the text enhancements as shown in the figure.

3. Press ⏎Enter after the first three lines in the memo heading. Press ⏎Enter three times after the subject line. Display the nonprinting symbols. Make sure you have only three paragraph symbols between the subject line and the first paragraph.

4. Save the document as `Health Benefits Memo` and print it.

5. Reverse the two paragraphs in the `Changes in Benefits` section.

6. Use the Cut and Paste commands to arrange the dates in chronological order.

7. Select the dates, press Tab⇥ to indent them, and apply red font to them.

8. Save the document as `Revised Health Benefits Memo` and print it.

4. Correcting Errors in a Letter

You work as an assistant for a real estate company. One of the agents wrote a letter to condominium owners who have expressed interest in selling their condominiums. The agent asked you to make necessary corrections. [L5, 7–9]

1. Open `WD1-0305` and save it as `Condominium Sales Letter`.

2. Start typing the date. When you see the ScreenTip of today's date, press ⏎Enter to complete it.

3. Double-click the book icon on the status bar to display the first spelling or grammatical error and correct it. Continue doing this until you correct all errors.

4. Select an appropriate synonym for `maximum` in the last paragraph.

5. Select the appropriate casing for the third paragraph. Manually capitalize any letters that should remain capitalized.

6. Select the four items below the third paragraph, press Tab⇥, and italicize them.

7. Select the first paragraph and bold it.

8. Select `Sincerely` and capitalize it.

9. Delete the first sentence in the first paragraph.

10. Click the drop-down arrow to the right of the Undo button. Select Undo actions starting with bolding text to the latest action.

11. Save the document and print it.

5. Enhancing and Editing a Welcome Letter

You live in a townhouse condominium complex in Amarillo, Texas. You are also on the welcome committee that greets new residents as they buy a townhouse. You have prepared a welcome letter and need to enhance and correct it. [L1–5, 7–8]

1. Open `WD1-0306` and save it as `Welcome New Owners`.

2. Start typing today's date at the top and press ⏎Enter when AutoComplete displays the full date.

3. Bold and apply Sea Green color to the first occurrence of `Madison Village`. Use Format Painter to apply these formats to the other `Madison Village` occurrences.

4. Select Title Case for each of these headings: `lawn care`, `snow removal`, `workout room`, and `swimming pool`.

5. Select `Lawn Care` and bold and underline it. Use Format Painter to copy these formats to the other three headings.

6. Move the `Swimming Pool` paragraph above the `Lawn Care` paragraph.

7. Move the `Snow Removal` paragraph below the `Workout Room` paragraph.

8. Check the spacing between paragraphs and make necessary adjustments.

9. Delete the `Snow Removal` paragraph; then undo the action.

10. Double-click the book icon on the status bar and correct all spelling and grammatical errors.

11. Save the document and print it.

Discovery Zone

Discovery Zone exercises require advanced knowledge of topics presented in *Essentials* lessons, application of skills from multiple lessons, or self-directed learning of new skills.

1. Enhancing and Correcting Errors in Minutes from a Meeting

You are the secretary for a condominium association. You need to enhance the minutes and correct errors in them. Open `WD1-0307` and save it as **Association Minutes**. Enhance the title by applying boldface and Violet font color to it. You need to enhance the headings by using underline and Violet font color. Use Format Painter to help copy the formats from one heading to the other headings. Use an appropriate Change Case option on the headings; make sure they are consistently formatted.

You believe that the `Condominium Dues` section should be placed before the `Parking Regulations` section. Make this change and adjust spacing between paragraphs if necessary; you should have one blank line between paragraphs.

You realize that the minutes contain spelling and grammatical errors. Instead of right-clicking the errors and correcting them, you want to use the Spelling and Grammar dialog box. Refer to Online Help to learn how to use this dialog box. In addition, use Online Help to learn about Thesaurus. It contains more choices than right-clicking a word and choosing Synonyms. Choose an appropriate replacement for `additional` in the `Condominium Dues` paragraph.

Create a custom dictionary named `WD1` and select to save the members' names so that Word doesn't indicate that they are misspelled. Set the grammar style to Formal to check and correct grammatical errors. Proofread the document and correct any grammatical errors that Word did not detect. Save the document with the changes and print it.

2. Creating AutoCorrect Entries

You really like how AutoCorrect can correct some errors as you type. After reading the Nice to Know in Lesson 6, Using "AutoCorrect," you want to create a couple of AutoCorrect entries. You want to be able to type an abbreviation and have Word automatically change it to full text.

Read the Nice to Know in Lesson 6 again and use onscreen Help to learn how to create and use AutoCorrect entries. You will create the following two entries:

- ccc for College Computer Club
- your initials for your full name

Be careful when creating the entry for your name. Some names may expand state abbreviations or simple words, which you don't want to do. For example, a person named `Ingrid Smith` should not use `is` as an AutoCorrect entry.

Create the document shown in Figure 3.25. Use your initials for Vice President and Activities Director instead of `xyz`. Word should automatically expand the abbreviations as you type them. Select the title and use the keyboard shortcut for changing the case to uppercase.

Ccc Officers	
The ccc officers for the 2000-01 academic year are listed below:	
President	Vicki Kamoreaux
Vice President	xyz
Secretary	Bryson Jorgenson
Treasurer	Gloria Rokovitz
Activities Director	xyz

Figure 3.25
Create the list of
computer club officers.

Make two more copies of the list so you have three copies of the list on one page. Save the document as `Computer Club Officers` and print it.

3. Compiling an Information Sheet by Using the Office Clipboard

You have a master file of workshop descriptions your training company provides to business people in the area. You need to prepare a custom workshop program for one of your clients. Open `WD1-0308`.

Refer to Lesson 4, "Moving and Copying Text," and onscreen Help to learn about the Office Clipboard and how to use it to collect and paste several items at once.

Display the Clipboard toolbar. Clear any existing items in the Clipboard, and copy the paragraphs to the Clipboard in this order: `Upgrade to Word 2000`, `Automating Your Work`, and `Collaborating on Documents`.

Press Ctrl+N to display a new document window and paste the entire Clipboard contents there. Save the document as `Bradshaw and Associates`. Type the intro paragraph at the beginning of the document, as shown in Figure 3.26. Save the document, and print it.

COMPUTER WORKSHOPS FOR BRADSHAW AND ASSOCIATES

We are pleased to provide the workshops you requested for individuals in your organization. According to our agreement, you may send up to 15 individuals to each session listed below. The workshops are scheduled for May 18 in your conference room. If you have additional questions, please call Taralyn VanBuren at 555-7843.

Figure 3.26
Create the Introductory
Information.

Change BRADSHAW AND ASSOCIATES to THE ROWLEY GROUP. Save the document as `The Rowley Group`. Delete the paragraphs about the workshops. Clear the Clipboard. Click `WD1-0308` on the status bar to go back to this document, and copy these paragraphs in this order to the Clipboard: `Basic Formatting with Word`, `Graphics Jamboree`, `Integrating Excel Data into Word`, and `Organizing Items in Tables`. Paste the entire Clipboard contents at the bottom of The Rowley Group document. Save the document and print it. Close all open documents.

[?] 4. Using Undo and Redo

You are confused about the Undo and Redo features. Use Online Help to learn how these features work and how they interact with each other. Print the Help topic.

Type a paragraph about these features. Apply text enhancements in various locations in the paragraph. Add and delete text to edit the paragraph. Now use Undo and Redo to see what happens as you continue using the features. Click the Undo and Redo drop-down list buttons to see a list of tasks you can reverse. After using these features, type a second paragraph that discusses examples of activities that you reversed with each feature. Save your document as **Undo and Redo** and print it.

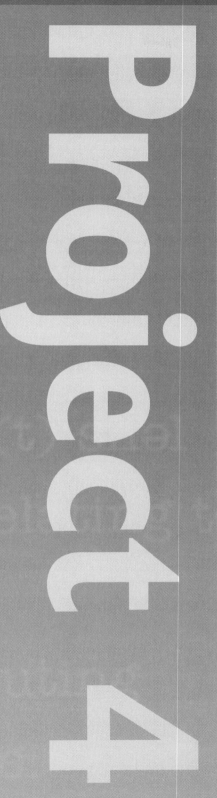

Formatting Documents

Objectives

In this project, you learn how to

➤ **Set Margins**

➤ **Change the Line Spacing**

➤ **Select Text Alignment**

➤ **Indent Text**

➤ **Change the Font and Font Size**

➤ **Create a Bulleted List**

➤ **Highlight Text**

➤ **Add a Border**

Key terms in this project include

- alignment
- border
- bullet
- bulleted list
- double indent
- double-space
- font
- font size
- hanging indent

- highlight
- indent
- line spacing
- margins
- sans serif font
- serif font
- shading
- single-space
- spinners

Why Would I Do This?

 o far, you've created documents using the default settings. Those settings are acceptable for some basic documents. However, you probably want to have control over the format settings used for different types of documents.

Visual Summary

In this project, you need to format a chief executive officer's (CEO's) letter to the stockholders. Some of the format settings you change include margins, line spacing, and fonts. Figure 4.1 shows the unformatted document, and Figure 4.2 shows the same document after it's been formatted. Notice how the formats make the second document look much more professional and inviting to read!

Figure 4.1
The unformatted document looks bland and uninviting to read.

Single-spaced text difficult to read

Quotation blends in with text

Special items not standing out

```
1999 Annual Report

Seatek Enterprises
January 2000

Corporate Overview
     The energy industry has seen dramatic change in the last
decade, due to deregulation and increased competition.
Despite these difficulties, industry analysts remain
optimistic about the future. In 1999, the warmest winter in
almost 100 years, combined with the sluggish economy resulted
in a substantial drop in prices.
1999 Management Changes
     In March 1999, Grant S. Keeper joined Seatek as its
Chief Financial Officer. Grant has an impressive record in
the energy industry accumulated over the past 33 years. He
was formerly Chief Financial Officer of Southwestern Power.
Grant adds strength to our management team. Mr. Keeper has
stated:
     2000 is the year we take the bull by the horns. Everyone
at Seatek must pull together and work toward our mutual
success. I'm counting on every employee to focus on our
common goals to improve the financial status of the Company.
Goals for 2000
     Fully implementing our strategic action plan will take
several years to complete and 2000 will be no less critical
than 1999. In pursuing the second year of our plan, we have
established several key goals for 2000:
Pursue innovative marketing techniques.
Increase usage of existing computer systems.
Implement an electronic project management program.
```

Unformatted title

Unformatted subtitle

Ragged right margin

Courier font

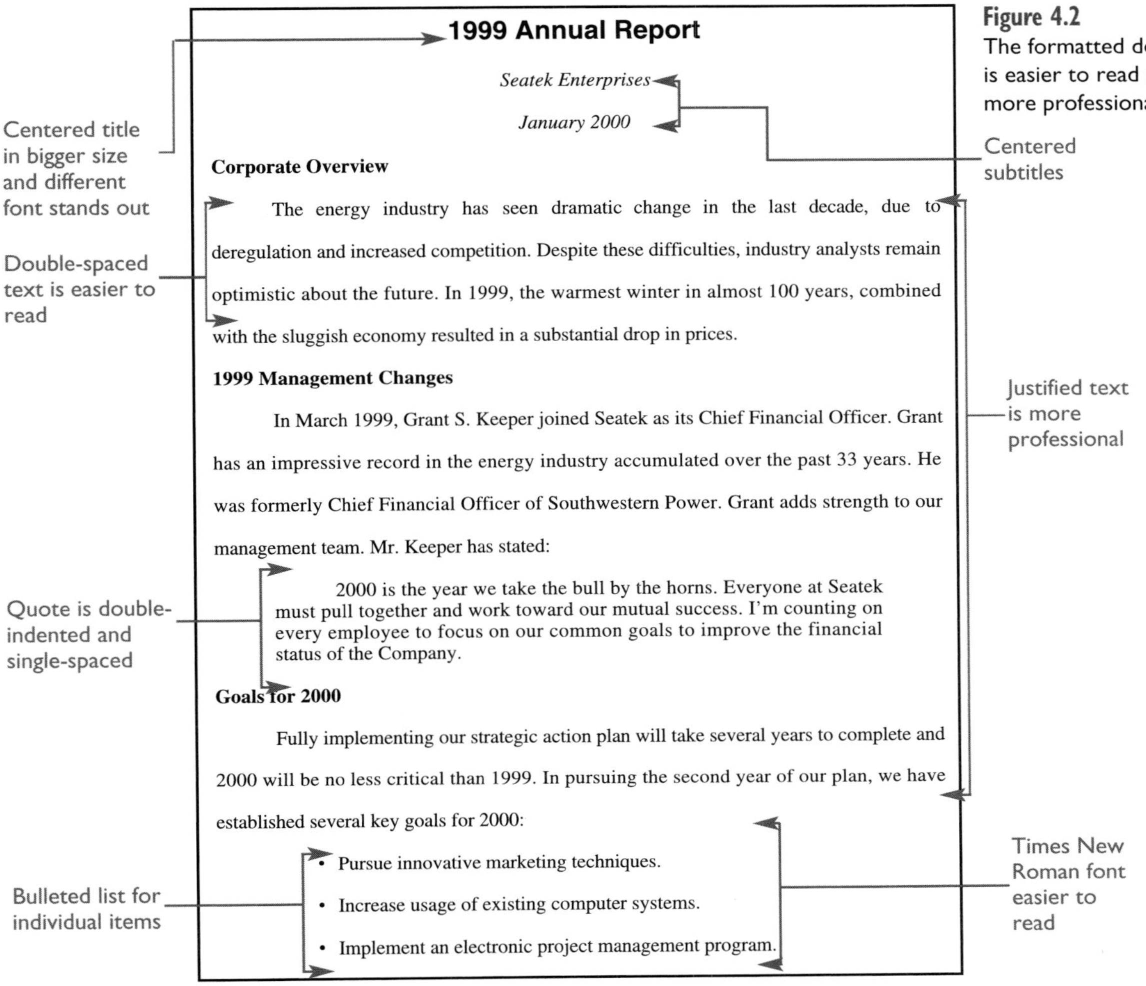
1999 Annual Report

Seatek Enterprises

January 2000

Corporate Overview

The energy industry has seen dramatic change in the last decade, due to deregulation and increased competition. Despite these difficulties, industry analysts remain optimistic about the future. In 1999, the warmest winter in almost 100 years, combined with the sluggish economy resulted in a substantial drop in prices.

1999 Management Changes

In March 1999, Grant S. Keeper joined Seatek as its Chief Financial Officer. Grant has an impressive record in the energy industry accumulated over the past 33 years. He was formerly Chief Financial Officer of Southwestern Power. Grant adds strength to our management team. Mr. Keeper has stated:

> 2000 is the year we take the bull by the horns. Everyone at Seatek must pull together and work toward our mutual success. I'm counting on every employee to focus on our common goals to improve the financial status of the Company.

Goals for 2000

Fully implementing our strategic action plan will take several years to complete and 2000 will be no less critical than 1999. In pursuing the second year of our plan, we have established several key goals for 2000:

- Pursue innovative marketing techniques.
- Increase usage of existing computer systems.
- Implement an electronic project management program.

Centered title in bigger size and different font stands out
Double-spaced text is easier to read
Quote is double-indented and single-spaced
Bulleted list for individual items
Centered subtitles
Justified text is more professional
Times New Roman font easier to read

Figure 4.2
The formatted document is easier to read and looks more professional.

Lesson 1: Setting Margins

A document's ***margins*** determine the amount of white space around the text. When you start a new Word document, the default top and bottom margins are 1" from the top and bottom edges of the page, and the default left and right margins are 1.25" from the left and right edges of the page. These margin settings are acceptable for many documents. However, you should change margins when doing so improves the appearance of your document. Sometimes a reference manual you are required to use specifies certain margin settings for particular documents.

In this lesson, you learn how to set different margin widths in a document.

To Set Margins

1 **Open WD1-0401 and save it as Annual Report.**
The report is currently formatted by the default margins.

2 **Choose File, Page Setup.**
The Page Setup dialog box appears, as shown in Figure 4.3. This dialog box has four tabs. By default, the Margins tab is positioned in front of the other tabs. The dialog box features a sample document page called the Preview area so that you can preview your changes before you apply them to the document.

Click a tab to display its options

Figure 4.3
The Page Setup dialog box contains the margins options.

Side margins

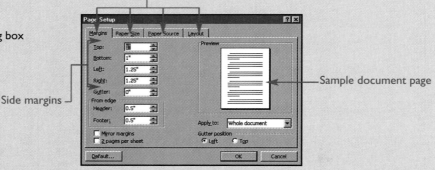

Sample document page

Displaying the Page Setup Dialog Box
You can double-click the ruler at the top of the document, to the left of the left margin, or to the right of the right margin to display the Page Setup dialog box. Make sure you double-click in the empty gray space at the ends of the ruler, not on the ruler itself.

3 **Click Margins if the margin options are not displayed.**

4 **Type 1.5 in the Top text box.**
Because the Top text box is selected when you first open the Page Setup dialog box, you simply type the margin setting you want; the number you type replaces the original setting.

Setting Margins
You don't have to type the inch mark (") when you set a margin. Word assumes you are specifying a setting in terms of inches. You can press Tab⇄ to go from one margin text box to another.

Instead of typing a margin setting, you can click the up and down arrows, called **spinners**, at the right side of each margin text box to increase or decrease the margin setting.

5 **Press Tab⇄.**
The Bottom text box is now active and ready for you to type a new setting for this margin.

6 **Type 1.25 and click OK.**

7 **Click the Print Layout View button to the left of the horizontal scrollbar.**

The 1.5" top and 1.25" bottom margins change the document, as shown in Figure 4.4.

Click and drag to set left margin

Click and drag to set right margin

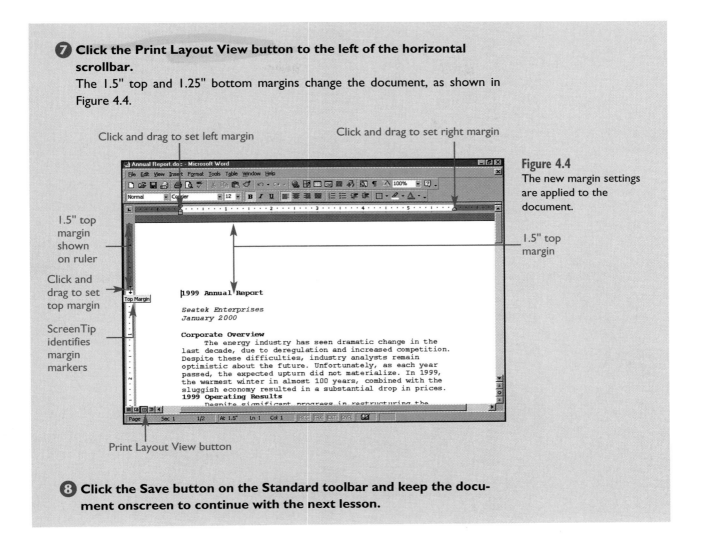

1.5" top margin shown on ruler

Click and drag to set top margin

ScreenTip identifies margin markers

Figure 4.4
The new margin settings are applied to the document.

1.5" top margin

Print Layout View button

8 **Click the Save button on the Standard toolbar and keep the document onscreen to continue with the next lesson.**

 Setting Margins on the Ruler

When you display the document in Print Layout view, you can set the margins on the ruler. You can set the left and right margins on the horizontal ruler and the top and bottom margins on the vertical ruler.

As shown in Figure 4.4 above, the white area on the ruler displays the typing area between the margins, and the dark gray area represents the margins. To change the margins, simply click and drag the margin markers on the ruler. You see a two-headed arrow as you click and drag the margin markers.

Lesson 2: Changing Line Spacing

Line spacing is the amount of vertical space from the bottom of one text line to the bottom of another. You use line spacing to control the amount of space between text lines in Word.

When you create a new document, Word **single-spaces** the document text, which means that text lines are close together with a small space to separate the lines. While some documents, such as letters, should be single-spaced, other documents look better double-spaced. For example, a long report is typically easier to read if it is double-spaced.

You can use the Line Spacing feature to change the amount of space between lines of text. When you set the line spacing, you decide whether to format the entire document or individual paragraphs. In this lesson, you change the line spacing to double.

To Change Line Spacing

1 **In the Annual Report file, position the insertion point at the beginning of the heading** `Corporate Overview.`
Before setting the line spacing, you must select the paragraphs that you want to format. In this document, you want to format all document text except the titles.

2 **Press** Ctrl+⇧Shift+End **to select text from the insertion point to the end of the document.**

3 **Choose F̲ormat, P̲aragraph.**
The Paragraph dialog box appears, as shown in Figure 4.5. Make sure the I̲ndents and Spacing tab is displayed.

Figure 4.5
Set the line spacing in the Paragraph dialog box.

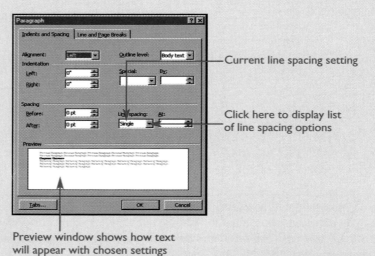

Current line spacing setting

Click here to display list of line spacing options

Preview window shows how text will appear with chosen settings

 Displaying the Paragraph Dialog Box
You can also display the Paragraph dialog box by right-clicking within a paragraph and choosing P̲aragraph from the shortcut menu.

4 **Click the drop-down arrow next to the Li̲ne spacing box.**
You see a list of line spacing options. Table 4.1 at the end of this lesson lists and describes the different line spacing options.

5 **Choose Double from the list; then click OK.**
The Double option double-spaces the selected text. When you *double-space* text, Word leaves one blank line between lines within a paragraph. Each hard return in the selected area is also doubled.

Keyboard Shortcuts for Changing Line Spacing
Use the following keyboard shortcuts to change line spacing for
selected text: Ctrl + 1 for single-spacing, Ctrl + 2 for double-spacing,
and Ctrl + 5 for 1.5 spacing.

6 **Click in the document window to deselect the text.**

7 **Press Ctrl + Home to return the insertion point to the beginning of the
document and deselect the text.**

8 **Click the Show/Hide ¶ button on the Standard toolbar.**
Your document should look like Figure 4.6.

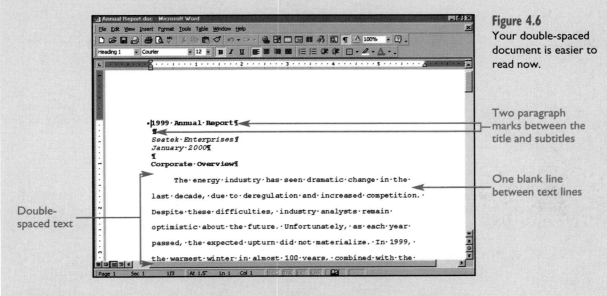

Figure 4.6
Your double-spaced
document is easier to
read now.

Two paragraph
marks between the
title and subtitles

One blank line
between text lines

Double-
spaced text

9 **Click the Save button to save your document. Leave the document
onscreen to continue with the next lesson.**

Table 4.1   Line Spacing Options

Spacing Option	Description
Single	Places text line immediately beneath the previous line.
1.5 Lines	Leaves one and one-half the amount of space of single-spacing.
Double	Doubles the amount of space between lines.
At Least	Specifies the minimum amount of spacing between lines, based on what you type as the value. Word adjusts the spacing as needed to make room for larger fonts or graphics.
Exactly	Specifies an exact spacing measurement. Word cannot adjust the line spacing to make room for larger elements.
Multiple	Specifies how much Word can adjust the line spacing (up or down) by a particular percentage. For example, 1.25 increases the space by 25 percent; .75 decreases the space by 25 percent. You can also enter full values, such as 3 to triple-space text.

Lesson 3: Selecting Text Alignment

Alignment refers to the placement of text between the left and right margins. The default alignment is Align Left, which aligns text with the left margin. Table 4.2 lists and describes the four alignment options.

Table 4.2 Alignment Options

Button	Option	Keyboard Shortcut	Description
▦	Align Left	Ctrl+L	Aligns text on the left margin only. The left side appears smooth, and the right side appears ragged.
▦	Center	Ctrl+E	Centers text between the left and right margins.
▦	Align Right	Ctrl+R	Aligns text at the right margin only. The right side appears smooth, and the left side appears ragged.
▦	Justify	Ctrl+J	Aligns text along the left and right margins, so both sides appear smooth. Inserts extra space between words to justify the text.

In this lesson, you decide to use the Justify option to make the paragraphs look more professional. The smooth edges on the left and right sides provide a cleaner look for the document. Also, you decide to use Center alignment to center the title between the margins.

To Change the Alignment

① In the Annual Report file, choose Edit, Select All.
Because you want to justify the text in the whole document, you must first select the entire document.

② Click the Justify button on the Formatting toolbar.
When you click the Justify button, Word inserts a small amount of space between the characters, so the text aligns at both the left and right margins. Notice, however, that you see one space symbol between words even in justified text. Justified text creates a more formal appearance than left-aligned text.

③ Click in the document window to deselect text.
You now want to center the title between the margins.

④ Position the insertion point within the title, 1999 Annual Report.

Changing Alignment for a Paragraph
When you want to change the alignment for a single paragraph, click within that paragraph (such as a title followed by a hard return) and click the alignment button. Only that paragraph's alignment changes.

⑤ Click the Center button on the Formatting toolbar to center the title between the left and right margins.

6 Select the two-line italicized subtitles, and then click the Center button on the Formatting toolbar to center them, as shown in Figure 4.7.

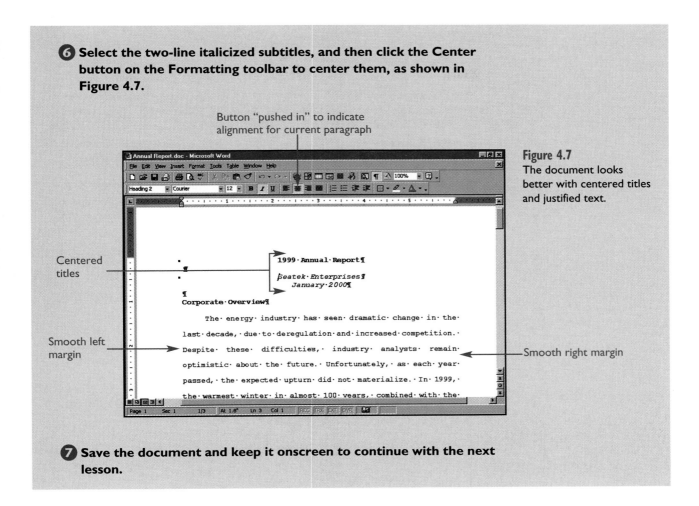

Button "pushed in" to indicate alignment for current paragraph

Centered titles

Smooth left margin

Smooth right margin

Figure 4.7
The document looks better with centered titles and justified text.

7 Save the document and keep it onscreen to continue with the next lesson.

Aligning New Text
In the previous exercise, you changed the alignment for existing text by selecting it first. You can also select alignment before typing a document. For example, you can select Center alignment and then type a document title, press ↵Enter two or three times, and then select Justify alignment. All new text from that point forward is automatically justified without selecting it first!

Lesson 4: Indenting Text

By now you know to press Tab⇄ to indent the first line of a paragraph. This format is typical in formal reports, letters, and legal documents. Sometimes, however, you might want to indent an entire paragraph from the left margin, or you might want to indent a paragraph from both margins. To indent an entire paragraph, you set options in the Indentation section of the Paragraph dialog box.

As you review the annual report, you see a quotation from the Chief Financial Officer, Grant Keeper, at the top of the third page. Often, you see a paragraph of quoted text indented from both margins. This is called a **double indent**. In addition, the paragraph is single-spaced. You need to apply both formats to the quoted paragraph in your document.

To Indent Text

1 **In the Annual Report file, position the insertion point within the following quotation that is found on page 3.**

2000 is the year we take the bull by the horns. Everyone at Seatek must pull together and work toward our mutual success. I'm counting on every employee to focus on our common goals to improve the financial status of the Company.

This quotation needs to be indented (see Figure 4.8). Because you are formatting a single paragraph, you don't need to select it first. Simply position the insertion point within the paragraph that you want to format.

Figure 4.8
Quotations that are full paragraphs should be double-indented and single-spaced.

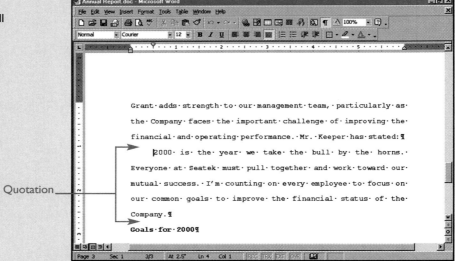

Quotation

2 **Choose Format, Paragraph to display the Paragraph dialog box.**
You need to change the settings in the Indentation section.

3 **In the Indentation section, click the Left increment button until you see 0.5" in the Left text box.**

4 **Click the Right increment button until you see 0.5'' in the Right text box.**

 Setting Indent Options from the Keyboard
You can also set the Left and Right indents from the keyboard. To set the Left indent, press ⟨Alt⟩+⟨L⟩ and type a measurement in the Left text box. To set a Right indent, press ⟨Alt⟩+⟨R⟩ and type a measurement in the Right text box.

5 **Click the Line spacing drop-down list arrow and choose Single to format the paragraph as single-spaced text.**

6 **Click OK.**
The quotation paragraph is indented on both sides and is single-spaced. The document should now look like Figure 4.9.

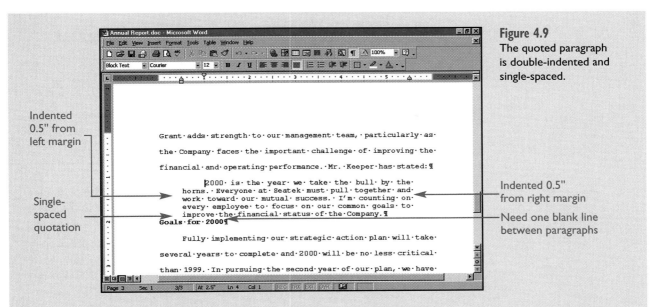

Figure 4.9
The quoted paragraph is double-indented and single-spaced.

Indented 0.5" from left margin

Single-spaced quotation

Indented 0.5" from right margin

Need one blank line between paragraphs

You only need one hard return before the quoted text, because double-spacing is in effect until the beginning of the quoted paragraph. You need two hard returns after the quoted paragraph, because single-spacing is in effect until you reach the beginning of the following paragraph.

7 Position the insertion point at the end of the quoted paragraph and press ⏎Enter.
Now the space around the quoted paragraph is correctly formatted, as shown in Figure 4.10.

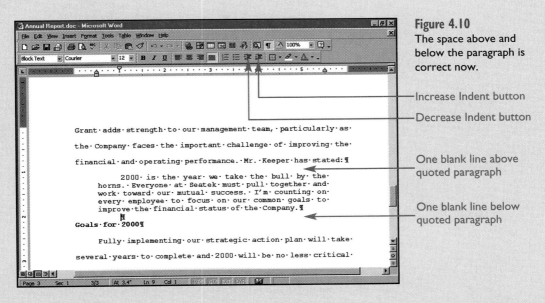

Figure 4.10
The space above and below the paragraph is correct now.

Increase Indent button

Decrease Indent button

One blank line above quoted paragraph

One blank line below quoted paragraph

8 Click the Show/Hide ¶ button to turn off the formatting marks.

9 Save the document and keep it onscreen to continue with the next lesson.

Indenting from the Left Side

If you need to *indent* text from the left side only, you can click the Increase Indent button on the Formatting toolbar. Every time you click this button, Word indents the paragraph one-half inch from the left margin.

The keyboard shortcut for indenting text from the left margin is Ctrl+M.

You can click the Decrease Indent button on the Formatting toolbar to decrease the amount of the indent one-half inch.

Create a Hanging Indent

Another important type of indent is the *hanging indent*, which keeps the first line of a paragraph at the left margin and indents the rest of the lines of that paragraph from the left margin.

To create a hanging indent, display the Paragraph dialog box, click the drop-down arrow below the Special option, and choose Hanging. Then in the By text box, specify the amount of space you want to indent the second and subsequent lines within the paragraph.

The keyboard shortcut for creating a hanging indent is Ctrl+T.

Lesson 5: Changing the Font and Font Size

Font refers to the style, weight, and typeface of a set of characters. In other words, think of font as the overall appearance of characters. With today's technology, you can choose from literally thousands of fonts. Fonts are available from a variety of sources. For example, printers come with built-in fonts they can produce. You can also purchase font software from companies such as Adobe. Fonts range in appearance from very professional to informal, fun fonts. Figure 4.11 illustrates some examples of different fonts.

Figure 4.11
Different fonts are appropriate for different occasions.

You should consider several factors when choosing a font. These factors include the font's readability, its suitability to the document's purpose, and its appeal to the reader. For example, Times New Roman is an appropriate font for the main text in correspondence and formal documents. Arial is appropriate for headings and titles. It makes them stand out from regular text. Designer fonts, such as Broadway and Comic, are appropriate for flyers, announcements, and other special-occasion documents that are less formal.

In addition to choosing the font, you should also consider the font size. **Font size** is the height of the characters, which is typically measured in points. One vertical inch contains about 72 points. You should use between 10-point and 12-point size for most correspondence and reports. Point sizes below 10 are difficult to read for detailed text, and point sizes above 12 are too big for regular paragraphs.

Currently, your document is formatted in Courier New 12-point size. You decide to use Times New Roman for the text and Arial for the title.

To Change the Font and Font Size

1 **In the Annual Report file, press** Ctrl + Home.

2 **Choose Edit, Select All.**
Because you want to change the font for the entire document, you must first select the text.

3 **Click the Font drop-down arrow on the Formatting toolbar.**
The Font menu displays the available fonts for the current printer (see Figure 4.12). You can scroll through the list to see all the available fonts.

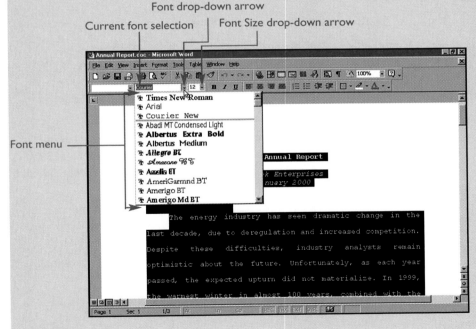

Font drop-down arrow

Current font selection   Font Size drop-down arrow

Font menu

Figure 4.12
Choose the font you want from the Font menu.

4 **Scroll down through the menu and choose Times New Roman.**

5 **Deselect the text.**
The document text appears in Times New Roman font (see Figure 4.13).

continues ▶

To Change the Font and Font Size   (continued)

Figure 4.13
The document reflects the font you selected.

Current font selected —

Times New Roman font applied to document —

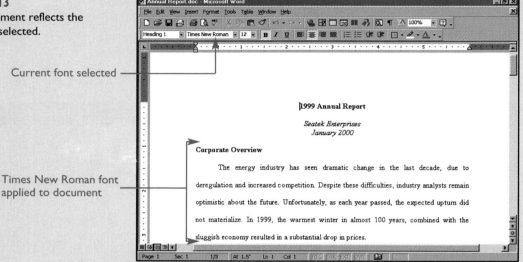

6️⃣ **Select the title** 1999 Annual Report.

7️⃣ **Click the Font drop-down arrow and choose** Arial.
Arial font helps the headings stand out from the regular text. With the title selected, you want to also increase the size of the title.

8️⃣ **Click the Font Size drop-down arrow.**
The Font Size menu displays a range of font sizes that are available for the currently selected font.

9️⃣ **Choose** 16 **from the Font Size menu.**
The title now appears in 16-point size. Titles are typically printed in a larger point size, but be careful that the title isn't too overpowering compared to the regular document text.

  Keyboard Shortcuts for Changing Font Size
Select text and press ⌃Ctrl+[to decrease the font size one point at a time, or press ⌃Ctrl+] to increase the font size one point at a time.

🔟 **Click within the document window to deselect the title.**
Your document should now look like Figure 4.14.

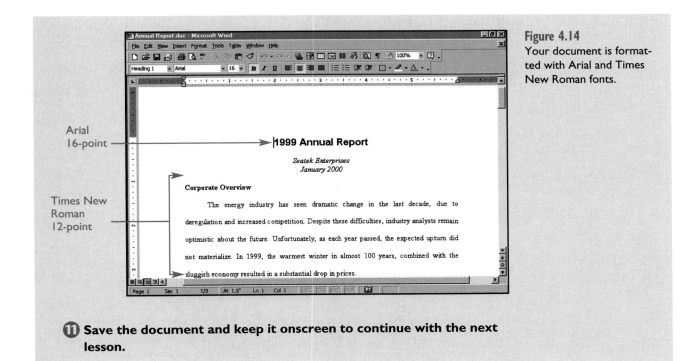

Arial
16-point

Times New
Roman
12-point

Figure 4.14
Your document is format-
ted with Arial and Times
New Roman fonts.

⑪ Save the document and keep it onscreen to continue with the next lesson.

Font Terminology

Most fonts, except for some designer fonts, are classified as serif or sans serif. A *serif font*, such as Times New Roman, has tiny lines at the ends of the charac-ters that help guide the reader's eyes across the line of text. Serif fonts should be used for text-intensive reading, such as paragraphs.

A *sans serif font*, such as Arial, does not have the tiny lines or extensions on the characters. Although a sans serif font has a cleaner look, it is difficult to read in large blocks of text, such as paragraphs. Use sans serif fonts for titles, head-ings, and other short blocks of text.

The Font dialog box contains options for changing the font and the font size (see Figure 4.15). The advantage of choosing fonts from within the dialog box is that you see a sample of how the font looks before you apply it to your document.

Furthermore, the Font dialog box contains other format options, such as superscript, strikethrough, and engrave. The Font dialog box also contains options to adjust the char-acter spacing and select text effects, such as Blinking Background.

To display the Font dialog box, choose Format, Font, or press Ctrl + D.

Figure 4.15
Use the Font dialog box
for more specific font
options.

Font list box

Special effects for
formatting characters

Preview of how selected
font options affect text

Font Size list box

Keyboard Shortcuts for Special Effects
You can choose the special effects from the Font dialog box or by using keyboard shortcuts. Table 4.3 shows the keyboard shortcuts.

Table 4.3   Special Effects Keyboard Shortcuts

Keyboard Shortcut	Effect
Ctrl+Shift+=	Superscript
Ctrl+=	Subscript
Ctrl+Shift+D	Double Underline
Ctrl+Shift+W	Underline Words Only
Ctrl+Shift+K	Small Caps
Ctrl+Shift+A	All Caps
Ctrl+Shift+H	Hidden Text

Lesson 6: Creating a Bulleted List

In word processing, a **bullet** is a special symbol used to attract attention to something on the page. People often use a **bulleted list** to itemize a series to make it stand out and be easy to read. For example, the objectives and terminology appear in bulleted lists on the first page of each project in this book. You can also create numbered lists. Use bulleted lists for listing items that can go in any order; use a numbered list for a list of items that must be in sequential order.

In this lesson, you create a bulleted list of goals for the coming year.

To Create a Bulleted List

1 **Press ⎈Ctrl+End to position the insertion point at the end of the document; then press ↑ once.**

This is where you want to create a bulleted list that itemizes the company's goals for the upcoming year.

2 **Click the Bullets button on the Formatting toolbar.**

Word indents the bullet, which is a round dot, and then indents from the bullet for you to type text.

> Word creates a bulleted list based on the last bullet type selected. If you see a different bullet shape, such as a check mark, choose F<u>o</u>rmat, Bullets and <u>N</u>umbering. Click the sample bulleted list with round bullets and click OK.

3 **Type the following paragraph and press ↵Enter after it.**

`Pursue innovative marketing techniques.`

Word inserts another bullet followed by an indent when you press ↵Enter (see Figure 4.16).

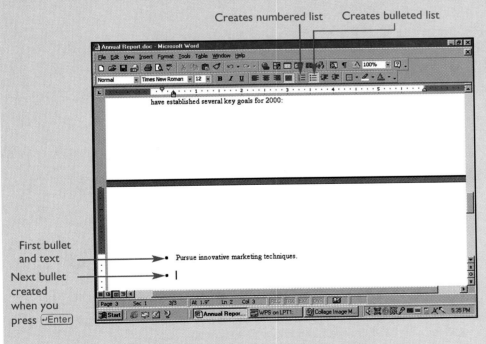

Creates numbered list   Creates bulleted list

First bullet and text

Next bullet created when you press ↵Enter

Figure 4.16
Using the Bullet feature helps you quickly create a bulleted list.

4 **Type the following paragraph and press ↵Enter.**

`Increase usage of existing computer systems by hiring in-house training personnel and establishing a continuing schedule of training classes.`

5 **Type the following paragraph and press ↵Enter.**

`Implement an electronic project management program in all business units and corporate headquarters.`

continues ▶

To Create a Bulleted List   (continued)

6 Type the following paragraph and press ⏎Enter.

Reduce the travel and expenditures for the Company by closely evaluating each request for viability.

Your document should look like Figure 4.17. You need to get rid of the bullet below the last item.

Figure 4.17
Your completed bullet list makes the items stand out.

Bulleted list ───

Need to delete extra bullet ───

Second line indents below text in first line

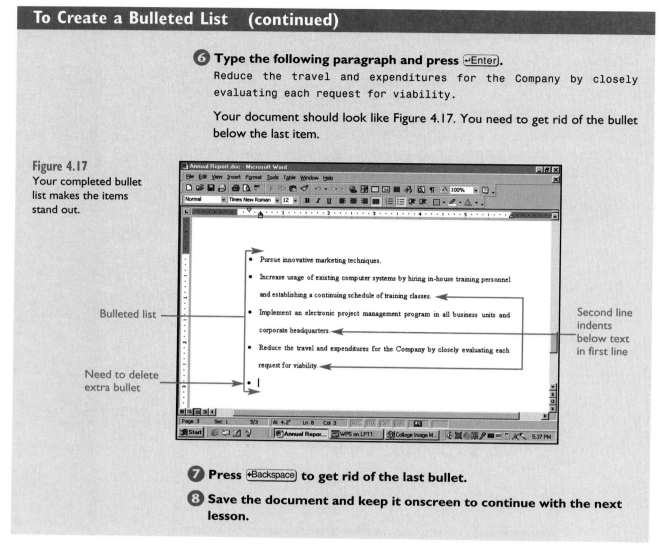

7 Press ⟵Backspace to get rid of the last bullet.

8 Save the document and keep it onscreen to continue with the next lesson.

 You can also create a numbered list by clicking the Numbering button on the Formatting toolbar. Word starts numbering the paragraphs as you type them.

You can also choose other bullet and number styles by choosing Format, Bullets and Numbering. When the Bullets and Numbering dialog box appears (see Figure 4.18), click the style you want and then click OK.

You can add or delete items within a bulleted or numbered list. When you do, the numbered list automatically renumbers itself.

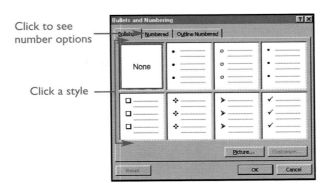

Figure 4.18
Select a different bullet or numbering style for your list.

Click to see number options

Click a style

You can use the Symbol dialog box (see Figure 4.19) to create bulleted lists with special symbols. To do this, complete the following steps:

1. Choose Insert, Symbol.
2. Select a category from the Font drop-down list. You can find special symbols in these font categories: Symbols, Wingdings, and WP Iconic Symbols.
3. Click a symbol to get a better view.
4. Click Insert; then click Close.
5. Press (Tab↹) and type the first item.
6. Press (↵Enter) to add another symbol and create your bulleted list.

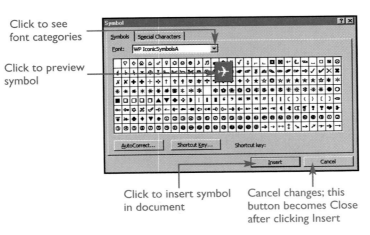

Figure 4.19
Select a symbol to create a bulleted list.

Click to see font categories

Click to preview symbol

Click to insert symbol in document

Cancel changes; this button becomes Close after clicking Insert

Lesson 7: Highlighting Text

People often use a highlighting marker to highlight important parts of textbooks, magazine articles, and other documents. You can use Word's **Highlight** feature to draw the reader's attention to important information within the documents you create.

After reviewing the annual report, you decide to highlight particular sections for the reader's benefit.

To Highlight Text

1 **With Annual Report open, press** Ctrl+Home **to position the insertion point at the beginning of the document.**

2 **Select the phrase** industry analysts remain optimistic about the future **in the first paragraph.**
You want to highlight this phrase so it will stand out.

> **X** If you have trouble clicking and dragging to select text, you can use keyboard shortcuts. First, position the insertion point at the beginning of industry, press F8, and press Ctrl+→ until you have selected the entire phrase.

 3 **Click the Highlight button on the Formatting toolbar.**
Word uses the default highlight color to highlight the text you selected. After you click the Highlight button, the text is deselected.

> **/!\ Highlight Color**
> The highlight color is the last color used. If you want to change the color, click the Highlight drop-down list arrow and click a different color.

4 **Scroll down to see the paragraph below the heading** 2000 Capital Expenditures.

5 **Select the phrase** increasing our competitiveness and efficiency in production.
You also want to highlight this phrase for your readers.

6 **Click the Highlight button to highlight the selected text.**
The phrase should be highlighted, as shown in Figure 4.20.

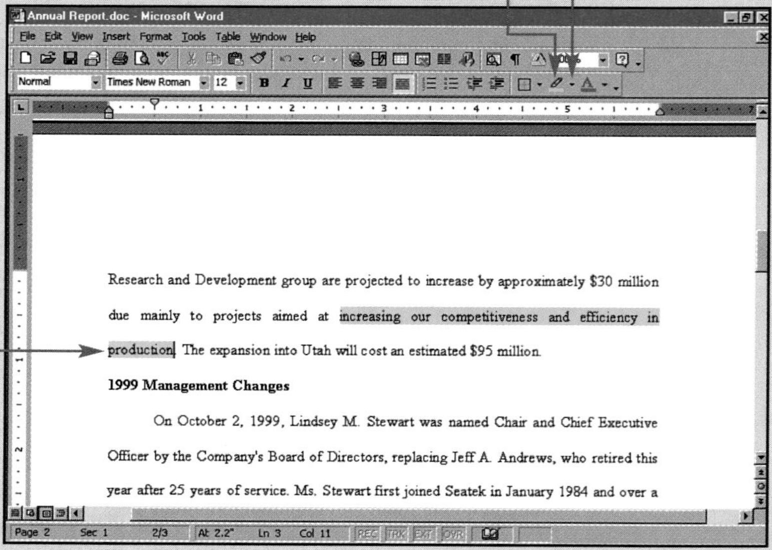

High-light button   Click to choose highlight color

Figure 4.20
Use the Highlight feature to point out important information.

Highlighted text

Research and Development group are projected to increase by approximately $30 million due mainly to projects aimed at increasing our competitiveness and efficiency in production. The expansion into Utah will cost an estimated $95 million.

1999 Management Changes

On October 2, 1999, Lindsey M. Stewart was named Chair and Chief Executive Officer by the Company's Board of Directors, replacing Jeff A. Andrews, who retired this year after 25 years of service. Ms. Stewart first joined Seatek in January 1984 and over a

7 **Save the document and keep it onscreen to continue with the next lesson.**

Using the Highlight Feature
You can click the Highlight button before selecting text. When you do this, the mouse pointer resembles a highlighting pen. You can then click and drag across text you want to highlight. The Highlight feature stays on, so you can highlight additional text. When you are through, click the Highlight button to turn it off. To remove highlight, select the highlighted text, click the Highlight drop-down arrow and choose None.

Printing Highlighted Text
If you have a color printer, you'll see the highlight colors on your printout. If you're using a black-and-white printer, the highlight will be shades of gray. Make sure you can easily read the text with the gray highlight. If not, select a lighter highlight color and print it again.

Lesson 8: Adding a Border

You can draw attention to an entire paragraph by putting a border around it. A **border** is a line that surrounds a paragraph or group of paragraphs. You can select the setting, line style, color, and width.

You decide to add a border around the double-indented paragraph.

To Add a Border

1 **In the Annual Report file, select the double-indented paragraph on page 2.**

2 **Choose Format, Borders and Shading.**
The Borders and Shading dialog box appears, as shown in Figure 4.21. This dialog box is where you select how you want the border to appear.

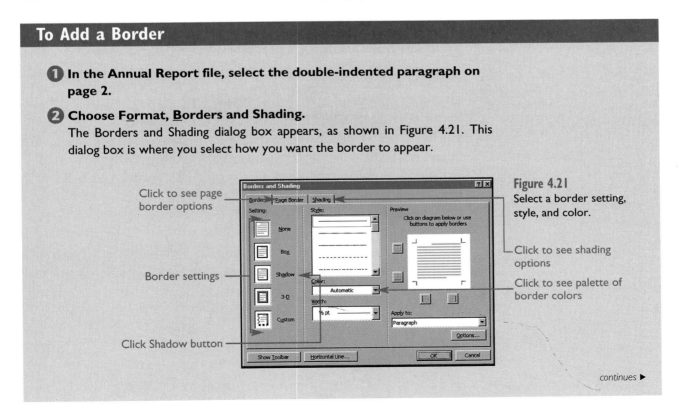

Click to see page border options

Border settings

Click Shadow button

Figure 4.21
Select a border setting, style, and color.

Click to see shading options

Click to see palette of border colors

continues ▶

To Add a Border (continued)

❸ Click the Sha̲dow setting to set the primary format of the border.

❹ Click the C̲olor drop-down arrow.
A color palette appears, so you can choose the color you want for the border (see Figure 4.22).

Figure 4.22
Choose a color from the color palette.

Shadow setting ————

Blue border ————

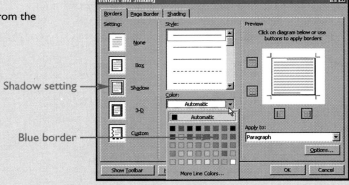

❺ Click Blue (the third color from the right on the second row).
The color palette closes, and you see the blue color displayed.

❻ Click OK and deselect the text.
Word applies a blue shadow border around the selected paragraph, as shown in Figure 4.23.

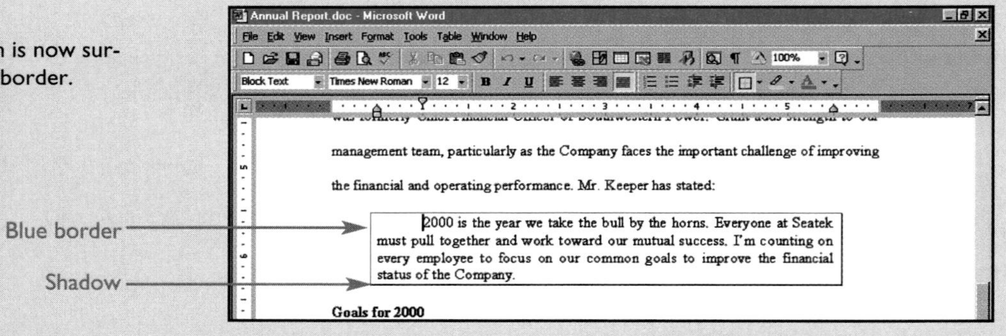

Figure 4.23
The paragraph is now sur-rounded by a border.

Blue border ————

Shadow ————

> 2000 is the year we take the bull by the horns. Everyone at Seatek must pull together and work toward our mutual success. I'm counting on every employee to focus on our common goals to improve the financial status of the Company.

❼ Save the document, print it, and close it.

Choosing a Page Border and Shading

You can also create a border for the entire page through the Borders and Shading dialog box. Simply click the **P**age Border tab at the top of the dialog box and choose the options you want.

You can add shading to paragraph and page borders. *Shading* is a colored background behind text within a border. Typically, you should color-coordinate the border and fill colors. For example, if you have a dark blue border, choose a complementary light blue fill color.

Another nice feature you can choose for page borders is A**r**t options. The A**r**t drop-down list provides images, such as hearts and stars, which form a page border.

Summary

In this project, you learned some exciting methods to enhance the appearance of your documents. You made the text easier to read by using double-spacing and appropriate fonts, inserting bullets, highlighting text, and adding a border. You also learned how to set margins, change the alignment, and indent text. All of these formatting techniques have dramatically improved your document.

Although these features are a great way to start improving your documents, Word offers a lot more enhancements. Use the Help feature to learn more about formatting options, especially those found in the Font, Paragraph, and Borders and Shading dialog boxes. There's no limit to what you can do with these features!

Checking Concepts and Terms

True/False

For each of the following, check *T* or *F* to indicate whether the statement is true or false.

__T __F   **1.** The default left and right margins are 1" each. [L1]

__T __F   **2.** To see the space for the left and right margins, you should view the document in Print Layout view. [L1]

__T __F   **3.** To double-space existing text, you must first select the text. [L2]

__T __F   **4.** You see additional space symbols between words when you select Justify alignment. [L3]

__T __F   **5.** You should select between 10- and 12-point font size for large bodies of text, such as paragraphs. [L5]

__T __F   **6.** To end a bulleted list, press Del to delete the extra bullet. [L6]

__T __F   **7.** If you click the Highlight button before selecting text, you can continue selecting and highlighting text without clicking the Highlight button each time. [L7]

__T __F   **8.** When you create a border, it applies to the paragraph that contains the insertion point. [L8]

__T __F   **9.** An effective border color combination would be a dark blue border with a light blue shading. [L8]

__T __F **10.** Sans serif fonts are more appropriate for paragraphs than serif fonts. [L5]

Multiple Choice

Circle the letter of the correct answer for each of the following.

1. What feature should you use to emphasize words or a phrase within a paragraph? [L7]

 a. border

 b. highlight

 c. bullets

 d. shading

2. What term refers to how text lines up at the left and right margins? [L3]

 a. line spacing

 b. margins

 c. justified text

 d. alignment

3. What format is appropriate for a long quotation within a document? [L4]

 a. indent

 b. double indent

 c. hanging indent

 d. double-spacing

4. What point size is most appropriate for a heading? [L5]

 a. 8

 b. 10

 c. 12

 d. 16

5. What format is most appropriate for emphasizing a list of items in random order? [L6]

 a. bulleted list

 b. numbered list

 c. border

 d. highlight

6. All of the following are border options except _____. [L8]

 a. style

 b. color

 c. setting

 d. position

Screen ID

Label each element of the Word screen shown in Figure 4.24.

Figure 4.24

A. Bullets

B. Center

C. double-spacing

D. Font

E. Font Size

F. Highlight

G. highlighted text

H. Justify

I. Top margin

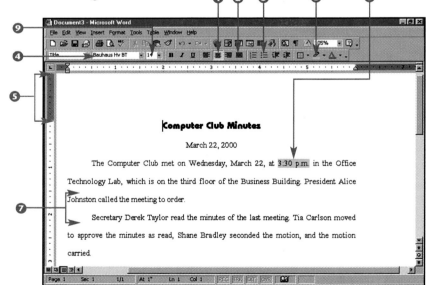

1. _____   4. _____   7. _____

2. _____   5. _____   8. _____

3. _____   6. _____   9. _____

Discussion Questions

1. Explain how margins and line spacing impact the readability of a document.

2. Display the Font dialog box. Scroll through the Font list box and look at the preview window for each font. Make a list of at least five sans serif fonts, five serif fonts, and five decorative fonts. Explain typical purposes for the three categories.

3. Think of advertising flyers you've seen on campus, in newspapers, and so on. Explain why bulleted lists can be more appropriate than paragraphs of text. Also explain how borders impact the effectiveness of flyers.

Skill Drill

Skill Drill exercises reinforce project skills. Each skill reinforced is the same, or nearly the same, as a skill presented in the project. Detailed instructions are provided in a step-by-step format.

1. Setting Margins

You've created a short report for a class and know that the report's appearance would be improved if the margins were changed. After checking a standard reference manual you decide to set a 1.5" top margin and a 1.25" bottom margin. [L1]

1. Open **WD1-0402** and save it as **Internet Report**.

2. Choose File, Page Setup.

3. Type **1.5** in the Top text box.

4. Press Tab⇥ to move to the Bottom text box.

5. Type **1.25** and click OK.

6. Save the document and leave it onscreen to continue to Exercise 2.

2. Changing Line Spacing

You decide to change the line spacing in your document to double-spacing to improve its readability. You decide to double-space all of the text except for the title. [L2]

1. In the Internet Report file, position the insertion point at the beginning of the first paragraph.

2. Select the paragraphs you want to format by pressing Ctrl+⇧Shift+End.

3. Choose Format, Paragraph.

4. Click the drop-down arrow next to the Line spacing box.

5. Choose Double from the list, and click OK.

6. Position the insertion point before the text **.edu** on page 2.

7. Select the lines listing the domain names.

8. Choose Format, Paragraph.

9. Click the drop-down arrow next to the Line spacing box.

10. Choose Single from the list, and click OK.

11. Save the document and keep it onscreen to continue to Exercise 3.

3. Selecting Text Alignment

After examining your report, you decide to justify the text for a more professional appearance. You also decide to use Center alignment to center the title and subtitles between the margins. [L3]

1. With Internet Report onscreen, choose Edit, Select All.

2. Click the Justify button on the Formatting toolbar.

3. Click in the document window to deselect text.

4. Position the insertion point within the title, `Using the Internet`, and click the Center button on the Standard toolbar.

5. Select the subtitle `Internet Protocol`; then click the Center button on the Formatting toolbar.

6. Repeat step 5 for these two subtitles: `Domain Names` and `Problems`.

7. Save the document and leave it onscreen to continue to the next exercise.

4. Indenting Text

Following standard procedures for quotations, you double-indent and single-space the quotation in your report. [L4]

1. In the Internet Report file, position the insertion point within the following quotation that is on the last page.

> `Given the tremendous economic opportunities of the Internet, and given the tremendous reliance that corporations and individuals place on the stability of their registered domain names, the court system and not the registration system should be the only authority for changing a properly registered domain name.`

2. Choose Format, Paragraph to display the Paragraph dialog box.

3. In the Indentation section, click the Left increment button until you see 0.5" in the Left text box.

4. Click the Right increment button until you see 0.5" in the Right text box.

5. Click the Line spacing drop-down arrow and choose Single.

6. Click OK.

7. Save the document and keep it onscreen to continue to the next exercise.

5. Changing the Font and Font Size

The font used in your document is Courier New 12-point size. For ease of reading you decide to use Garamond for the body text and Univers font for an attention-getting title. [L5]

1. With Internet Report onscreen, press (Ctrl)+(Home).

2. Choose Edit, Select All.

3. Click the Font drop-down arrow on the Formatting toolbar.

4. Scroll down through the menu and choose Garamond.

5. Deselect the text.

6. Select the title `Using the Internet`.

7. Click the Font drop-down arrow and choose Univers.

8. Click the Font Size drop-down arrow and choose 14 from the Font Size menu.

9. Click within the document window to deselect the title.

10. Save and keep the document onscreen to continue to the next exercise.

6. Creating a Bulleted List

The list of domain conventions is difficult to read. You determine that including a bullet before each will improve both the appearance and readability of the list. [L6]

1. With the Internet Report onscreen, position the insertion point before the text `.edu` on page 2.

2. Select the list of domains.

3. Click the Bullets button on the Formatting toolbar.

4. Save the document and keep it onscreen to continue to the next exercise.

7. Highlighting Text

While proofreading the report, you decide that highlighting would add emphasis to important concepts. [L7]

1. With the Internet Report onscreen, position the insertion point before the second sentence in the second paragraph on page 1.

2. Select the sentence `An IP address is the numeric address the Internet needs to send e-mail and other data between computers.`

3. Click the Highlight button on the Formatting toolbar.

4. Scroll down to see the sentence `Domain names developed as a method for Internet users to reach desired sites quickly without memorizing IP addresses.` Click the Highlight button on the Formatting toolbar.

5. Save the document, print it, and close it.

Challenge

Challenge exercises expand on or are somewhat related to skills presented in the lessons. Each exercise provides a brief narrative introduction followed by instructions in a numbered step format that are not as detailed as those in the Skill Drill section.

1. Formatting an Invitation to a Halloween Party

You are having a Halloween party at your home and decide to create your own invitations. You create the text first and then wish to improve it by changing fonts, changing text alignment, creating a fun bulleted list, and adding a page border. [L1–3, 5–6, 8]

1. Open `WD1-0403` and save it as `Halloween Party`.

2. Set a 2.5" top margin and 2" left and right margins.

3. Set the line spacing to double-spacing.

4. Make the first line of the invitation, `Hey! You're Invited to a Halloween Party!`, larger and bolder by using the Font dialog box. Because this is a fun invitation, try a different font, such as Chiller, Dauphin, Desdemona, or Cooperplate Gothic Bold. Apply your font choice to the last line of the invitation so both lines have the same appearance.

5. Pick another font for the body of the invitation. Try to find one that coordinates with the one you used for the title.

6. Center the first line of the invitation. Left-align the body of the invitation and the bulleted list. Center the last line of the invitation.

7. Select the `When`, `Where`, `Why`, and `RSVP` lines. Choose Format, Bullets and Numbering. When the Bullets and Numbering dialog box appears, select the Bulleted tab. Click the Customize button to select a bullet related to your Halloween theme. When the Customized Bulleted List dialog box appears, click the Font button and choose the Webdings font with the size set at 22 points. Next, click the Bullet button and select either the spider symbol or the spider web symbol from the Symbol dialog box. Return to your document by clicking OK in each dialog box.

8. Select a Halloween theme page border from the Art drop-down list. Select an appropriate page border color.

9. Save the document and print it.

2. Formatting a Letter to Attendees of an International Symposium

You are organizing the annual International Symposium on Cultural Diversity in Business. The letter you are sending out to invite participants needs formatting. Because this is a business letter, you want the body of the letter single-spaced, but you would like additional spacing between the paragraphs. [L1–2, 5]

1. Open the file WD1-0404 and save it as **Symposium**.
2. Insert the date at the top of the letter; leave four blank lines between the date and the salutation.
3. Set all four margins to 1.5".
4. Select the body of the letter and change the paragraph spacing before and after options to 6 points.
5. Add four blank lines to the end of the document and type your name and title.
6. Save the document and print it.

3. Editing a Welcome Letter

You composed a letter to welcome new members to an organization of which you are president. You use several of the formatting techniques you leaned in this project to improve the appearance of the letter. [L1, 5]

1. Open WD1-0405 and save it as **Welcome Letter**.
2. Insert the correct date at the top of the letter.
3. Type your name and address for the inside address. Edit the salutation to reflect your name.
4. Set 2" top and bottom margins. Use your judgment to set the left and right margins. Make sure the text looks balanced on the page.
5. Change the font for the entire document to 11-point Garamond.
6. Save the document and print it.

4. Formatting a Research Paper

You are formatting a lengthy research paper for submission to a scholarly journal. To create a more professional appearance you plan to format the paper for text alignment, enhanced headings and subheadings, adjusted line spacing, and formatted quotations. You decide to enhance the quotation further by applying a paragraph border. Finally, you call attention to important points by highlighting the text. [L1–5, 7–8]

1. Open WD1-0406 and save it as **Research Paper**.
2. Set a 1.5" top margin and a 1.25" bottom margin.
3. Position the insertion point at the beginning of the first paragraph. Select the body text and choose double-spacing.
4. With the body text still selected, change alignment to Justify.
5. On page 3 of the document, format the quotation It is abundantly clear that whatever information occurs first has disproportionate influence on the final outcome of interviews. Indent the quotation one inch on both the left and right sides. Single-space the quotation.

6. With the insertion point still within the quotation, format the paragraph with a blue shadow border.

7. Increase the font size of the major headings to 14-point Arial.

8. Change the font for the secondary headings to Arial. Leave the font size at 12 points.

9. Highlight the following phrases.

   `Personal interviewing continues to be the most widely used method for selecting employees and is often used in conjunction with other techniques such as reference checking, weighted application blanks, skill tests, and psychological testing.`

   `the validity of the interview rests on the interviewer`

10. Save the document and print it.

5. Formatting a Loan Proposal

You want to apply for a loan from a local bank. You prepare a loan proposal to facilitate the process. [L1–5]

1. Open `WD1-0407` and save it as `Loan Proposal`.

2. Set 1.25" top and bottom margins.

3. Select double-spacing for the body of the document.

4. Increase the size of the heading `Loan Proposal` and center align it on the page.

5. Indent the expense list by selecting it and choosing a 2" left indention in the Paragraph Format dialog box. Change the list to single-spacing. Highlight the total amount of anticipated expenses.

6. Repeat the above process with the net profits list.

7. Adjust the spacing as needed. You might need to delete some extra blank lines to prevent the lists from separating between pages.

8. Save the document and print it.

Discovery Zone

Discovery Zone exercises require advanced knowledge of topics presented in *Essentials* lessons, application of skills from multiple lessons, or self-directed learning of new skills.

1. Formatting a Permission Slip

As a PTA volunteer at the local elementary school, you have been asked to create a permission slip to be used for an upcoming field trip. Open `WD1-0408` and save it as `Permission Slip`.

Set a 1.5" top margin. Center the three-line heading at the top of the document and emphasize it by changing font size and applying bold. Choose a font and font size for the body text. The font should be appropriate for an elementary school. (*Hint*: Make the font large enough so curious children can easily read it.) Use 1.5 line spacing.

To format the return slip, apply a border to the text. After applying the border, apply a Gray-15% shading. Also apply an appropriate page border with an appropriate border color. Then save and print it.

[?] 2. Creating a Health Information Sheet

As part of an assignment in a Health class, you create an information sheet on Osteoarthritis to share with your classmates.

Open **WD1-0409** and save it **Osteoarthritis**. Apply the formats as indicated in Figure 4.25.

Figure 4.25
Use this example to help you format your document.

Shading, line spacing, and Bookman Old Style font

12-point Antique Olive with 6-point spacing above and below paragraph

Use Bullets and Numbers dialog box to create numbers for both lists

1.5"

16-point Antique Olive, centered

Use this page border

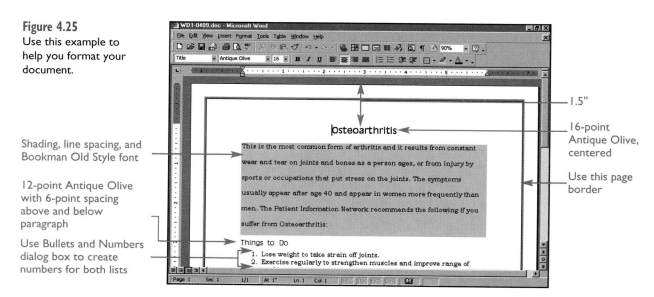

Use onscreen Help to learn how to set spacing before and after paragraphs. Also use Help to learn about text enhancements, so you can apply Blinking Background to **Exercise regularly**.

Use the Format Painter to copy the **Things to Do** formats to the next heading. Make sure the other regular text matches the font you used in the first paragraph. Each numbered list should start with **1**. Save the document and print it.

[?] 3. Formatting a Course Description Document

Use Figure 4.26 to create a course description document. Set appropriate margins so the document looks nice on the page. Use Format Painter when applicable. Use Help to learn about customizing bulleted lists; then create a customized bulleted list that uses the disk symbol in the Wingdings font. Save the document as **Course Descriptions** and print it.

Sans serif font such as Kabel Md BT

Black 3-point width border, shading, and sans serif font

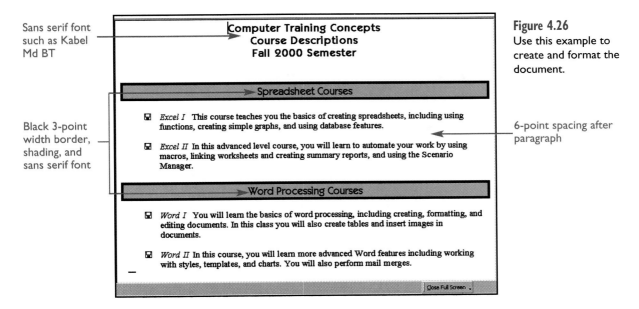

Figure 4.26
Use this example to create and format the document.

6-point spacing after paragraph

Edit your document by using course descriptions for computer courses at your school or training center. Look at course catalogs to create your descriptions. Save the revised document with a filename such as **UVSC Course Descriptions**.

Formatting Longer Documents

Objectives

In this project, you learn how to

- ➤ Center Text Vertically on a Page
- ➤ Insert Page Numbers
- ➤ Insert Page and Section Breaks
- ➤ Prevent Text from Separating Across Pages
- ➤ Insert a Nonbreaking Space
- ➤ Create Footnotes
- ➤ Create Headers and Footers
- ➤ Create a Hanging Indent Paragraph

Key terms in this project include

- endnote
- footer
- footnote
- footnote reference mark
- footnote text
- hard page break
- header
- nonbreaking hyphen
- nonbreaking space
- orphan
- section break
- soft page break
- suppress
- vertical alignment
- widow

Why Would I Do This?

n the last project, you learned some important formatting elements, such as margins, alignment, and line spacing. But Word offers additional format features that improve the appearance of your documents.

In this project, you learn how to center text vertically on a title page, insert page numbers, create footnotes, and format a hanging paragraph. You will also manipulate page and section breaks and create headers in a report.

Visual Summary

Figure 5.1 illustrates a centered title page.

Figure 5.1
The title page is centered horizontally and vertically.

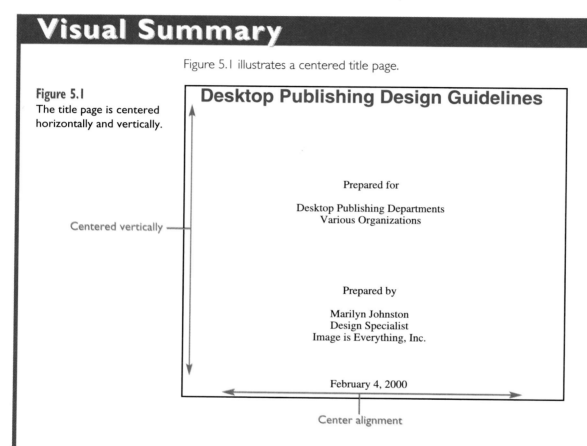

Figure 5.2 illustrates bibliographic entries.

Figure 5.2
Use the hanging indent format for bibliographic entries.

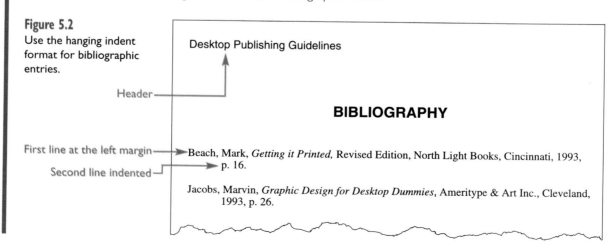

Figure 5.3 illustrates footnotes. By the time you complete this project, you'll be able to apply these types of formats.

Entire bulleted list
wraps to top of page

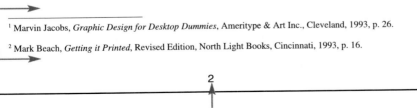

Figure 5.3
This page contains an entire bulleted list on one page and footnotes to document sources.

Desktop Publishing Guidelines

- Times New Roman
- Bookman
- Garamond
- Palatino

Use a sans serif font for titles, headings, and graphics captions. The clean look of a sans serif font is a nice change of pace for the reader. The reader can easily locate headings on a page because the sans serif font stands out from the serif font. Typical sans serif fonts include Arial, Helvetica, and Avant Garde.[1]

When you choose a font, make sure it has about four font styles. A font style is a variation of the actual font. The four primary font styles are regular, bold, italic, and bold italic. Use one of the last three font styles to help enhance text instead of selecting additional font faces.[2]

Footnote number

Weight

When selecting font faces, you should also look at its weight. The weight of a font refers to the degree of thickness of the font face. *Regular* weight is appropriate for basic document text. You don't want a font that is too light (thin) or too heavy (thick) for paragraphs of text.

Headings, however, typically have a heavier weight than regular document text. When choosing a sans serif font, be careful that it is not too heavy. Some heavy-weight fonts are difficult to read, because the characters seem to run into each other.

[1] Marvin Jacobs, *Graphic Design for Desktop Dummies*, Ameritype & Art Inc., Cleveland, 1993, p. 26.

[2] Mark Beach, *Getting it Printed*, Revised Edition, North Light Books, Cincinnati, 1993, p. 16.

2

Footnotes at
bottom of page

Page number

Lesson 1: Centering Text Vertically on a Page

Typically the first page in a document or research paper is the title page. The standard format is to center it horizontally and vertically. In the last project, you learned to use the Center alignment option to center text horizontally. In this lesson, you learn to center text vertically on a page. You use the *vertical alignment* option in the Page Setup dialog box to position text between the top and bottom edges of a page.

The report you work with in this project contains a section break after the title page. You use a *section break* to mark the end of a section in a document. By using section breaks in a document, you can format a single section without formatting the entire document. For example, in this lesson, you select center vertical alignment for section 1, which contains only the title page. The rest of the document, which is in section 2, maintains the original document formats. You learn more about section breaks in Lesson 3.

To Center Text Vertically on a Page

1 Open **WD1-0501** and save it as **Desktop Publishing Guidelines**. **Notice that the insertion point is at the beginning of the document.**

2 Choose **File**, **Page Setup**.
The Page Setup dialog box appears with the margin options displayed. You need to display the layout options.

3 Click the **Layout** tab.
The layout options appear, as shown in Figure 5.4. The default vertical alignment places text at the top of the page.

Figure 5.4
The Layout tab contains the option to select vertical alignment.

Current vertical alignment

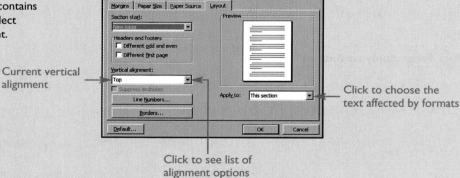

Click to choose the text affected by formats

Click to see list of alignment options

4 Click the **Vertical** alignment drop-down arrow.

5 Choose **Center**.
The **Vertical** alignment option now displays Center. The Apply to option displays This section.

6 Click **OK**.

7 Click the **Print Layout View** button, click the **Zoom** drop-down arrow, and choose **Two Pages**.
The title page is now centered vertically on the page, as shown in Figure 5.5. In this document, the remaining pages use top vertical alignment because they are in a different section.

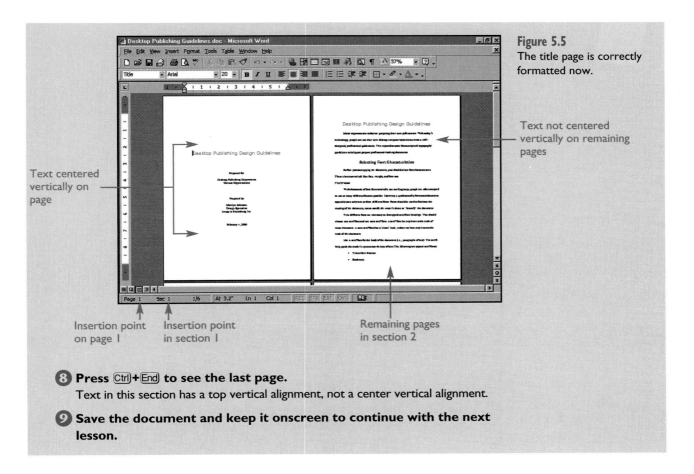

Figure 5.5
The title page is correctly formatted now.

Text centered vertically on page

Text not centered vertically on remaining pages

Insertion point on page 1

Insertion point in section 1

Remaining pages in section 2

8 **Press Ctrl+End to see the last page.**
Text in this section has a top vertical alignment, not a center vertical alignment.

9 **Save the document and keep it onscreen to continue with the next lesson.**

When you select options in the Page Setup dialog box, you specify the amount of text to which you wish to apply the formats. Table 5.1 lists and describes the Apply to options.

Table 5.1   Page Setup Apply to Options

Option	Description
Whole Document	Applies formats to the entire document, regardless of where the insertion point is when you access the dialog box.
This Point Forward	Applies formats from the current page to the end of the document.
This Section	Applies formats to the current section only; other sections retain their formats.
Selected Text	Applies formats to only the text you selected prior to accessing the Page Setup dialog box.

Vertical Alignment with Page and Section Breaks
Depending on the page breaks in your document, the only Apply to options in the Page Setup dialog box might be Whole Document and This Point Forward. In most situations, you don't want to center text vertically for the whole document for all pages after the title page.

To make sure you vertically center only the current page, you must have a section break after the title page. When you have a section break, Word lets you choose to apply formats to a single section only.

Lesson 2: Inserting Page Numbers

Imagine that you have a printed research paper in a file folder. You are rushing to class to submit your research paper when you drop the folder. All of the pages go in every direction. Can you imagine the frustration of trying to put the report back together in order if you have not included page numbers in the document? Page numbers help make sure the document is assembled in the correct order.

Page numbers are essential in long documents. They serve as a convenient reference point for the writer and the reader. Without page numbers in a long document, you would have a difficult time trying to find text on a particular page or trying to tell someone else where to locate a particular passage in the document.

You can use the Page Numbers feature to automatically insert page numbers throughout your document. This feature lets you select the position of the page number, such as top of the page, and the alignment, such as on the right side. Word not only inserts page numbers for you but also updates the numbers when you add or delete pages. In this lesson, you insert page numbers in your report.

Insert Page Numbers

❶ In the Desktop Publishing Guidelines file, position the insertion point at the top of the document and make sure you are displaying the document in Print Layout view with the Two Pages zoom option. While selecting page numbering options, you need to instruct Word not to number the title page.

⚠ Using Page Numbers in Sections
Although your document is divided into two sections, one for the title page and one for the report, Word applies page numbering to the entire document, continuing page numbers from one section to the next. To prevent a page number from appearing on the title page, you need to position the insertion point on that page before you access the Page Numbers feature.

❷ Choose Insert, Page Numbers.
The Page Numbers dialog box appears, as shown in Figure 5.6. The dialog box contains options to let you choose the position and alignment of the page numbers.

Figure 5.6
Choose the position and alignment of your page numbers.

Deselect for no page number on first page

Click to change alignment

Click to set additional options

You want to display the page numbers at the bottom of the pages between the left and right margins.

❸ Click the Alignment drop-down arrow and choose Center.
This option centers the page numbers between the left and right margins, similar to the Center alignment command you used in Project 4, "Formatting Documents."

4 **Click the <u>S</u>how number on first page check box to deselect this option.**

By deselecting <u>S</u>how number on first page, you *suppress*, or "hide," the page number. The page is still counted as page 1, but the page number does not appear.

 First Page in Each Section

The page numbering feature applies throughout the document. When you deselect <u>S</u>how number on first page, Word suppresses the page number on the first page of every section.

5 **Click OK.**

Word does not show a page number on the title page or the next page because both pages are the first page in their respective section (see Figure 5.7).

First page in section 1   First page in section 2

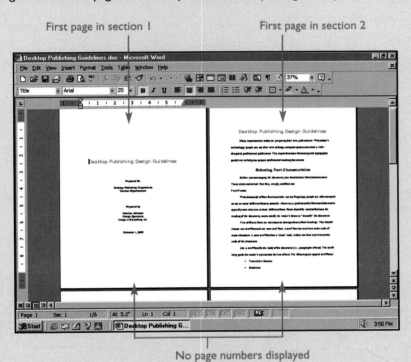

No page numbers displayed

Figure 5.7
Page numbers don't appear on the first page in each section.

 Viewing Page Numbers

Word automatically switches to Print Layout view, so you can see page numbers. Normal view does not display page numbers.

6 **Click the Zoom drop-down arrow and choose 100%.**

7 **Scroll to the bottom of page 3.**

In Print Layout view, you see the page number at the bottom of the third page. It is centered between the left and right margins, as shown in Figure 5.8.

continues ▶

To Insert Page Numbers   (continued)

Figure 5.8
In Print Layout view, the page number displays. Here it is centered at the bottom of the page.

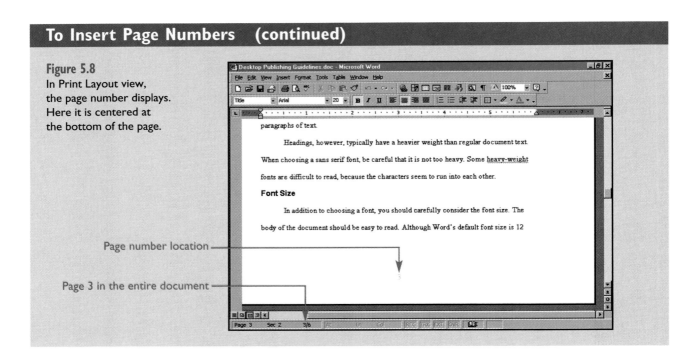

Page number location

Page 3 in the entire document

The page numbers actually appear, starting with the second page within section 2. Word, however, counts the title page as page 1 and the first page of section 2 as page 2. Typically, you should count the first page of the body of the report as page 1. Therefore, in the next exercise, you position the insertion point at the beginning of section 2 and restart the section page numbers at 1 again.

To Restart Page Numbers in Section 2

1 **Position the insertion point at the top of page 2, the first page of the body of the document.**
The first page of the body of the report—not the title page—should count as page 1. Therefore, you must change the page number value back to one on this page.

2 **Choose Insert, Page Numbers.**

3 **Make sure the Alignment chosen is Center and that Show number on first page is deselected.**

4 **Click Format to display additional options.**
The Page Number Format dialog box appears (see Figure 5.9). You need to start the page number back at 1 for this section.

Figure 5.9
Change the page number back to 1 for section 2.

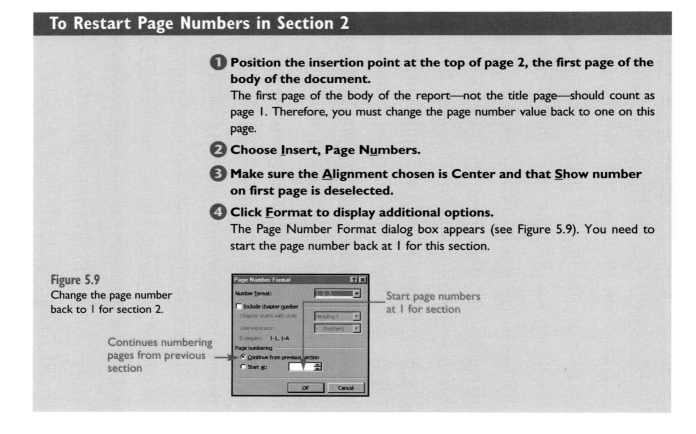

Start page numbers at 1 for section

Continues numbering pages from previous section

5 **Click the Start at option button and type 1.**

6 **Click OK; then click OK in the Page Numbers dialog box.**

The first page in section 2 is counted as page 1 within its section (see Figure 5.10).

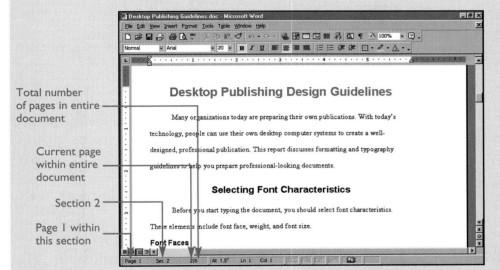

Total number of pages in entire document

Current page within entire document

Section 2

Page 1 within this section

Figure 5.10
The status bar shows that you are on page 1 in section 2.

7 **Scroll to the bottom of page 2 within section 2.**

The page number is page 2 in section 2. It is the third page in the entire document (see Figure 5.11).

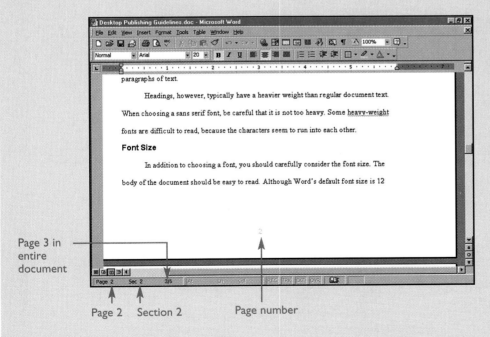

Page 3 in entire document

Page 2   Section 2   Page number

Figure 5.11
The page number is now page two.

8 **Save the document and leave it onscreen to continue with the next lesson.**

Changing the Page Number Position
If you decide you want page numbers in a different location, simply access the Page Numbers dialog box and choose another position and alignment.

Lesson 3: Inserting Page and Section Breaks

In Lesson 1, you learned that a section break divides a document into different sections that can contain different formats. Although page numbering affects the entire document, other formats, such as margins, can affect an individual section.

At times, you might want to start a new page within a section. Instead of pressing ⏎Enter several times to get to a new page, insert a **hard page break** to immediately start a new page. Insert a hard page break in your document to start the Setting the Spacing section on a new page.

 Section and Page Breaks
If you want to have different formats, such as page numbers and vertical alignment, throughout your document, insert a section break by choosing Next page in the Break dialog box.

Inserting a page break starts a new page within the section. You can insert a page break as long as you plan to use the same formats in that section, regardless of the page break.

To Insert a Hard Page Break

① **In the Desktop Publishing Guidelines file, position the insertion point at the beginning of the line that contains the title Setting the Spacing on page 3.**
You want to start a new page for this information.

② **Choose Insert, Break.**
The Break dialog box appears (see Figure 5.12). This dialog box lets you insert page and section breaks.

Figure 5.12
Use the Break dialog box to create a page or section break.

Starts a new page →

Starts a new section →

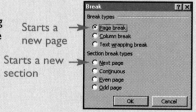

③ **Make sure Page break is selected and click OK.**
Word inserts a page break at the insertion point location. The title is now located at the top of the new page.

 If the page break occurs in the middle of the title, click the Undo button to undo the page break action. Then position the insertion point at the beginning of the title and insert the page break again.

4 **Click the Normal View button and scroll up to see the page break.**

In Normal view, you see a dotted line with the words `Page Break` to indicate a hard page break (see Figure 5.13). A section break has two dotted lines with the words `Section Break (Next Page)`. A regular page break is simply a dotted line.

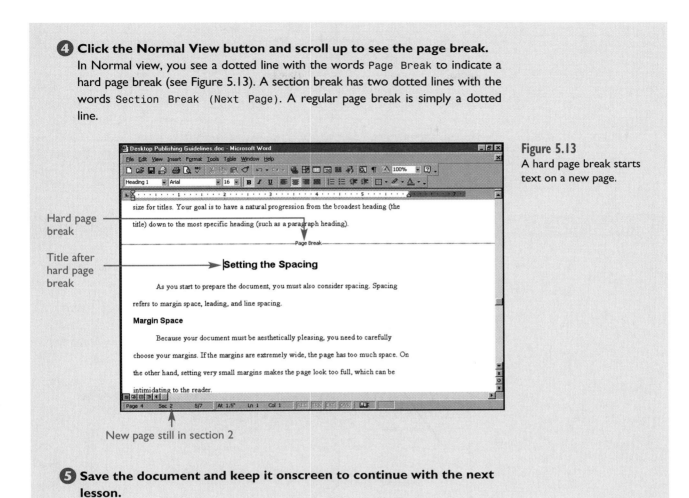

Hard page break

Title after hard page break

New page still in section 2

Figure 5.13
A hard page break starts text on a new page.

5 **Save the document and keep it onscreen to continue with the next lesson.**

 Hard Page Break Keyboard Shortcut
You can insert a hard page break quickly by pressing Ctrl+↵Enter.

Lesson 4: Preventing Text from Separating Across Page Breaks

As you continue typing a document, Word automatically continues to another page when you fill up a page. These page breaks, often called *soft page breaks*, are adjusted as you add and delete text in a document.

To achieve a professional appearance, certain types of text should not separate between pages. For example, your document should not contain widows or orphans. A *widow* is the last line of a paragraph that appears by itself at the top of a page. An *orphan* is the first line of a paragraph that appears by itself at the bottom of a page. However, you don't have to worry about widows and orphans, because Word's Widow/Orphan Control feature is a default option.

Another problem that might occur is when a heading falls on the last line on the page with the following paragraph on the next page. Most of the time, Word keeps headings from being isolated at the bottom of a page.

Word, however, lets other text separate between pages. For example, it does not keep bulleted lists or tabulated text together on a page. Your document has a bulleted list on pages 1 and 2. Inserting a page break before the bulleted list will ensure the bulleted list stays together; this approach, however, is not desirable. You might later add or delete text on page 1, causing a gap at the bottom of the page where the bulleted list could then fit. In this lesson you select the bulleted list and use the Keep with ne<u>x</u>t option in the Paragraph dialog box.

To Keep Text from Separating Across Page Breaks

1 **In the Desktop Publishing Guidelines file, make sure the document is displayed in Normal view.**

2 **Scroll through the document so you see the bottom of page 1 and the top of page 2 in section 2.**
You see two bulleted items at the bottom of page 1 and the remaining bulleted list on the next page (see Figure 5.14).

Figure 5.14
The bulleted list is separated on two pages.

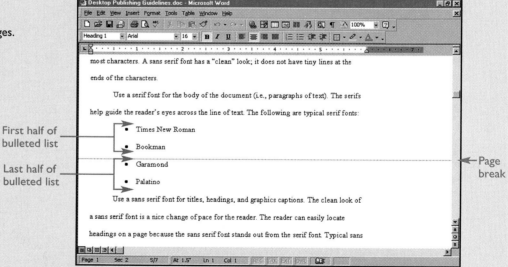

First half of bulleted list

Last half of bulleted list

Page break

3 **Click and drag to select the entire bulleted list, which spans both pages.**
You need to select the text that you want to keep from separating across pages.

4 **Choose F<u>o</u>rmat, <u>P</u>aragraph to display the Paragraph dialog box.**

5 **Click the Line and <u>P</u>age Breaks tab.**
The Widow/Orphan Control option is selected; however, though it can keep at least two lines of a paragraph together on each page, it does not keep lines together that end with a hard return. You need to select the Keep with ne<u>x</u>t option (see Figure 5.15).

Click to keep your bulleted list together

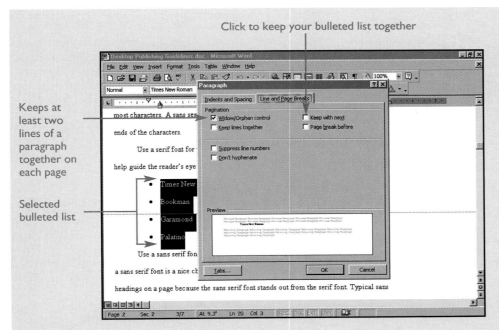

Keeps at least two lines of a paragraph together on each page

Selected bulleted list

Figure 5.15
Select options to keep text together between breaks.

6 Click the Keep with next check box and click OK.
Word now keeps the entire bulleted list together, as shown in Figure 5.16. Because the bulleted list can't fit at the bottom of page 1, it appears at the top of page 2.

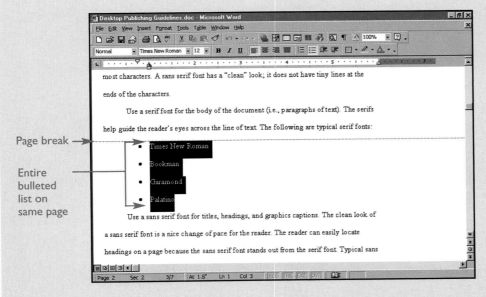

Page break

Entire bulleted list on same page

Figure 5.16
The bulleted list stays together on the same page now.

 If the entire bulleted list does not appear at the top of page 2, switch to Print Layout view and then back to Normal view.

7 Save the document and keep it onscreen to continue with the next lesson.

> ## (i) Widow and Orphan Control
> Word can identify widows and orphans because lines within a paragraph end in a soft return. The Widow/Orphan Control can't keep bulleted list items together, however, because each line ends with a hard return instead of a soft return.

Lesson 5: Inserting a Nonbreaking Space

By now you know that the word-wrap feature wraps a word to the next line if it doesn't fit at the end of the current line. Occasionally, word-wrapping between certain types of words is undesirable; that is, some words should be kept together. For example, the date `March 31` should stay together instead of separating between lines. Other items that should stay together include names, such as `Ms. Stevenson`, and page references, such as `page 15`.

To prevent words from separating due to the word-wrap feature, insert a **nonbreaking space**. Some people might refer to a nonbreaking space as a hard space.

As you review your document, you notice that the words `12` and `point` word-wrap between the two words. You want to keep `12 point` together on the same line.

To Insert a Nonbreaking Space

1 In the Desktop Publishing Guidelines file, click the Show/Hide ¶ button on the Standard toolbar.

2 Position the insertion point at the end of the second line in the first paragraph on page 3.
Notice that the word `point` in the phrase `12 point` wraps to the next line (see Figure 5.17).

Figure 5.17
You need to keep
`12 point` together.

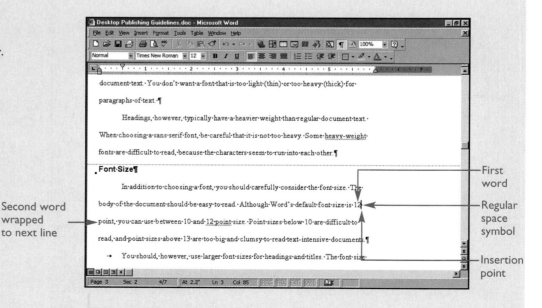

Second word
wrapped
to next line

First word

Regular space symbol

Insertion point

3 Press **Backspace** to delete the regular space.
This brings `12 point` together without any space between the two words.

4 **Press** Ctrl + ⬆Shift + Spacebar.

Word now keeps 12 point together (see Figure 5.18). Notice the difference in the nonbreaking space symbol and the regular space symbol.

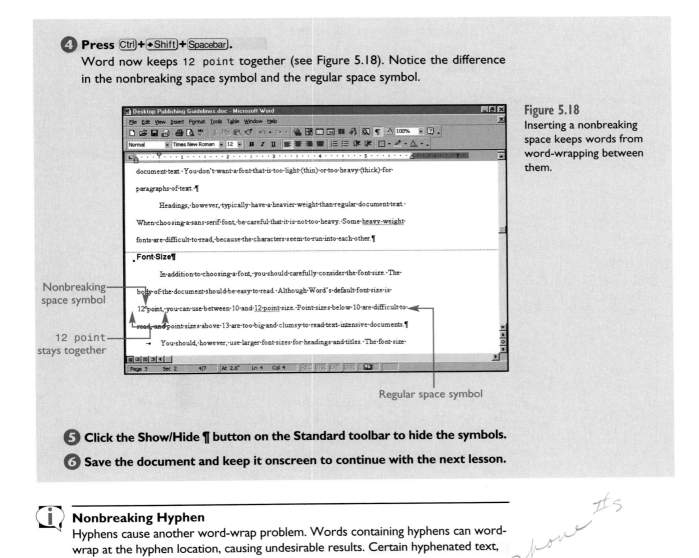

Figure 5.18
Inserting a nonbreaking space keeps words from word-wrapping between them.

Nonbreaking space symbol

12 point stays together

Regular space symbol

5 **Click the Show/Hide ¶ button on the Standard toolbar to hide the symbols.**

6 **Save the document and keep it onscreen to continue with the next lesson.**

ⓘ **Nonbreaking Hyphen**

Hyphens cause another word-wrap problem. Words containing hyphens can word-wrap at the hyphen location, causing undesirable results. Certain hyphenated text, such as phone numbers, should stay together.

To keep hyphenated words together, replace the regular hyphen with a nonbreaking hyphen. A **nonbreaking hyphen** keeps text on both sides of the hyphen together. To insert a nonbreaking hyphen, press Ctrl + ⬆Shift + - .

When you display the formatting symbols, a regular hyphen looks like a hyphen. A nonbreaking hyphen appears as a wider hyphen.

Lesson 6: Creating Footnotes

Footnotes provide references for information obtained from another source for your document. People also use footnotes to provide additional information, such as a definition or commentary, about a topic in their document. Footnotes appear at the bottom of the page where you create them. Instead of creating footnotes, you can create **endnotes** that appear at the end of the document.

When you create footnotes, Word automatically numbers them for you. If you add or delete footnotes, Word renumbers them. In this lesson, you create two footnotes and then edit one of them.

Footnote Keyboard Shortcut
The keyboard shortcut for creating a footnote is Alt+Ctrl+F.

To Create Footnotes

1 **In the Desktop Publishing Guidelines file, click the Print Layout View button.**

2 **Position the insertion point at the end of the first full paragraph on page 2 in section 2.**
The insertion point should be after the period ending with Avant Garde.

3 **Choose Insert, Footnote.**
The Footnote and Endnote dialog box appears (see Figure 5.19).

Figure 5.19
Specify whether you want to create footnotes or endnotes.

Select footnote

——Click here to set additional options

4 **Make sure the Footnote option is selected and click OK.**
Word inserts a superscript 1 in the document and displays the footnote area at the bottom of the page. You see a separator line that separates the body of the document from the footnotes.

5 **Type the following footnote text and press ↵Enter after the footnote.**
Marvin Jacobs, Graphic Design for Desktop Dummies, Ameritype & Art Inc., Cleveland, 1993, p. 26.

When you create another footnote, Word places it on the next line by default. However, you need to press ↵Enter after typing a footnote to leave a blank line between footnotes.

Your footnote should look like the one shown in Figure 5.20.

Figure 5.20
The footnote provides a reference to where you obtained the information.

Separator line —

Footnote text at bottom of page

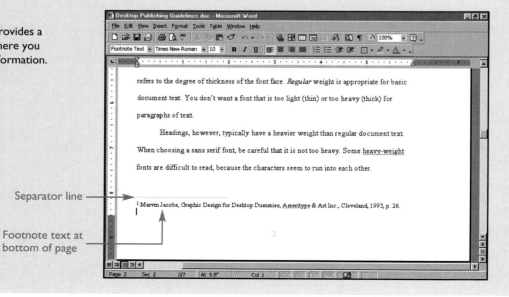

6 **Click anywhere in the document window after you type the footnote.**
A footnote consists of two parts: the footnote reference mark and the corresponding footnote text. The *footnote reference mark* appears in the body text where you placed the insertion point. The *footnote text* appears at the bottom of the page.

7 **Position the insertion point at the end of the paragraph immediately before the `Weight` heading on page 3.**

8 **Choose** **I**nsert, Foot**n**ote and click **OK.**

9 **Type the following footnote text, making sure you italicize the book name, `Getting it Printed`.**
`Mark Beach, Getting it Printed, Revised Edition, North Light Books, Cincinnati, 1993, p. 16.`

You have one blank line between the footnotes because you pressed ⏎Enter in step 5 to separate the footnotes (see Figure 5.21).

Footnote reference mark →

First footnote →

Second footnote →

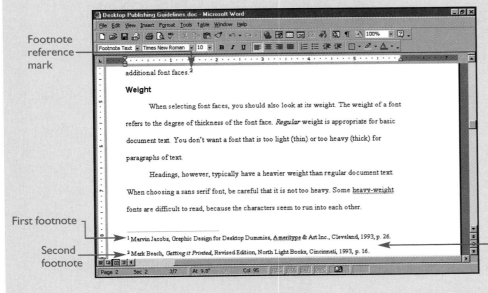

Figure 5.21
Two footnotes appear at the bottom of the page.

← Blank line between footnotes

10 **Click anywhere in the document when you finish the footnote.**

 Pressing ⏎Enter After Footnotes
Typically, you should press ⏎Enter after typing text in a footnote. If, however, you know that you do not want any more footnotes on a particular page, do not press ⏎Enter after typing the last footnote on that page.

 View Modes and Footnotes
Footnotes, similar to page numbers, appear in Print Layout view but not in Normal view. You can still work with footnotes even in Normal view, however, by double-clicking the footnote reference mark.

After creating a footnote, you may decide that you need to change it. For example, you might have left out some information or noticed an error you need to correct. In the next exercise, you need to edit the first footnote by italicizing the book title. Let's change to Normal view so you can see how to work with footnotes in this view mode.

To Edit a Footnote

❶ Click the Normal View button to the left of the horizontal scrollbar; then scroll up to see the first footnote reference mark.

❷ Position the mouse pointer directly on top of the footnote reference mark.

You first see a little box by the mouse pointer, and a ScreenTip appears to show you the text you created for the footnote (see Figure 5.22).

Figure 5.22
The ScreenTip shows the footnote text you created.

Shows footnote text ⎯

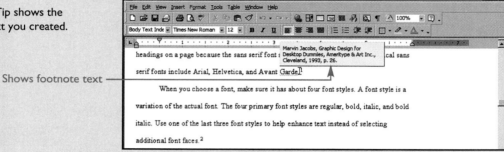

❸ Double-click the footnote reference mark.

Word displays a separate window below the document window (see Figure 5.23). This is how the footnotes appear in Normal view. You can now edit your footnote.

Figure 5.23
The screen displays footnotes in a separate window when you are in Normal view.

Document window ⎯

Click to close footnote window when done editing ⎯

Footnote window ⎯

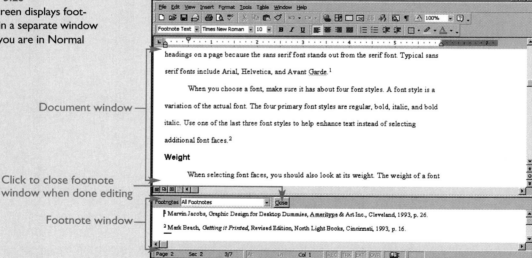

❹ Select `Graphic Design for Desktop Dummies` and click the Italic button on the Formatting toolbar.

Now the title is correctly formatted.

❺ Click the Close button on the toolbar above the footnote to close the footnote window.

❻ Save the document and keep it onscreen to continue with the next lesson.

Editing Footnotes in Print Layout View

To edit a footnote in Print Layout view, scroll to the bottom of the page to see the footnotes. Then click within the footnote to edit it.

Moving, Copying, and Deleting Footnotes

If you create a footnote in the wrong location, you can move the footnote reference marker to the correct location. If you need to cite the same source later, you can copy the footnote reference marker instead of typing the same information again. Finally, you can delete the footnote reference marker to delete the footnote text itself.

To perform any of these tasks, first click and drag across the footnote reference marker within the body of the document; then perform the task you need (that is, cut, copy, or delete).

Changing Font Size for Footnotes

The default font and font size for footnotes is 10-point Times New Roman. To change the font size for all footnotes, follow these steps to modify the Footnote Text style.

1. Choose F̲ormat, S̲tyle.

2. Select All styles from the L̲ist drop-down list.

3. Select the Footnote Text style from the S̲tyles list and click M̲odify.

4. Click F̲ormat and choose F̲ont from the menu.

5. Select the size and click OK in the Font dialog box.

6. Click OK in the Modify Style dialog box.

7. Click the close button to close the Style dialog box.

Lesson 7: Creating Headers and Footers

A **header** contains document information at the top of every page. You can insert text, page numbers, dates, and filenames in a header. You can also create a footer for the same type of information. A **footer** appears at the bottom of every page. Headers and footers are typically used in long documents, such as reports, legal briefs, medical transcripts, and proposals.

Each section in a document can have different information in a header. For example, the header in your book changes to reflect the project discussed in that section.

In this lesson, you create a header containing the title of the report.

To Create Headers

1 **In the Desktop Publishing Guidelines file, press Ctrl+Home to position the insertion point at the top of the document.**
Although you don't want a header to display on the title page, you must follow this sequence of steps to prevent a header from displaying on this page.

continues ▶

To Create Headers   (continued)

② Choose <u>V</u>iew, <u>H</u>eader and Footer.

Word switches to the Print Layout view. The Header and Footer toolbar appears in the middle of the screen (see Figure 5.24). The header area is outlined at the top of the screen. Word displays information that the header will appear on the first page in section 1.

Figure 5.24
You type in the header area and use the toolbar buttons to customize the header.

Indicates header for section 1

Header area

Header and Footer toolbar

Show Next button

③ Click the Show Next button on the Header and Footer toolbar.

This tells Word to omit a header for section 1 and display section 2, so you can create a header there. You now see the first page of section 2. The note above the header area tells you that you're creating a header for section 2 now (see Figure 5.25). You see a note that tells you that this header is the same as the header in the previous section.

Figure 5.25
You are now seeing the header area for section 2.

Note indicating header in section 2 is same as header in section 1

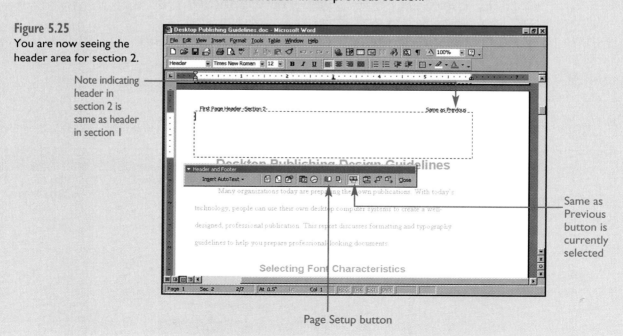

Same as Previous button is currently selected

Page Setup button

4 Click the Page Setup button on the Header and Footer toolbar.
Clicking this button displays the Page Setup dialog box with the layout options on top. Refer to Figure 5.4 earlier in the project.

5 Click the Different first page check box to deselect it. Then click OK.
When the Different first page check box is marked, Word lets you create a different header for the first page of the section from the rest of that section or document. You deselect this check box to use the same header for all of section 2.

6 Click the Same as Previous button to deselect it.
The note above the header window no longer says Same as Previous. This disconnects the header in section 2 from the empty header in section 1. Otherwise, the headers would be identical from section to section.

7 Type Desktop Publishing Guidelines.
This is the text that appears in the header for all of section 2 (see Figure 5.26).

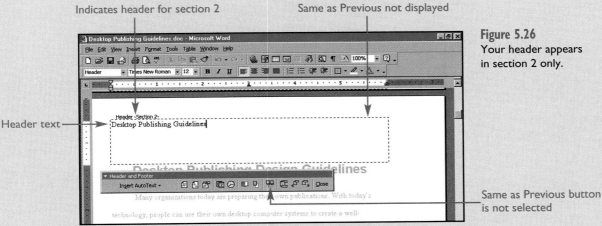

Indicates header for section 2

Same as Previous not displayed

Header text

Figure 5.26
Your header appears in section 2 only.

Same as Previous button is not selected

8 Click the Close button on the Header and Footer toolbar.
Headers and footers do not appear in Normal view. To see them, you must switch to Print Layout view.

9 Click the Print Layout View button and scroll through the document to see the header in section 2.
The header is not shown on the title page, but it appears on all pages within section 2.

10 Save the document and keep it onscreen to continue with the next lesson.

 Header and Footer Options
Use the toolbar buttons to insert the date, filename, and page number in a header or footer. You can also toggle between a header and a footer. When you position the mouse pointer on a button, a ScreenTip appears telling you the name of the button.

You can even create different headers and footers for odd- and even-numbered pages. Click the Page Setup button and click the Different odd and even button.

Lesson 8: Creating Hanging Indent Paragraphs

The last page in your document contains a bibliography. You need to format the bibliographic entries. The standard format is a hanging indent, which keeps the first line of the paragraph at the left margin and indents the remaining lines in the paragraph.

To Create Hanging Indent Paragraphs

1 **With the Desktop Publishing Guidelines file open, use the Go To command to go to the top of page 6.**
This is the page that contains the bibliography. The bibliographic entries are not currently formatted, as shown in Figure 5.27.

Figure 5.27
You need to use the hanging indent format for each entry.

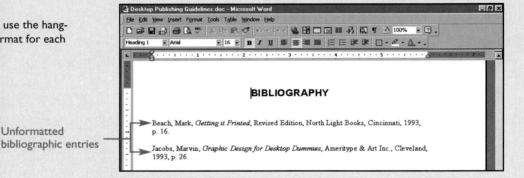

Unformatted bibliographic entries

2 **Click in the first bibliographic entry.**

3 **Choose Format, Paragraph, and click the Indents and Spacing tab.**
You see the Paragraph dialog box that you worked with in Project 4. Make sure the Indents and Spacing options are displayed.

4 **Click the Special drop-down arrow, choose Hanging, and click OK.**
The first line remains at the left margin, and the second line is indented.

 If you use Spacebar to indent the second line, you will have problems if you later edit the paragraph. Use the hanging indent option to correctly format bibliographic entries.

5 **Click in the second paragraph.**

6 **Choose Format, Paragraph.**

7 **Click the Special drop-down arrow, choose Hanging, and click OK.**

 Selecting Text and Applying Hanging Indents
You can also select consecutive paragraphs and use the Hanging option to apply a hanging indent to several paragraphs at one time.

Now both bibliographic entries are formatted with the hanging indent feature (see Figure 5.28).

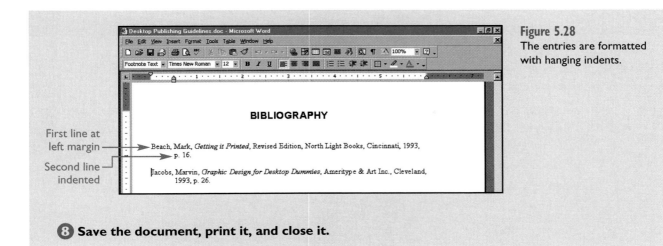

Figure 5.28
The entries are formatted with hanging indents.

First line at
left margin

Second line
indented

8 Save the document, print it, and close it.

Hanging Indent Keyboard Shortcut
You can also press Ctrl+T to quickly create a hanging indent for the current paragraph.

Sorting Bibliographic Entries
If you didn't type bibliographic entries in alphabetical order, you can select the single entries and have Word alphabetize them for you. To do this, follow these steps:

1. Select the bibliographic entries.
2. Choose Table, Sort. The options are set to sort by paragraphs in ascending order.
3. Click OK.

If you have authors with the same last name, however, these entries may not be further alphabetized by first name. In any case, sorting can help you quickly arrange the bibliographic entries.

Summary

You learned a lot of valuable formatting features in this project. Now you can center text vertically on a page, insert page numbers, create headers, and insert page breaks. In addition, you learned how to create footnotes to document your sources in a research paper and how to use hanging indents for bibliographic entries. Plus, your documents will look professional when you correctly insert nonbreaking spaces and keep certain text, such as bulleted lists, from separating across page breaks.

You can now expand your knowledge and skills of these and related features by using Help. For example, you might want to learn more about section breaks and the other buttons on the Header and Footer toolbar. In addition to using Help, complete the following exercises to reinforce and expand your skills.

Checking Concepts and Terms

True/False

For each of the following, check *T* or *F* to indicate whether the statement is true or false.

__T __F   **1.** If you have a document with regular page breaks instead of section breaks, selecting center vertical alignment only affects the current page. [L1]

__T __F   **2.** When you turn on page numbers, Word displays page numbers for all sections, not just the current section. [L2]

__T __F   **3.** Page numbers appear in both Normal view and Printout view. [L2]

__T __F   **4.** A hard page break starts text on a new page. [L3]

__T __F   **5.** If a bulleted list separates between two pages, you should insert a hard page break before the first bulleted item. [L4]

__T __F   **6.** Use a nonbreaking space to keep two single-spaced lines together. [L5]

__T __F   **7.** You should press ⏎Enter after typing footnote text to insert a blank line between it and the next footnote you create. [L6]

__T __F   **8.** By default, footnotes have the same point size that body text does. [L6]

__T __F   **9.** When the Same as Previous button is active on the Header and Footer toolbar, the header in the current section is identical to the header in the last section. [L7]

__T __F   **10.** The hanging indent format indents text from the right margin. [L8]

Multiple Choice

Circle the letter of the correct answer for each of the following.

1. Assume you have section breaks in a document. All of the following formats continue through sections by default except: [L1–3, 7]

   a. headers

   b. page numbers

   c. footers

   d. vertical alignment

2. Which of the following is not a true statement about page numbering? [L2]

   a. You can choose whether page numbers appear at the top or bottom of the page.

   b. Page numbers appear on every new document you create.

   c. By default, page numbers appear on the first page of the document.

   d. The page number alignment option specifies where the page number appears between the left and right margins.

3. If you want a section to have its own page numbers, what should you do? [L2]

   a. Do not start numbering pages until you get to that section.

   b. Select the pages in the section prior to displaying the Page Numbers dialog box.

   c. Manually type page numbers at the top of the pages in that section.

   d. At the beginning of that section, change the Page Numbering Start at option to 1.

4. Which view mode shows dotted lines indicating the different types of page and section breaks? [L3]

   a. Normal view

   b. Print Layout view

   c. Web Layout view

   d. Zoom Two Pages

5. Assume the current page is half full. What should you do to start typing text on the next page? [L3]

   a. Insert a hard page break.

   b. Press ⏎Enter until you are on the next page.

   c. Create a section break.

   d. Click the Next Page button below the vertical scrollbar.

6. Word does not prevent which situation from presenting itself? [L4]

a. a single line of a paragraph from appearing at the top of a page

b. a heading being isolated at the bottom of the page, whereas the following paragraph is on the next page

c. a numbered or bulleted list from separating across page breaks

d. an orphan from appearing at the bottom of a page

7. You should insert a nonbreaking space between each set of words, except: [L5]

a. May 18

b. before 2000

c. Mr. Shivey

d. page 14

8. Identify the correct default for footnotes. [L6]

a. Footnotes appear in 12-point Times New Roman.

b. The first line of each footnote is indented.

c. Footnotes appear at the bottom of the page.

d. Word automatically inserts one blank line between footnotes.

9. What types of items can you put into a header or footer? [L7]

a. page numbers

b. text

c. date

d. all of the above

10. What is the keyboard shortcut for creating a hanging indent? [L8]

a. Ctrl + T

b. Tab ↹

c. Ctrl + H

d. Ctrl + ⇧Shift + Spacebar

Screen ID

Label each element of the Word screen shown in Figure 5.29.

Figure 5.29

A. footnote

B. footnote reference mark

C. header text

D. indicates current physical page

E. indicates page number within current section

F. indicates total number of pages in entire document

G. page number that will print

H. separator line

I. third section

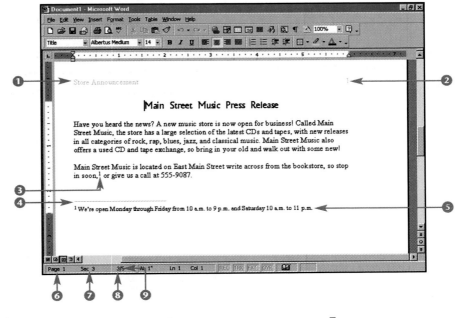

1. _____   4. _____   7. _____

2. _____   5. _____   8. _____

3. _____   6. _____   9. _____

Discussion Questions

1. Explain section breaks and how formatting works with them.

2. Why would you want to deselect the Same as Previous button on the Header and Footer toolbar?

3. Look at the location of page numbers in this text-book. What position and alignment options would you choose to produce this effect?

4. Why does Word prevent widows and orphans but not keep bulleted list items together on a page?

5. Explain what a nonbreaking space is. List examples of when you should insert a nonbreaking space. (Think of other examples not provided in this book.)

Skill Drill

Skill Drill exercises reinforce project skills. Each skill reinforced is the same, or nearly the same, as a skill presented in the project. Detailed instructions are provided in a step-by-step format.

1. Creating a Title Page

You have created a research paper for your business communication class. Before submitting it you create a title page. You use the section break feature, so the remaining document maintains its original settings.

1. Open **WD1-0502** and save it as **Interview Paper**.

2. Choose File, Page Setup and click the Layout tab.

3. Click the Vertical alignment drop-down arrow and choose Center.

4. Check to see that the Apply to option displays This Section. Click OK.

5. Click the Print Layout View button. Click the Zoom drop-down arrow, and choose Two Pages.

6. Save the document and leave it onscreen as you continue to Exercise 2.

2. Inserting Page Numbers

You decide to insert page numbers in your document so your readers can easily locate specific sections of the paper. You want page numbers to begin with the main document and not the title page.

1. In the Interview Paper file, position the insertion point at the top of the document (the title page).

2. Make sure you are displaying the document in Print Layout view with the Two Pages zoom option.

3. Choose Insert, Page Numbers.

4. Click the Alignment drop-down arrow and choose Center.

5. Click the Show number on the first page check box to deselect this option.

6. Click OK.

7. Click the Zoom drop-down arrow and choose 100%. Scroll to the bottom of page 3 to check the placement of the page number.

8. Save the document and keep it onscreen to continue to Exercise 3.

3. Restarting Page Numbers

When you review the Interview document, you notice that the page numbers are starting on the title page. You need to restart them so the body of the document begins with page 1.

1. With Interview Paper onscreen, position the insertion point at the top of page 2, the first page of the body of the document.

2. Choose Insert, Page Numbers.

3. Click the Format button to display additional options.

4. Click the Start at option button and type **1**.

5. Click OK and then click OK in the Page Numbers dialog box.

6. Scroll to the bottom of the page and check to see that the page number has changed to **1**.

7. Save the document and leave it onscreen to continue to the next exercise.

4. Inserting Page Breaks

Because you have three main sections in your document, you decide to begin each section on a new page.

1. With the Interview Paper onscreen, position the insertion point at the beginning of the centered title `II. Pre-interview Impression Effects` on page 1.

2. Choose Insert, Break.

3. Choose Page Break and click OK.

4. Click the Normal View button and scroll up to check the page break.

5. Repeat this process with the remaining heading `III. Perception in the Interview`.

6. Save the document and keep it onscreen to continue to the next exercise.

5. Preventing Text from Separating Across Page Breaks

While proofreading, you notice that when you created page breaks the headings were separated from their paragraph text. You use the Keep with Next option to correct this problem.

1. In the Interview Paper file, make sure the document is displayed in Normal view.

2. Scroll through the document so you see the bottom of page 2 and the top of page 3 in section 2.

3. Drag across the heading `The Bias of Information Processing` and the first two lines of the following paragraph. Choose Format, Paragraph to display the Paragraph dialog box.

4. Click the Line and Page Breaks tab.

5. Click the Keep with next check box and click OK. If the heading does not appear at the top of page 3, click the Print Layout View button, and then click the Normal View button again.

6. Repeat this process with any other headings that have separated incorrectly.

7. Save the document and keep it onscreen to continue to the next exercise.

6. Inserting a Nonbreaking Space

You notice that a nonbreaking space should be inserted within the text.

1. With Interview Paper onscreen, locate the second section, `Pre-interview Impression Effects`. Within the first paragraph of this section you see the three interview phases proposed by Dipboye. You notice that the second phase has split from its number.

2. Press (Del) to delete the regular space between `2.` and `The Interview Phase`.

3. Press (Ctrl)+(▲Shift)+(Spacebar) to keep this text from breaking.

4. Save the document and keep it onscreen to continue to Exercise 7.

7. Inserting a Footnote

You decide to create footnotes that supplement the text contained in paragraphs.

1. With the Interview Paper file open, display the first page in section 2.

2. Position the insertion point after `skill tests,` in the second paragraph.

3. Choose Insert, Footnote and click OK.

4. Type the following footnote text:

   `Skill tests provide valuable information to see if an applicant possesses a certain`

   `skill. For example, word processing applicants typically take a skill test to see if they can correctly format documents in a timely manner.`

5. Click outside the footnote to close it.

6. Save the document and keep it onscreen to continue to Exercise 8.

8. Create a Header

You decide to add a header to your document. You want to use the name of the document and your name in the header, but you don't want the header to appear on the title page.

1. With Interview Paper onscreen, position the insertion point at the beginning of the document.

2. Choose View, Header and Footer.

3. Click the Show Next button on the Header and Footer toolbar.

4. Deselect the Same as Previous button on the Header and Footer toolbar.

5. Type `The Personal Interview`, press Tab twice, and type your name.

6. Click the Close button on the Header and Footer toolbar.

7. Save the document, print it, and close it.

Challenge

Challenge exercises expand on or are somewhat related to skills presented in the lessons. Each exercise provides a brief narrative introduction followed by instructions in a numbered step format that are not as detailed as those in the Skill Drill section.

[?] 1. Creating Endnotes in a Report

You create an endnote page containing three endnotes for a long report on Desktop Publishing Design Guidelines.

1. Open `WD1-0503` and save it as `DTP Guidelines`.

2. Position the insertion point after the period ending the second sentence in the third paragraph in the `Font Faces` section, `The serifs help guide the reader's eyes across the line of text.` Create the following endnote using regular number format. Use Help to learn how to create an endnote and how to select endnote number format.

   `Linda I. Studer and Marvin Jacobs, Graphic Design For 21st Century Desktop Publishers, North Olmsted, Ohio, 1999, p. 23.`

3. Position the insertion point at the end of the paragraph immediately before the `Weight` heading. Create the following endnote:

   `Ibid., p. 22.`

4. Position the insertion point at the end of the paragraph immediately before the `Setting the Spacing` heading. Create the following endnote:

   `Dan Poynter, ` *`The Self-Publishing Manual: How to Write, Print and`* *`Sell Your Own Book,`* ` Ninth edition, revised, Para Publishing, Santa Barbara, p. 106.`

5. If you didn't press `Enter` after the first and second endnotes, edit them now. You need one blank line between endnotes.

6. Save the document and print it.

2. Formatting a Loan Proposal with a Title Page

Format a small business loan proposal to meet the requirements of a local bank. You need to create a title page, number the pages, and keep text together.

1. Open WD1-0504 and save it as `Deli Proposal`. Create a title page by inserting a section break after `Fort Walton Beach, Florida`.

2. Apply centered vertical alignment to the title page. Choose 24-point Garamond font for the entire document.

3. Include page numbering. The title page and first page of the proposal should not be numbered. All others should be numbered in the top right corner of the page. Make sure that section 2 starts back at page 1.

4. Starting in section 2, change the top and bottom margins to 1.5" and justify the text.

5. Check the lists for net profits. If necessary, use the Keep with ne<u>x</u>t command to keep the listed items together on one page.

6. Save the proposal and print it.

[?] 3. Formatting a Status Report

You composed a status report for division managers concerning an upcoming Information Technology Training Conference. You open it and make a few changes before sending it out.

1. Open WD1-0505 and save it as `Status Report`.

2. Create a title page from the first three lines. Space the lines out, use a larger font size and sans serif font, and include your name and the current date in 12-point Times New Roman.

3. Create a separate page for each of the sections of the status report. Delete the extra hard returns between each section break and the heading.

4. Emphasize the headings of each section by changing the font, centering the headings, and applying a border and shading. Be consistent with the sans serif font you used on the three-line title on the title page. Use Format Painter to copy the style from one heading to another.

5. On every page but the title page, insert a header with the name of the conference, `Information Technology Training Conference`, on the left and your name on the right. Insert a footer with `Status Report for Division Managers` on the left and the page number on the right. Use Help for more information about creating a footer and inserting the page number at the right side of a header or footer.

6. Save the document, print it, and close it.

[?] 4. Formatting a Research Paper

A research paper you have created and want to publish has to be formatted to the guidelines of the scholarly journal to which you are submitting it.

1. Open **WD1-0506** and save it as **Domain Name**.

2. Set 1.25" top and bottom margins. Apply 12-point Times New Roman to the entire document.

3. Edit the title font so it is Indigo, 16-point AvantGarde Md BT. Edit the subheading **Internet Protocol** so it is Indigo, 14-point AvantGarde Md BT. Use the Format Painter to copy the **Internet Protocol** formats to the remaining subheadings.

4. Insert a header with your name on the left and the current date on the right. Insert a footer with the page number centered. Start the header on page two. Use Help to learn about centering text in a header or footer and how to make sure the header is different on the first page.

5. Position your insertion point at the end of the document and insert the following footnote.

   `Mikki Barry (Internet Policy Consultants), Internet article, http://www.mids.org/legal/dispute.html, 1996.`

6. Save the document, print it, and close it.

5. Creating a Reference List

You've been asked to speak to the local student business organization. You decide to provide the students with a list of references you used to prepare your topic on desktop publishing and proofreading.

1. Set a 2" top margin. Key the title **REFERENCE LIST** in all capital letters centered directly below the top margin. Apply Arial and bold to the title.

2. Triple-space after the title. Single-space each reference. Set your font size to 8 points after spacing the paragraphs.

3. Create the following references using hanging indents:

   Anderson, Laura Killen. *Handbook for Proofreading*, Lincolnwood, Illinois: NTC Business Books, 1996.

   Beach, Mark. *Getting it Printed*, revised edition, Cincinnati: North Light Books, 1993.

   Smith, Debra A. and Helen R. Sutton. *Powerful Proofreading Skills: Tips, Techniques and Tactics*, Menlo Park, California: Crisp Publications, Inc. 1994.

   Studer, Linda I and Marvin Jacobs. *Graphic Design for 21st Century Desktop Publishers*, North Olmsted, Ohio: Words & Pictures Publishing, 1999.

4. Save the document as **Reference**. Print and close the document.

6. Formatting the Center Street Deli Sign

You decide to use some formatting techniques to improve the appearance of the flyer for Center Street Deli.

1. Open **WD1-0507** and save it as `Deli Sign`.

2. Center the document vertically. Insert hard returns between lines for attractive placement.

3. Center the first line.

4. Type and center the two-line address:

   ```
   250 East Main
   Bowling Green, Ohio
   ```

5. Create a header and a footer that center your deli motto, `Come in and see how good freshness tastes!`

6. Select one unique font for the flyer and change the font size for each section of the flyer.

7. Select the Daily Menu Specials heading and each of the listed items. Apply a one-inch left and right indent. Apply a border and complementary shading.

8. Save your document, print it, and close it.

Discovery Zone

Discovery Zone exercises require advanced knowledge of topics presented in *Essentials* lessons, application of skills from multiple lessons, or self-directed learning of new skills.

1. Formatting an Endnotes Page

You are asked to create an endnotes page for a report you have written for your Advanced Word Processing class. An endnotes page places the endnotes on a separate page at the end of the body of a report.

Open **WD1-0508** and save it as `Endnotes Page`. Insert your name and the current date on the title page.

Before creating the endnotes, you need to research endnote options to learn about the line that separates the notes from the text.

Use Figure 5.30 to create the following endnotes in their respective locations listed below. Before closing the first endnote, change to Normal view, review your notes about changing the separator line, and delete the separator line.

- First Endnote: end of the third paragraph
- Second Endnote: end of the fourth paragraph
- Third Endnote: end of the last paragraph

Create a new section page before the endnotes. Apply the formats as indicated in Figure 5.30. Insert page numbers in the bottom center of pages. Do not number the title page. Start numbering over on page 1 in section 2. Do not number the first page of section 2.

Figure 5.30
Create the endnotes page with the required formats.

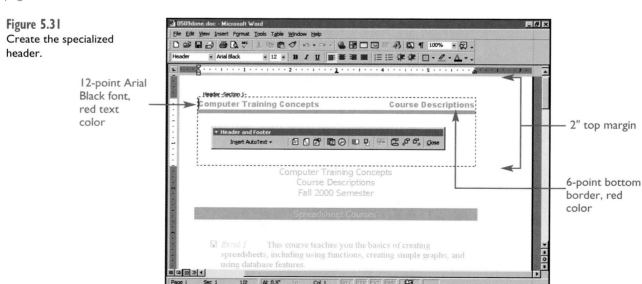

Triple-space after the heading

Tab before endnotes

Double-space between endnotes

1.5" top margin

Arial bold

12-point Times New Roman

Save the report again and print the final copy.

2. Formatting the Course Descriptions Document

Now that you know how to use headers and footers and page numbering, you decide to use them to add identifying information to the Course Descriptions document you created in Project 4. Open **Course Descriptions** and save it as **Revised Course Descriptions**.

Insert a page break above the Word Processing Courses heading so this section appears on a separate page. Include page numbers at the bottom of the document. Add a header. Type **Computer Training Concepts** on the left side of the header, and **Course Descriptions** along the right side. Explore the Page Setup Option under Headers and Footers and insert a 6-point border to the bottom of the header. Use Help for additional assistance and information.

Apply the formats as indicated in Figure 5.31 and insert small lowercase Roman numeral page numbers.

Figure 5.31
Create the specialized header.

12-point Arial Black font, red text color

2" top margin

6-point bottom border, red color

Save the document and print it.

3. Formatting a Reunion Letter

To improve the appearance of your reunion letter, you decide to use some of the formatting techniques you learned in this project. Open **WD1-0509** and save it as **Reunion Letter**. Change the line spacing of the list of choices to 1.5 and add bullets before each choice. Add a hard page break above the last list of choices, the activities. Create a footer that centers **Richards Family Reunion** on both pages. Insert a header to the second page that contains today's date and the page number. Center the pages vertically.

At the end of the first paragraph, type **Let's plan the reunion between June 5-August 19**. Include appropriate spaces and hyphens to make sure the text doesn't wrap incorrectly.

Save and print the letter.

Using Tables

Objectives

In this project, you learn how to

➤ **Create a Table**

➤ **Enter Text in a Table**

➤ **Insert Rows and Columns**

➤ **Delete Rows and Columns**

➤ **Adjust Column Width and Row Height**

➤ **Format a Table**

➤ **Apply Shading and Borders**

➤ **Move and Position a Table**

Key terms in this project include

- border
- cell
- column
- column headings
- column width
- gridlines
- row
- row height
- shading
- table
- table alignment

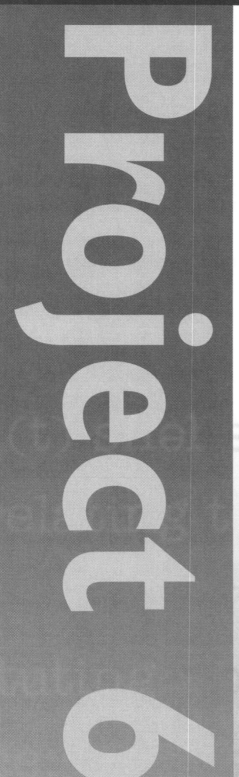

Why Would I Do This?

Sometimes you might want an easy way to organize a series of data in a columnar list format. Although you could align text with tabs, you have more format control when you create a table. A **table** is a series of rows and columns that neatly organize data. Each **row** presents data going across the table (left to right), and each **column** presents data vertically in the table. The intersection of a row and column is called a **cell**.

You can create tables to store customer names and addresses, phone lists, personal inventories, calendars, project forms, and so on. After you complete this project, you'll probably think of additional ways you can use tables in your own documents.

Visual Summary

Figure 6.1 shows the structure of a table.

Figure 6.1
Learning table terminology helps you understand how to format the table.

Columns run vertically

Rows run horizontally

Gridlines

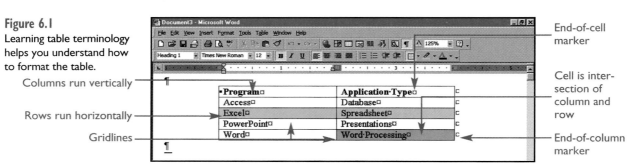

End-of-cell marker

Cell is intersection of column and row

End-of-column marker

Figure 6.2 shows a table inserted within a business letter. You will create this table by completing the lessons in this project.

Figure 6.2
The table organizes the information in an easy-to-read format.

Table shading

Taller row height

Wide column

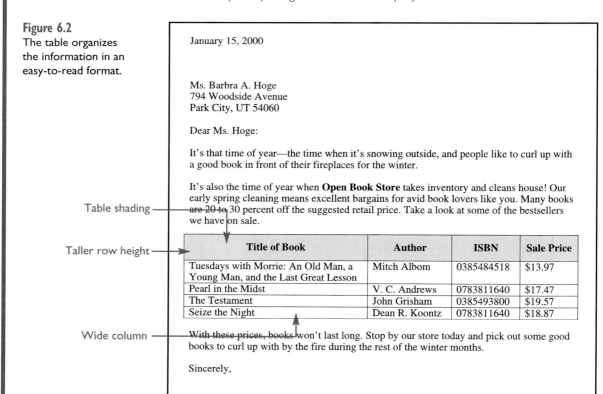

Lesson 1: Creating a Table

You can create a table between paragraphs in a letter, memo, or report; or you can create a table as a separate document. Before you create a table, you should think about what data you want to include and how you want to organize it. Doing so helps you create an appropriate table structure from the beginning, but you can always change the table later.

In this lesson, you work for a local bookstore named Open Book Store. Your manager, Gabriel Thompson, has asked you to insert a table that lists some books that are on sale this month. You decide to create a table to include book titles, authors' names, ISBN numbers, and sale prices. You also decide to list four books that are on sale. Your table will consist of four columns and four rows.

To Create a Table

1 Open **WD1-0601** and save it as **Book Sales Letter**.

2 **Position the insertion point on the blank line after the last paragraph before the closing.**
You need to position the insertion point where you want to create the table. Although you really want the table between the second and third paragraphs, you'll insert the table after the third paragraph and then learn how to move it in a later lesson.

3 **Click the Insert Table button on the Standard toolbar.**
Word displays a table grid. You click and drag through the grid to specify how many columns and rows you want in your table.

4 **Position the mouse pointer on the fourth cell down in the fourth column.**
The grid shows that you are creating a table with four rows and four columns (see Figure 6.3).

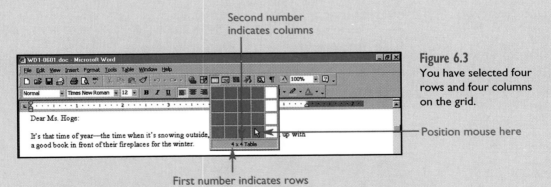

Second number indicates columns

Figure 6.3
You have selected four rows and four columns on the grid.

Position mouse here

First number indicates rows

5 **Click the mouse button in the cell.**
You now have a new table in your document (see Figure 6.4). By default, Word creates evenly spaced columns between the left and right margins. Your table contains **gridlines**, lines that separate cells within the table.

continues ▶

To Create a Table   (continued)

Figure 6.4
Your newly created table is
below the last paragraph.

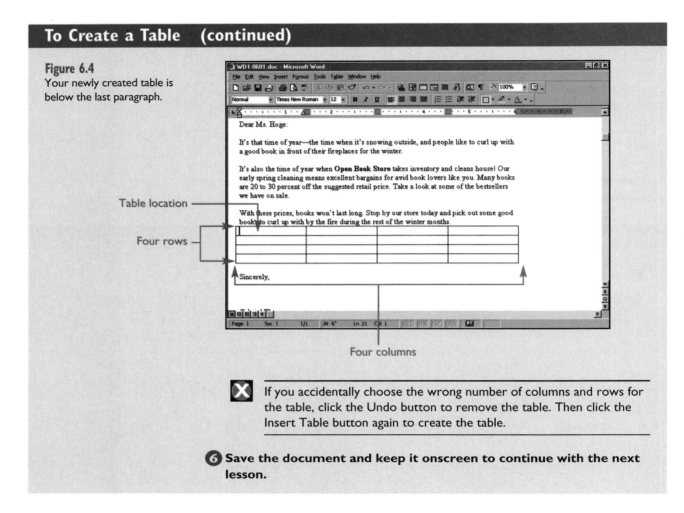

Table location

Four rows

Four columns

 If you accidentally choose the wrong number of columns and rows for
the table, click the Undo button to remove the table. Then click the
Insert Table button again to create the table.

6 **Save the document and keep it onscreen to continue with the next
lesson.**

ⓘ Creating a Table
You can also create a table from the Insert Table dialog box (see Figure 6.5).
To do this, choose Table, Insert, Table. Specify the number of columns and rows
you want and click OK.

Figure 6.5
Use the Insert Table dialog
box to create a table.

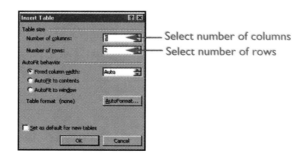

Select number of columns
Select number of rows

Lesson 2: Entering Text in a Table

After creating a table, you are ready to enter text into the cells. Type directly in the cell,
letting text word-wrap within that particular cell. When you are ready to type in the next
cell, press Tab.

You are now ready to type book titles, author names, ISBN numbers, and sale prices in
your table. The insertion point is in the first cell, so you can start typing the first item now.

To Enter Text in a Table

1 **In the Book Sales Letter file, type the following book title in the first cell.**

Tuesdays with Morrie: An Old Man, A Young Man, and the Last Great Lesson

The book title wraps within the same cell, making the first row taller.

Pressing ⏎Enter in a Table
Do not press ⏎Enter within the cell. Let Word word-wrap text within the cell. Inserting a hard return can cause problems when you adjust the column widths later.

2 **Press Tab⇄ to move the insertion point to the next cell to the right on the same row.**

3 **Type Mitch Albom in the cell.**

4 **Press Tab⇄ and type 0385484518.**

5 **Press Tab⇄ and type $13.97.**
You are ready to type text on the next row. Instead of pressing ⏎Enter to get to the next row, press Tab⇄. When you press Tab⇄ in the last cell on a row, Word moves the insertion point to the first cell on the next row.

6 **Type the rest of the table text shown in Figure 6.6. Do not press Tab⇄ after typing $12.00 in the last cell.**

Type this data in your table

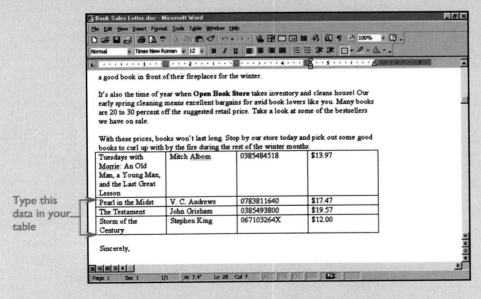

Figure 6.6
Finish typing text in your table.

If you accidentally press Tab⇄ in the last cell and create a new row at the end of the table, click the Undo button to remove the extra row.

7 **Save the document and keep it onscreen to continue with the next lesson.**

Table 6.1 lists different methods for moving around in a table.

Table 6.1   Moving the Insertion Point in a Table

To Move to the	Press
Next cell to the right	`Tab`
Cell to the left	`Shift`+`Tab`
First cell in column	`Alt`+`PgUp`
Last cell in column	`Alt`+`PgDn`
First cell in current row	`Alt`+`Home`
Last cell in current row	`Alt`+`End`

Lesson 3: Inserting Rows and Columns

After creating the table, you might decide to add another row or column. For example, you might realize that you left out information in the middle of the table, or you might want to create a row for **column headings**, text that appears at the top of each column describing that column.

In this lesson, you decide to add a row at the top of the table to type in column headings. Before inserting a row, however, you need to position the insertion point on the row below or above where you want to insert the new row.

To Insert a Row

❶ **In the `Book Sales Letter` file, position the insertion point within any cell on the first row.**
Remember that rows go across, not down. You will insert a row in the wrong place if the insertion point is not on the first row.

❷ **Choose T̲able, I̲nsert to display the Table Insert menu options for inserting columns and rows (see Figure 6.7).**

Figure 6.7
Use the Table Insert menu to insert columns or rows.

Black box represents current cell

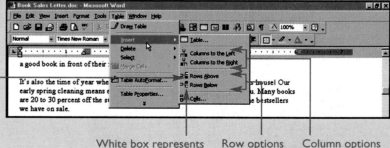

White box represents where new row or column goes

Row options   Column options

3 Choose Rows Above.

Word inserts a new row above the current one. The new row is currently selected.

4 Click in the first cell.

5 Type the following data in cells on the first row:

Title of Book

Author

ISBN

Sale Price

Your table now contains all the data you want to include (see Figure 6.8).

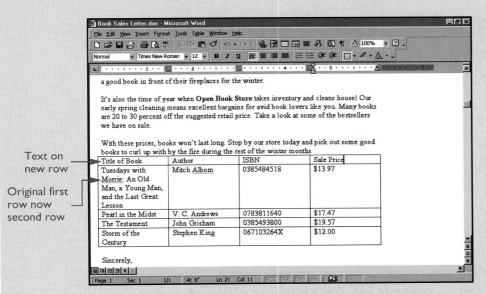

Figure 6.8
Your table now contains column headings.

Text on new row

Original first row now second row

6 Click in the last cell on the last row, the cell containing $12.00.

You want to add a row below the last row for another book that's on sale.

7 Press Tab.

Pressing Tab in the last cell on the last row creates a new row below the original last row.

8 Type the following information on the last row:

Seize the Night

Dean R. Koontz

0783811640

$18.87

Your table contains data on the new row at the bottom of the table (see Figure 6.9).

continues ▶

To Insert a Row (continued)

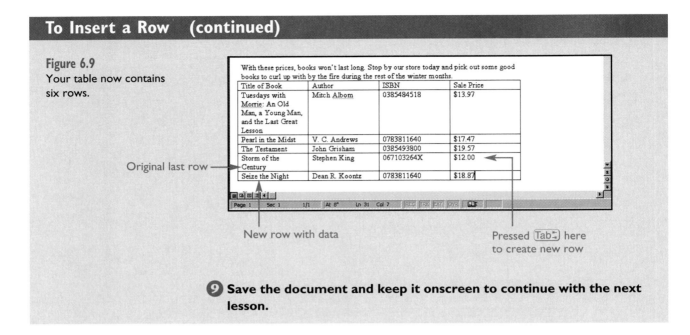

Figure 6.9
Your table now contains six rows.

Original last row ⟶

New row with data

Pressed Tab⇥ here to create new row

9 **Save the document and keep it onscreen to continue with the next lesson.**

Inserting Columns
You can also insert columns in a table. You can choose to insert a new column to the left or right of the column containing the insertion point. For example, if the insertion point is in the second column and you insert a column to the left, the new column becomes the second column, and the original second column becomes the third column. When you insert a column, the existing columns decrease in width to make room for the new column.

Lesson 4: Deleting Rows and Columns

After creating a table, you might decide that you no longer need a particular row or column. You can delete a row or column just as easily as you insert rows and columns. In this lesson, you realize that your bookstore only has one copy of *Storm of the Century* and will not receive more for another month. Therefore, you decide to remove this book from your list of sale items.

To Delete a Row

1 **In the Book Sales Letter file, position the insertion point in the fifth row, the row that contains the *Storm of the Century* information.**
You must first position the insertion point in any cell on the row that you want to delete.

2 **Choose Table, Delete.**
The Delete options include Table, Columns, Rows, Cells.

3 **Choose Rows.**
Word deletes the row containing the insertion point (see Figure 6.10).

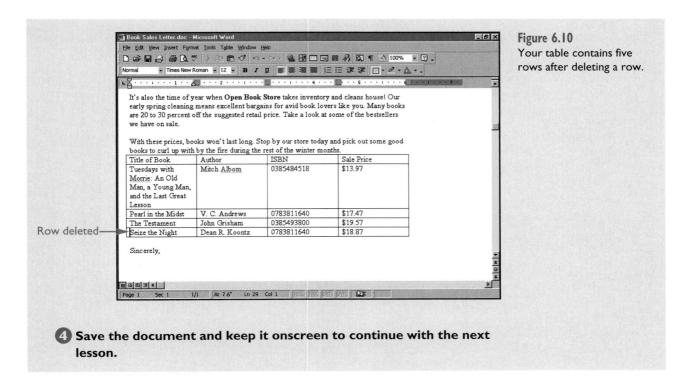

Figure 6.10
Your table contains five rows after deleting a row.

Row deleted

4 **Save the document and keep it onscreen to continue with the next lesson.**

Deleting Cell Contents
Instead of deleting a row or column, you might want to keep the table structure but delete the text in the cells. To delete just the text, select the cells containing text you want to delete and then press Del. This leaves empty cells in which you can type new text.

Lesson 5: Adjusting Column Width and Row Height

When you create a table, Word creates evenly spaced columns. **Column width** is the horizontal space or width of a column. You may, however, need to adjust the column widths based on the type of data you type in the column. For example, the book title column should be wider, and the sale price column should be narrower in your current table.

Furthermore, you might want to adjust the row height. **Row height** is the vertical distance from the top of the row to the bottom of the row. By default, Word expands the row height when text word-wraps within a cell on that row. To make the column headings on the first row stand out, you want to make this row taller.

To Adjust Row Height and Column Widths

1 **In the Book Sales Letter file, make sure you're displaying the document in Print Layout view at 100% zoom.**

2 **Position the mouse pointer on the gridline that separates the first and second rows.**
You see a two-headed arrow. This indicates that you can adjust the height by clicking and dragging the gridline (see Figure 6.11).

continues ▶

To Adjust Row Height and Column Widths   (continued)

Move Table Column markers

Figure 6.11
Click and drag the
gridline when you see
a two-headed arrow.

Adjust Table Row markers

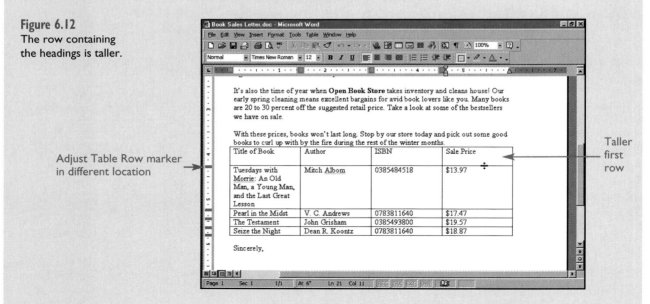

Mouse pointer on gridline

  Using the Markers to Adjust Width and Height
You can click and drag the Adjust Table Row marker to change the
row height and the Move Table Column marker to change a column
width.

❸ **Click and drag the gridline down to make the row about twice its
original size, as shown in Figure 6.12.**

Figure 6.12
The row containing
the headings is taller.

Adjust Table Row marker
in different location

Taller
first
row

You now need to adjust the column widths. The first column needs
to be wider, whereas the remaining columns need to be narrower.

④ Position the mouse pointer on the vertical gridline on the right side of the sales price column.

The mouse pointer is a two-headed arrow, indicating that you can change the column width (see Figure 6.13).

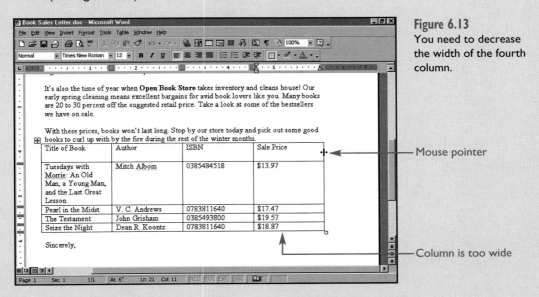

Figure 6.13
You need to decrease the width of the fourth column.

Mouse pointer

Column is too wide

⑤ Double-click the gridline.

Double-clicking a vertical gridline adjusts the column width based on the text in that column. The fourth column is now narrower.

⑥ Double-click the vertical gridline between the third and fourth columns to decrease the width of the third column.

⑦ Double-click the vertical gridline between the second and third columns.

The last three columns look better than they did when they were wider (see Figure 6.14). Now you can increase the width of the first column.

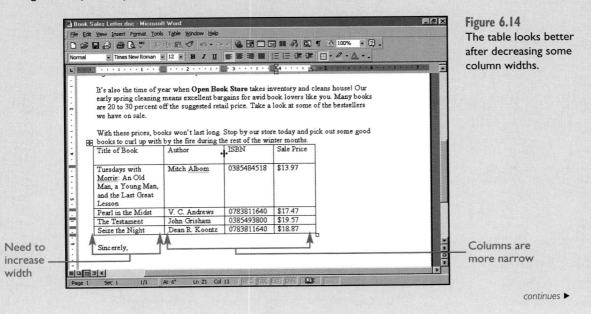

Figure 6.14
The table looks better after decreasing some column widths.

Need to increase width

Columns are more narrow

continues ▶

To Adjust Row Height and Column Widths (continued)

⑧ Double-click the vertical gridline between the first and second columns.

The first column is wider to accommodate the text in that column (see Figure 6.15).

Figure 6.15
The table looks better after adjusting column widths.

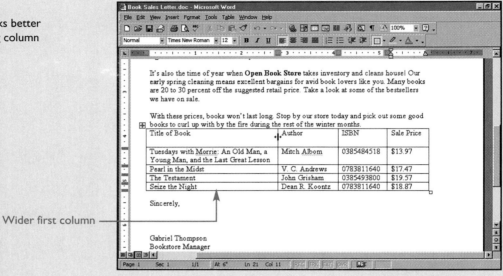

Wider first column

⑨ Save the document and keep it onscreen to continue with the next lesson.

 Adjusting Column Widths

Before making a column wider, you should adjust other columns that need to be narrower. If you make one wider and then decrease other column widths, you may have to go back and increase the first column width again.

You can also specify an exact measurement for column widths. To do this, choose Table, Table Properties. Then click the Column tab, click the Preferred width check box, and set a specific setting (see Figure 6.16).

Figure 6.16
Set a specific column width.

Indicates current column

Select this option

Click to set previous column

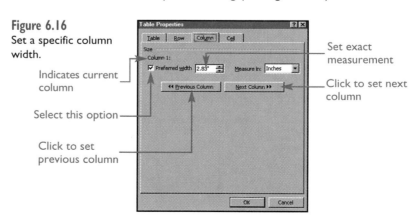

Set exact measurement

Click to set next column

If you want to set the same width for all columns, click the Table tab in the Table Properties dialog box and set the Preferred width there.

Lesson 6: Formatting the Table

After creating a table, entering data, and adjusting the structure, you need to format the table. You want the headings to stand out, so you decide to use center alignment, boldface, and center vertical alignment for the first row.

To Format the Table

1 **In the Book Sales Letter file, choose View, Toolbars, Tables and Borders.**
The Tables and Borders toolbar appears as a floating palette by the table.

2 **Position the mouse pointer between the left gridline and the text in the first cell on the first row.**

 Moving the Toolbar
You might need to move the Tables and Borders toolbar so you can position the mouse pointer between the gridline and text. To do this, simply click and drag the toolbar to another location on your screen.

The mouse pointer looks like a solid black arrow (see Figure 6.17).

Tables and Borders toolbar

Mouse pointer

Click to select text alignment within cells

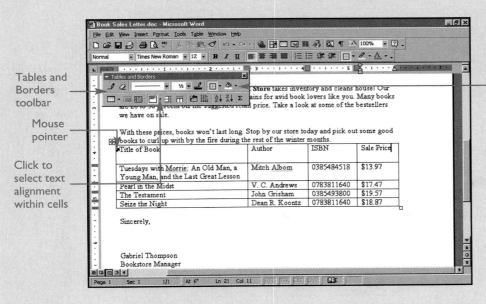

Figure 6.17
You want to format the first row of the table.

Click to see Shading Color palette

3 **Double-click to select the entire row.**
Double-clicking the mouse when it appears as the black solid arrow selects text on the current row. Single-clicking selects the current cell's text.

4 **Click the Bold button on the Formatting toolbar.**

5 **Click the drop-down arrow to the right of the Alignment button on the Tables and Borders toolbar.**
You see a palette of alignment styles (see Figure 6.18). The default is Align Top Left, which aligns text in the top left corner of the cell.

continues ▶

To Format the Table   (continued)

Click here to
see alignment options

Figure 6.18
Select how you want text
aligned in the selected
cells.

Align Top Left,
default option

Align Center, centers
horizontally and vertically

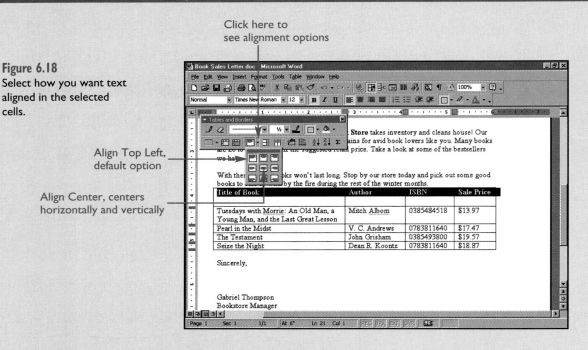

6 **Click the Align Center button; then, click in the first cell to deselect the text.**

The text on the first row is boldface, centered horizontally, and centered vertically, as shown in Figure 6.19.

Figure 6.19
The first row is now
formatted.

Indicates center alignment
for current cell

Formatted row

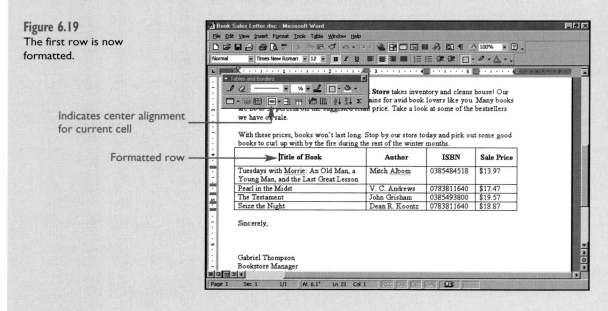

7 **Save the document and keep it onscreen to continue with the next lesson.**

Formatting Tables

You can also change text color, font, and font size for cells within a table. These options can help enhance the appearance of your table. To apply these attributes, select the cell or cells you want to format; then choose options in the Font dialog box or from the Formatting toolbar.

 In addition to changing the horizontal and vertical alignment of text in cells, you can also change the direction. Click the Change Text Direction button to rotate text 90 or 270 degrees (with the top of the text facing the left or right). Continue clicking this button to change the direction.

Lesson 7: Applying Shading and Borders

You can also enhance the appearance of a table by selecting shading and border options. **Shading** refers to the background color within a cell or group of cells. Table shading is similar to the Highlight feature that places a color behind text. **Border** refers to the line style around each cell in the table. The default line style is a single line.

You decide to further enhance your table by shading the first row so it will stand out.

To Select Table Shading

❶ In the Book Sales Letter file, make sure the Tables and Borders toolbar is displayed.

❷ Select the text on the first row of the table.

❸ Click the drop-down arrow to the right of the Shading Color button 🎨▾ on the Tables and Borders toolbar.
You see the Shading Color palette, as shown in Figure 6.20.

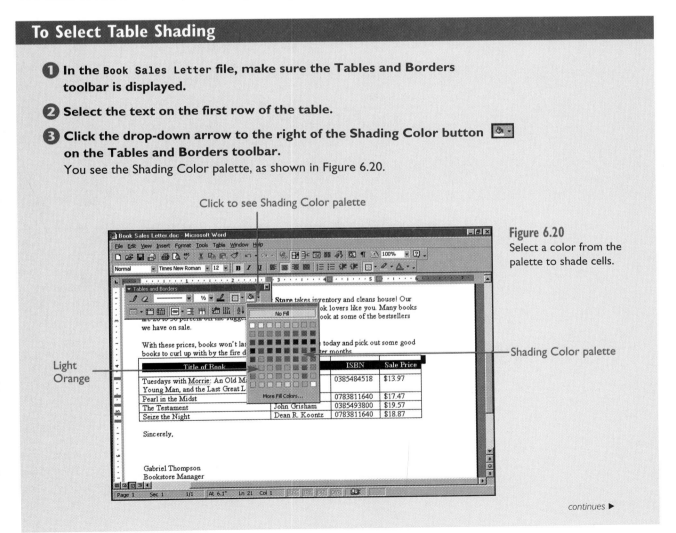

Figure 6.20
Select a color from the palette to shade cells.

To Select Table Shading   (continued)

> **Selecting a Color**
> When you position the mouse pointer on a color, Word displays a
> ScreenTip that tells you the exact name of the color, such as Sky Blue.

④ Click the Light Orange color.

⑤ Deselect the row to see the color.
The first row contains a Light Orange shading color, as shown in Figure 6.21.

Figure 6.21
The first row stands out
with a bright color.

Light Orange shading

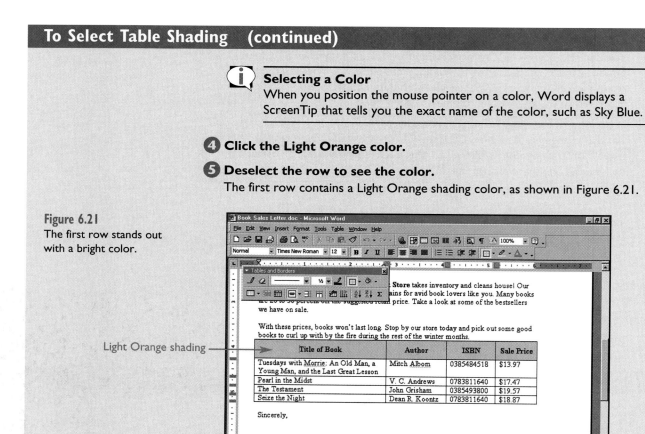

**⑥ Save the document and keep it onscreen to continue with the next
lesson.**

> **Borders**
> In Project 4, "Formatting Documents," you learned how to insert a border around
> a paragraph. Although you see borders for your table, you can customize the
> borders. To do this, choose Table, Table Properties. Then, click the Borders and
> Shading button. You'll see options similar to those you used for paragraph borders.
>
> Remember that some colors do not print well or may cause text to be difficult
> to read on a black-and-white printout.

Lesson 8: Moving and Positioning a Table

After you create a table, you might decide to move it to a different location. In your current letter, you want the table above, not below, the last paragraph. In this lesson, you
learn how to position the table. You also need to make sure you have a blank line before
and after the table. Doing so helps separate the table from the preceding and following
text, which makes the printout look more professional.

To Move the Table

 1 **In the Book Sales Letter file, make sure the insertion point is inside the table; then position the mouse pointer on the table marker.**
You should see a four-headed arrow, indicating that you can move the entire table.

2 **Click and drag the table marker straight up above the last paragraph.**
As you drag the table marker, you see a dotted line indicating where you're moving the table. When you release the mouse, Word moves the table to that location (see Figure 6.22). The top left corner of the table is positioned where you see the four-headed mouse pointer.

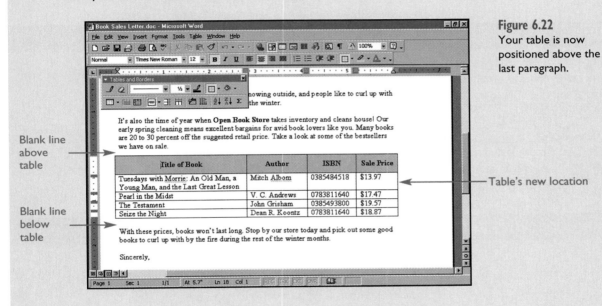

Figure 6.22
Your table is now positioned above the last paragraph.

Blank line above table

Blank line below table

Table's new location

3 **Make sure you have one blank line above and below the table.**

4 **Save the document and print it.**

Positioning a Table
Table alignment refers to the location of a table between the margins. If the table does not fill the space between the left and right margins, Word positions the table at the left margin. You can choose to center the table itself between the margins or allow text to wrap around the table. To adjust the table alignment, choose Table, Table Properties, and click the Table tab (see Figure 6.23). Click the desired Alignment option and Text Wrapping option. You can also click Positioning to see additional options.

Figure 6.23
Select where you want
to position the table.

Click to center
table between margins

Choose desired Text
Wrapping option

Click to select additional
positioning options

Summary

After completing these lessons, you know how to create a table, adjust the structure, and format the data. You can create exciting tables that look professional by centering text, shading cells, and positioning the table. In addition, you know how to move a table to a new location.

You probably noticed a lot of different buttons on the Tables and Borders toolbar. To learn more about these buttons, point to the button to see the ScreenTip displaying the button's name. Then access onscreen Help to learn about these additional table buttons.

Checking Concepts and Terms ✔

True/False

For each of the following, check *T* or *F* to indicate whether the statement is true or false.

__T __F **1.** You can create a table with more columns and rows by clicking the Insert Table button than you can from within the Insert Table dialog box. [L1]

__T __F **2.** After you type text within a cell, you should press ↵Enter to be able to type in the next cell in that column. [L2]

__T __F **3.** When you insert a column to the left of the first column, the original first column becomes the second column. [L3]

__T __F **4.** To delete an entire row, you must select it and press Del. [L4]

__T __F **5.** Double-clicking a vertical gridline adjusts the column width based on the largest item in that column. [L5]

__T __F **6.** When text word-wraps within a cell, Word increases the height of the entire row accordingly. [L2]

__T __F **7.** You can select an alignment option that centers text both horizontally and vertically for the current cell. [L6]

__T __F **8.** When you use an alignment option, Word applies that alignment to the entire row. [L6]

__T __F **9.** Shading refers to changing the color of the text within a table. [L7]

__T __F **10.** By default, Word centers a table between the left and right margins if it does not span the space between the margins. [L8]

Multiple Choice

Circle the letter of the correct answer for each of the following.

1. Creating a table would be appropriate for all of the following except: [L1]

   a. a phone list

   b. an inventory of collectibles

   c. a daily calendar

   d. a memo

2. Assume you created a table with the names of the months in the first column. Each row lists data for that particular month. The insertion point is in the first cell on the third row. This row lists goals for April. You realize that you left out the goals for March. What should you do? [L3]

   a. Choose Table, Insert, Columns to the Left.

   b. Choose Table, Insert, Columns to the Right.

   c. Choose Table, Insert, Rows Above.

   d. Choose Table, Insert, Rows Below.

3. What happens when you press (Tab⇅) when the insertion point is in the last cell in the last row? [L3]

   a. Word inserts a new row above the current row.

   b. Word inserts a new row below the current row.

   c. The insertion point appears in the paragraph below the table.

   d. The insertion point stays in the cell because it's already in the last cell of the table.

4. If the insertion point is in the last cell on the first row, what key(s) should you press to go to the first cell on the next row? [L2]

   a. (Ctrl)+(G)

   b. (⬆Shift)+(Tab⇅)

   c. (Alt)+(Home)

   d. (Tab⇅)

5. If you want to create labels that explain what is in each column, where should you place these headings? [L3]

   a. in the first column

   b. in the first row

   c. at the beginning of your document

   d. on the blank line immediately above the table

6. Refer to Figure 6.22 in Lesson 8. If the insertion point is in the cell that contains $13.97 and you choose Table, Delete, Rows, what happens? [L4]

   a. You delete just the text $13.97.

   b. You delete the Sale Price column.

   c. You delete the entire second row.

   d. You delete the entire fourth row.

7. If you make a row taller, what should you do to center text vertically in that row? [L6]

   a. Select the text and click the Center button on the Formatting toolbar.

   b. Choose Align Top Center from the Tables and Borders toolbar.

   c. Press (↵Enter) before the text in the cell to push it down to the center of the cell.

   d. Choose Align Center from the Tables and Borders toolbar.

8. If you create a table that lists people's names, office numbers, and phone numbers in columns, for which column(s) should you decrease the width? [L5]

   a. office numbers and phone numbers

   b. office numbers only

   c. people's names only

   d. phone numbers and names

9. All of the following help make the first row stand out except _____. [L6–7]

   a. shading

   b. boldface

   c. taller height

   d. smaller font size

10. If you want to move a table to another location that you can see onscreen, what should you do? [L8]

    a. Select the table, cut it, and then paste it in its new location.

    b. Select the table, choose Table, Delete, Table. Then position the insertion point in the new location and click the Undo button.

    c. Click and drag the table marker to where you want the table to be positioned.

    d. all of the above

Screen ID

Label each element of the Word screen shown in Figure 6.24.

Figure 6.24

A. Adjust Table Row marker

B. Column

C. Mouse pointer on horizontal gridline

D. Shading

E. Shading Color button

F. Table marker

G. Tables and Borders toolbar

H. Alignment drop-down arrow

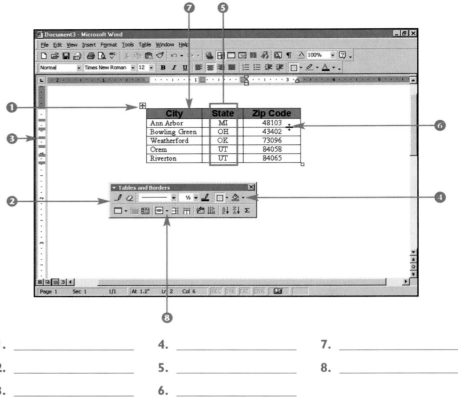

1. _____	4. _____	7. _____
2. _____	5. _____	8. _____
3. _____	6. _____	

Discussion Questions

1. Look through magazines, brochures, reports, and other documents that contain tables. Discuss the types of data conveyed in the tables. Evaluate the effectiveness of the table designs and formats. Provide suggestions for improving the tables.

2. What types of formatting can you do to enhance the appearance of a table?

3. Assume you have a table in which the column headings are centered. The last column lists amounts of money. What can you do to make the column of numbers look good below the column heading?

Skill Drill

Skill Drill exercises reinforce project skills. Each skill reinforced is the same, or nearly the same, as a skill presented in the project. Detailed instructions are provided in a step-by-step format.

1. Adding a Table to a Loan Proposal

Additional information is needed in the loan proposal you have been formatting in previous projects. You decide the information would be better organized in table form. In this exercise you create the basic structure of the table. [L1]

I. Open `WD1-0602` and save it as `Enhanced Proposal`.

2. Position the insertion point between the first and second paragraphs in the main body of the proposal. (You will reposition the table in a later exercise.)

3. Click the Insert Table button on the Standard toolbar.

4. Click and drag through the grid to specify two columns by four rows.

5. Save the document and leave it onscreen as you continue to exercise 2.

2. Entering Data in the Table

You are now ready to enter the anticipated expenses in the table structure you created in Exercise 1. [L2]

I. With Enhanced Proposal displayed, type `Demolition` in the first cell.

2. Press `Tab` to move to the next cell and type `$10,000`.

3. Press `Tab` to move the insertion point to the first cell on the next row.

4. In the remaining cells, type the following data:

```
Construction      $10,500
Landscaping       $ 3,000
Decorating        $ 2,500
```

5. Save the document and keep it onscreen to continue to exercise 3.

3. Adding Rows to the Table

You decide you want column headings to identify the data in the table. You need to add a row to the top of the table. You also need to add a row at the bottom of the table for a Total row. [L3]

I. With Enhanced Proposal on the screen, position the insertion point in either cell on the first row.

2. Choose Table, Insert.

3. Choose Rows Above.

4. Click in the first cell.

5. Type the following data in cells on the first row:

```
Expense
Amount
```

6. Click in the last cell on the last row, the cell containing `$2,500`.

7. Press `Tab`.

8. Type `Total` in the first cell of the new row.

9. Save the document and keep it onscreen to continue to exercise 4.

4. Deleting a Row

You review the costs of your project and decide to postpone the expense of landscaping for now. You need to delete the row containing the landscaping information from the table you have created. [L4]

I. With Enhanced Proposal on the screen, position the insertion point in the fourth row, the row that contains the `Landscaping` information.

2. Choose Table, Delete.

3. Choose Rows.

4. Save the document and keep it onscreen to continue to exercise 5.

5. Adjusting Row Height and Column Width

You decide to call attention to the column headings in your table by adjusting the height of the row in which the headings appear. You also decide your table will look better if you adjust the column widths. [L5]

1. With Enhanced Proposal on the screen, change your view to display the document in Print Layout View at 100% zoom.

2. Position the mouse pointer on the gridline that separates the first and second rows.

3. Click and drag the gridline down to make the row about twice its original size.

4. Position the mouse pointer on the vertical gridline on the right side of the Expense column.

5. Double-click the gridline to adjust the column width to the amount of text in the column.

6. Position the mouse pointer on the vertical gridline on the right side of the Amount column and double-click.

7. Save the document and keep it onscreen to continue to Exercise 6.

6. Formatting A Table

Changing the Row Height makes the column headings stand out, but you decide they will look more professional if they are horizontally and vertically aligned and bolded. [L6]

1. In the Enhanced Proposal file, choose View, Toolbars, Tables and Borders.

2. Select the first row by positioning the mouse pointer between the left gridline and the text in the first cell and double-clicking.

3. Click the drop-down arrow to the right of the Alignment button on the Tables and Borders toolbar.

4. Click the Align Center button.

5. Click the Bold button on the Formatting toolbar; then click in the first cell to deselect the text.

6. Save the document and keep it onscreen to continue to Exercise 7.

7. Applying Shading and Borders to a Table

To further enhance the first row, you want to apply a light blue color behind the text. [L7]

1. In the Enhanced Proposal file, make sure the Tables and Borders toolbar is displayed.

2. Select the text on the first row of the table.

3. Click the drop-down arrow to the right of the Shading Color button on the Tables and Borders toolbar.

4. Click the Light Blue color.

5. Deselect the row to see the color.

6. Save the document and keep it onscreen to continue to Exercise 8.

8. Moving and Positioning a Table

While proofreading your proposal, you realize that the table is in the wrong position. You need to move the table. [L8]

1. In the Enhanced Proposal file, position the mouse pointer on the table marker.

2. When you see the four-headed arrow, click and drag the table marker straight down and position the table between the second and third paragraphs.

3. Make sure you have one blank line above and below the table.

4. Save, print, and close the document.

Challenge

Challenge exercises expand on or are somewhat related to skills presented in the lessons. Each exercise provides a brief narrative introduction followed by instructions in a numbered step format that are not as detailed as those in the Skill Drill section.

1. Creating a Schedule of Activities

Create a schedule of activities for an upcoming International Symposium on Cultural Diversity.

1. Open WD1-0603 and save it as Activities Schedule.

2. Create the table shown in Figure 6.25.

7:30 – 8:00 a.m.	Breakfast	Breakfast	Breakfast
8:00 – 9:00 a.m.	Round Table	Panel	Lecture
9:00 – 12:00 p.m.	Panel	Demonstration	Panel
12:00 – 1:30 p.m.	Lunch	Lunch	Lunch
1:30 – 3:00 p.m.	Seminar	Seminar	Seminar
3:00 – 5:30 p.m.	Free	Free	Free
5:30 – 7:00 p.m.	Reception	Free	Dinner
7:00 – 10:00 p.m.	Free	Free	Dance

Figure 6.25
Create the activities schedule table.

3. Insert a row at the top of the table and enter the following column headings:

Time

Tuesday

Wednesday

Thursday

4. Insert a column for Monday's activities after the Time column. Enter the column heading and the following activities:

Breakfast

Panel

Round Table

Lunch

Seminar

Free

Reception

Free

5. Delete the word Free in each of the cells in which it appears.

6. Change the row height in the first row to approximately double its original size. Apply center alignment, boldface, and center vertical alignment to the same row.

7. Save the document and print it.

2. Creating an Invoice

You want to create an invoice using the Tables feature.

1. Open WD1-0604 and save it as Invoice.

2. Create a table with the data shown in Figure 6.26.

Figure 6.26
Create the invoice table.

Date	Description	Amount
1/14/2000	Word 2000 Intro	$200
2/14/2000	Excel 2000 Intro	$200
3/14/2000	Front Page	$200
4/14/2000	Internet Explorer	$200

3. In the Table Properties dialog box, specify exact measurements for column widths: 1" for Column 1, 2" for Column 2, and 1" for Column 3.

4. Change the row height in the first row to approximately double its original size. Apply center alignment, italics, and center vertical alignment to the same row.

5. Apply Rose shading to the column headings row.

6. Save the document and print it.

3. Adding a Table to the Computer Training Concepts Letter

You want to use what you have learned about tables to improve the appearance of the letter to be sent to those who request information from Computer Training Concepts.

1. Open WD1-0605 and save it as Concepts Letter.

2. Add a table to the second page of the letter listing the course descriptions. Include the information shown in Figure 6.27.

Figure 6.27
Create the table of course offerings.

Excel I	This course teaches you the basics of creating spreadsheets, including using functions, creating simple graphs, and using database features.
Excel II	In this advanced level course, you will learn to automate your work by using macros, linking worksheets, and creating summary reports, and using the Scenario Manager.
Word I	You will learn the basics of word processing, including creating, formatting, and editing documents. You also learn how to create professional-looking tables.
Word II	In this course, you will learn more advanced Word features. You will create and use styles, create mail merge documents, and create charts.
PowerPoint	This course teaches you the basics about creating simple slide shows with graphics, transitions, and sound.

3. Adjust column widths as needed.

4. Customize the borders of the table using the Table Properties dialog box. Click the Borders and Shading button and apply the Box Setting.

5. Apply Align Center Left to the cells with the course names.

6. Apply Sky Blue Shading to the cells with the course names.

7. Save the document and print it.

4. Adding a Table to the Membership Renewal Document

You decide to add a table to the Membership Renewal document to explain the annual membership fees.

1. Open WD1-0606 and save it as Membership Rates.

2. Add the following sentence to the end of the first paragraph:

See the enclosed table explaining our membership rates.

3. Create a table on the second page of the document using the information shown in Figure 6.28.

Type of Membership	Annual Dues	Annual Dues Less 10% Discount
Basic	$600	$540
Basic Plus	$800	$720
Extended	$1000	$900

Figure 6.28
Create the membership information table.

4. Add a row to the table for **Premier Membership**. Its annual dues are **$1,200**. Its annual dues after subtracting the ten percent discount are **$1,080**.

5. Apply Align Bottom Center formatting to the column headings row.

6. Use the Custom setting and the Preview diagram options available in the Borders and Shading dialog box to apply borders like those in Figure 6.28.

7. Save the document and print it.

5. Creating a Table in a Flyer

Create a flyer advertising free workshops sponsored by a school.

1. Open **WD1-0607** and save it as **Workshops**.

2. Create a table with two columns and four rows between the **Free Workshops** heading and the **Sponsored By** subheading. Use the information shown in Figure 6.29 to complete the table.

Student Success Workshops	Writing Workshops
Taking Notes	Using Proper Punctuation
Reading Textbooks	Writing Creatively
Improving Concentration	Correcting Common Mistakes
Managing Time	Streamlining Prose
Taking Tests	Analyzing Text

Figure 6.29
Create the table of workshops.

3. Emphasize the column headings by changing the font, adjusting row height, setting alignment, and selecting yellow shading for the row.

4. Insert a row after the fourth row. Type **Overcoming Test Anxiety** in the first column. Type **Revising Globally** in the second column.

5. Vertically align the flyer text and table on the page. Apply a page border.

6. Save the document and print it.

6. Adding Tables to a Reunion Planning Letter

To improve the appearance of the reunion letter you plan to send out, you decide to add tables to the lists of options.

1. Open **WD1-0608** and save it as **Reunion Letter Questionnaire**.

2. Change the format of each list of options so that it displays in a table. The first column should contain the option text, whereas the second column should be blank so that the recipient can check the appropriate options.

3. Adjust the width of the second column so that it is 1" wide.

4. Adjust the page margins so that the letter fits on one page.

5. Save the document and print it.

Discovery Zone

Discovery Zone exercises require advanced knowledge of topics presented in *Essentials* lessons, application of skills from multiple lessons, or self-directed learning of new skills.

1. Creating a Class Schedule

You've been asked to create a flyer advertising the Spring Class Open House for a local craft store. Use Help to research how to merge cells into one cell in a table. Open **WD1-0609** and save it as **Checkerboard Square**. Apply appropriate formatting (such as shading, fonts, merged cells, and so on) as indicated in Figure 6.30. Use onscreen Help, if needed, to learn more about table options. Save and print your document.

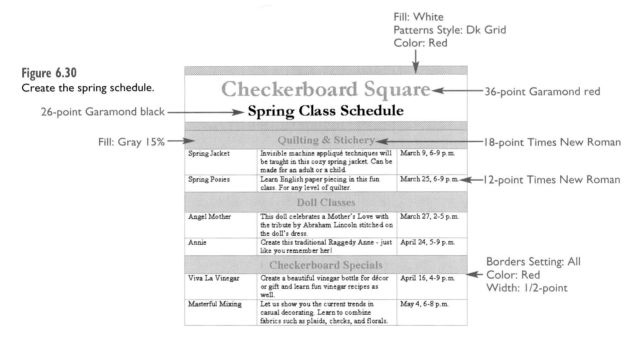

Figure 6.30
Create the spring schedule.

2. Calculating Totals in the Proposal

The loan proposal you are submitting to the bank requires a table showing quarterly net profits over the past year and your forecast for the coming year. Open **WD1-0610** and save it as **Loan Proposal with Totals**.

Using Figure 6.31, create a table between the fourth and the fifth paragraphs. The total is also necessary. Use the Help feature to find out how to total the numbers in each column using AutoSum and how to use AutoFormat. Select the Professional AutoFormat style.

	This Year	Next Year
Quarter 1	$20,000	$25,000
Quarter 2	22,000	26,000
Quarter 3	23,000	27,000
Quarter 4	24,000	28,000
Totals		

Figure 6.31
Create the quarterly table.

Save and print your document.

3. Creating a Table of Potential Computer Systems

Your supervisor has asked you to research six different computer systems and provide the following details in a table: brand name, model number, hard-drive capacity, RAM, megahertz, other features, and price. Choose one major computer retailer, such as CompUSA, to complete your research. Choose models with similar features so the comparison will be appropriate.

Write a memo to your supervisor that explains where you got the research and create a table that compares the computer systems. Apply appropriate formatting, such as shading, column widths, and so on, to make the table look good. If needed, select the table and choose a smaller point size. Sort the table in ascending order by price, but do not sort the heading row. Explore the Tables and Borders toolbar. Use Help to learn how to sort text in a table.

Save your document as `Computer Systems Memo` and print it.

Project 7

Project 7

Using Graphic Elements

Objectives

In this project, you learn how to

> ➤ **Insert an Image**
> ➤ **Move an Image**
> ➤ **Size an Image**
> ➤ **Wrap Text Around an Image**
> ➤ **Create a Text Box**
> ➤ **Use Fills and Borders**
> ➤ **Create WordArt**

Key terms in this project include

- border
- clip art
- Clip Gallery
- fill
- gradient

- sizing handles
- text box
- tight wrap
- WordArt
- wrapping style

Why Would I Do This?

Some of the most exciting features of Word are its graphics capabilities. You can insert ***clip art***—graphic images or drawings— in any document. Use clip art to enhance flyers, brochures, newsletters, and announcements. Another exciting feature is ***WordArt***, a feature that creates interesting shapes for text. Finally, you can use a ***text box*** to insert text to grab the reader's attention.

Visual Summary

Figure 7.1 illustrates clip art, WordArt, and a text box. You'll learn how to create these graphic elements in this project.

Figure 7.1
Graphic elements enhance documents by making them more interesting and appealing.

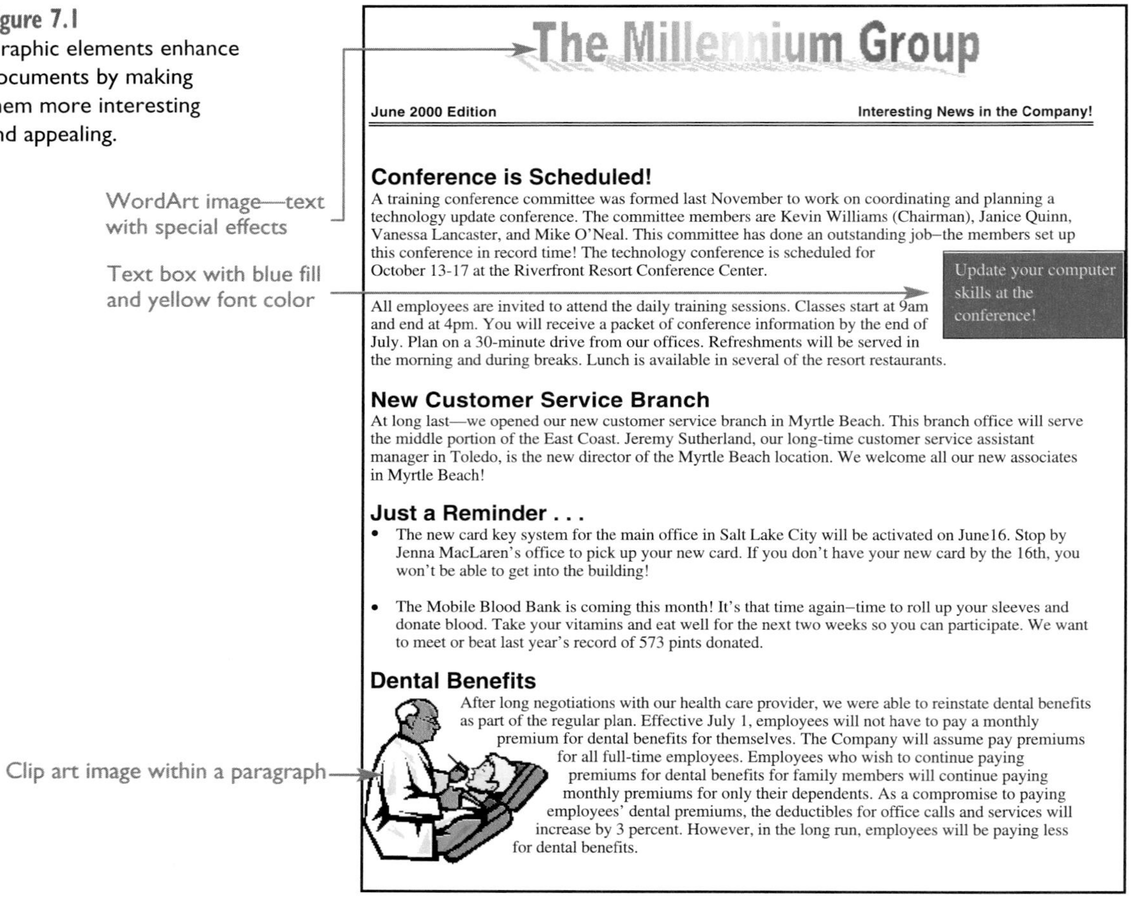
WordArt image—text with special effects
Text box with blue fill and yellow font color
Clip art image within a paragraph

The Millennium Group

June 2000 Edition | Interesting News in the Company!

Conference is Scheduled!
A training conference committee was formed last November to work on coordinating and planning a technology update conference. The committee members are Kevin Williams (Chairman), Janice Quinn, Vanessa Lancaster, and Mike O'Neal. This committee has done an outstanding job–the members set up this conference in record time! The technology conference is scheduled for October 13-17 at the Riverfront Resort Conference Center.

Update your computer skills at the conference!

All employees are invited to attend the daily training sessions. Classes start at 9am and end at 4pm. You will receive a packet of conference information by the end of July. Plan on a 30-minute drive from our offices. Refreshments will be served in the morning and during breaks. Lunch is available in several of the resort restaurants.

New Customer Service Branch
At long last—we opened our new customer service branch in Myrtle Beach. This branch office will serve the middle portion of the East Coast. Jeremy Sutherland, our long-time customer service assistant manager in Toledo, is the new director of the Myrtle Beach location. We welcome all our new associates in Myrtle Beach!

Just a Reminder . . .
- The new card key system for the main office in Salt Lake City will be activated on June16. Stop by Jenna MacLaren's office to pick up your new card. If you don't have your new card by the 16th, you won't be able to get into the building!
- The Mobile Blood Bank is coming this month! It's that time again–time to roll up your sleeves and donate blood. Take your vitamins and eat well for the next two weeks so you can participate. We want to meet or beat last year's record of 573 pints donated.

Dental Benefits
After long negotiations with our health care provider, we were able to reinstate dental benefits as part of the regular plan. Effective July 1, employees will not have to pay a monthly premium for dental benefits for themselves. The Company will assume pay premiums for all full-time employees. Employees who wish to continue paying premiums for dental benefits for family members will continue paying monthly premiums for only their dependents. As a compromise to paying employees' dental premiums, the deductibles for office calls and services will increase by 3 percent. However, in the long run, employees will be paying less for dental benefits.

Lesson 1: Inserting an Image

Office 2000 comes with an enormous number of clip art images. You can find images representing people, animals, special occasions, and more! Depending on how Office 2000 was installed on your computer, you may have just a few or all of these images. In addition to using these images, you can obtain clip art from Microsoft's Web page at `www.microsoft.com` or purchase clip art packages at a computer supply store.

In this lesson, you insert clip art in a company newsletter. You will search through the Clip Gallery to locate a particular image that corresponds with text in the document. The **Clip Gallery** is a collection of images, sound clips, and motion clips.

Appropriate Uses of Images
Be sure to read about the legal uses of clip art images, whether you're using Microsoft's clip art or other clip art you've purchased. Whereas some clip art is acceptable for use in an educational environment, it may not be legal to use in some advertising situations.

To Insert an Image

① **Open** WD1-0701 **and save it as** Company Newsletter.

② **Position the insertion point at the end of the heading** Dental Benefits.

③ **Choose** Insert, Picture, Clip Art.
The Insert ClipArt dialog box appears, as shown in Figure 7.2. The dialog box displays the Clip Gallery, so you can select pictures, sound, or motion clips. The Pictures tab organizes images into categories, such as Animals, Entertainment, and Seasons.

Back available after clicking through categories

Forward available after going back through images

Click to get additional clips from Web site

Image categories

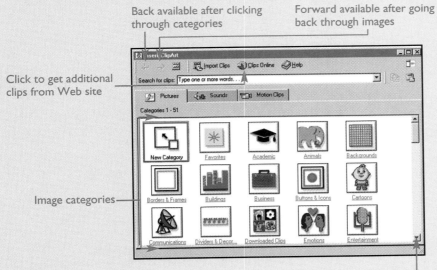

Figure 7.2
Select a category of images.

Scroll to see additional categories

You want to select a dental image, which can be found in the Healthcare and Medicine category.

④ **Scroll through the picture categories and click Healthcare & Medicine to see a gallery of healthcare images (see Figure 7.3).**

continues ▶

To Insert an Image (continued)

Category name

Figure 7.3
The gallery shows ten
healthcare images.

Number of images
in category

Click to copy
image to Clipboard

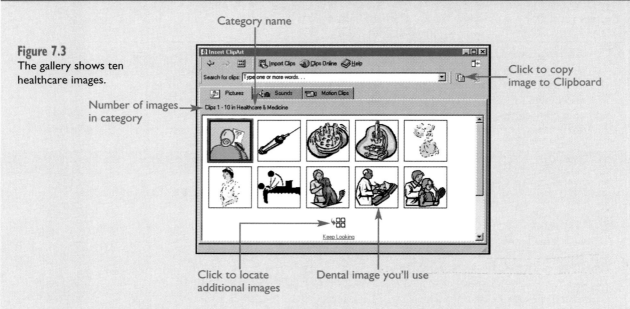

Click to locate
additional images

Dental image you'll use

5 **Right-click the dental image and choose <u>I</u>nsert.**
Word inserts the image at the insertion point location. You need to close the
dialog box to see the image in your document.

> **Other Ways to Insert Images**
> You can use the Copy and Paste commands to insert an image. Simply
> click an image and click the Copy button within the dialog box. Then
> click in your document and click the Paste button on the Standard
> toolbar.
>
> You can also click the image to see a palette of four buttons. Click the
> Insert Clip button to insert the image.

6 **Click the Close button in the upper-right corner of the dialog box.**
The image appears at the end of the heading Dental Plan (see Figure 7.4).

Figure 7.4
The image appears in your
document.

Image
location

Text moves
down

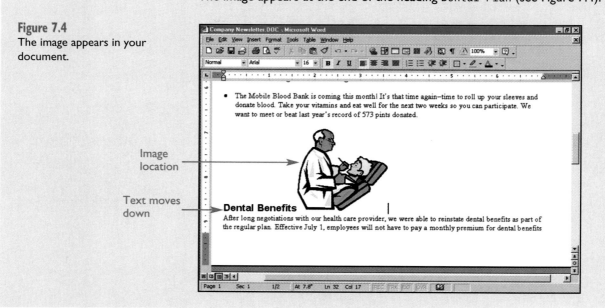

Save the document and keep it onscreen to continue with the next lesson.

 Using Other Images

You can insert almost any type of image by choosing Insert, Picture, From File. Some image file types you can use include Joint Photographic Experts Group (.jpg), Windows Bitmap (.bmp), Graphics Interchange Format (.gif) and Windows Metafile (.wmf). Word can insert these types of files without any special conversion.

If you want to insert other types of graphics files, such as a WordPerfect (.wpg) graphics image, you must install the graphics filters from the installation CD first.

 Scanning a Picture

If you have a scanner attached to your computer, you can scan a picture to use as an image within Word. Choose Insert, Picture, From Scanner or Camera. Refer to the Help topic Scan a picture and insert it in a document for more information about inserting an image into your document by using a scanner.

Lesson 2: Moving an Image

After inserting an image, you might want to move it around on the page until you are satisfied with its location. If you want to move an image to another area that you currently see on the screen, you can click and drag the image there.

In this lesson, you move the image below the heading and position it in the left margin.

Moving an Image to an Unseen Area

If you can't see the part of the document to which you want to move the image, you should not click and drag. Doing so might cause your screen to scroll so quickly through the document that you won't be able to stop at the place you want to drop the image.

Instead, click the image to select it. Then click the Cut button. Position the insertion point where you want the image to appear and click the Paste button. This is easier than clicking and dragging the image from page to page.

To Move an Image

1 **In the Company Newsletter file, click the image to select it.**

Word displays **sizing handles**, little black boxes that appear around the image so you can adjust the image's size and move it elsewhere (see Figure 7.5).

continues ▶

To Move an Image   (continued)

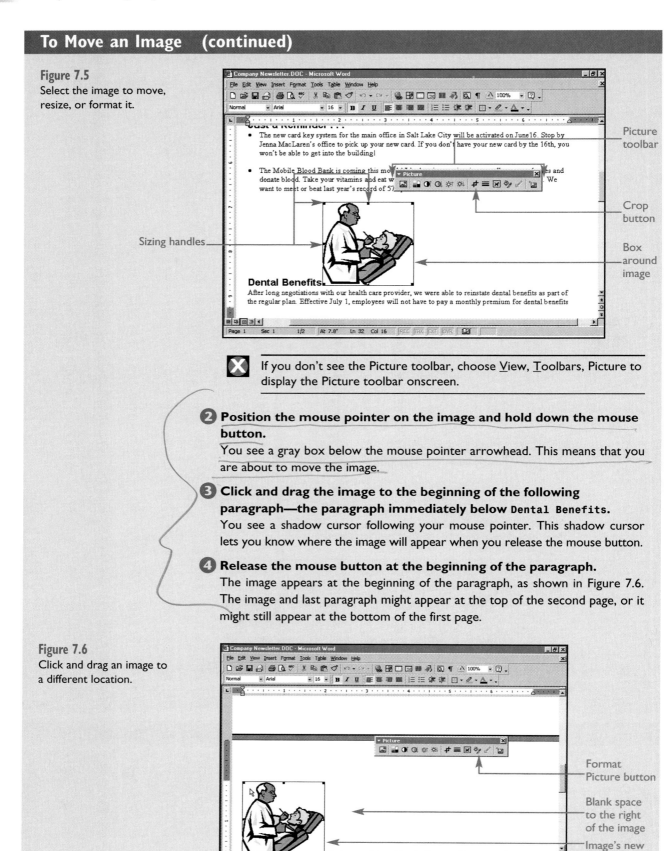

Figure 7.5
Select the image to move, resize, or format it.

Picture toolbar

Crop button

Box around image

Sizing handles

> If you don't see the Picture toolbar, choose <u>V</u>iew, <u>T</u>oolbars, Picture to display the Picture toolbar onscreen.

② Position the mouse pointer on the image and hold down the mouse button.
You see a gray box below the mouse pointer arrowhead. This means that you are about to move the image.

③ Click and drag the image to the beginning of the following paragraph—the paragraph immediately below Dental Benefits.
You see a shadow cursor following your mouse pointer. This shadow cursor lets you know where the image will appear when you release the mouse button.

④ Release the mouse button at the beginning of the paragraph.
The image appears at the beginning of the paragraph, as shown in Figure 7.6. The image and last paragraph might appear at the top of the second page, or it might still appear at the bottom of the first page.

Figure 7.6
Click and drag an image to a different location.

Format Picture button

Blank space to the right of the image

Image's new location

5 **Click outside the image.**
Clicking outside the image deselects it so you can work elsewhere in your document.

6 **Save the document and keep it onscreen to continue with the next lesson.**

Lesson 3: Sizing an Image

When you insert an image in a document, it comes in at a predetermined size. Most of the time, you need to adjust the image's size so that it fits better within the document.

In this lesson, you decide on a specific size for the image. You want it to be 1.7" tall and 1.8" wide. To set a specific size, you need to access the Format Picture dialog box.

To Change the Image's Size

1 **In the Company Newsletter file, click the dental image to select it.**
The Picture toolbar should appear. If it doesn't, right-click the Standard toolbar and choose Picture.

2 **Click the Format Picture button on the Picture toolbar.**
The Format Picture dialog box appears. You use this dialog box to select the format settings for your images.

3 **Click the Size tab.**
You see the options for setting the size of your image (see Figure 7.7).

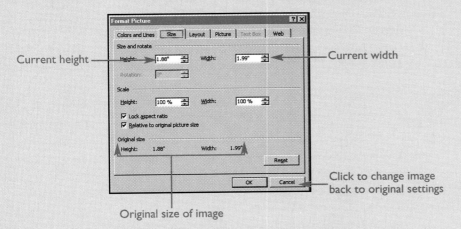

Figure 7.7
Use the Format Picture dialog box to specify an exact size for your image.

4 **Click and drag across 1.88" in the Height box.**

5 **Type 1.7.**
When you select the current setting and type, the new setting replaces the old setting. Also, you don't have to type the inch mark.

6 **Press Tab↹ to make the Width box active.**
The width should automatically change to 1.8".

continues ▶

To Change the Image's Size   (continued)

7 **Click OK.**

8 **Scroll to the bottom of page 1.**

The picture and part of the last paragraph now fit at the bottom of page 1. The image is slightly smaller, as shown in Figure 7.8.

Figure 7.8
The image is smaller.

1.7" height —

1.8" width —

9 **Click outside the image, save the document, and keep it onscreen to continue with the next lesson.**

ⓘ Using the Sizing Handles

If you don't need an exact size, you can click and drag the sizing handles to adjust the image's size. Table 7.1 describes how to use the sizing handles.

Table 7.1   Adjusting the Image's Size with the Sizing Handles

Desired Result	Click and Drag This
Increase the width	Click and drag either the middle-left or middle-right sizing handle away from the image.
Decrease the width	Click and drag either the middle-left or middle-right sizing handle toward the image.
Increase the height	Click and drag the upper-middle or bottom-middle sizing handle away from the image.
Decrease the height	Click and drag the upper-middle or bottom-middle sizing handle toward the image.
Adjust the height and width at the same time	Click and drag a corner sizing handle at an angle to adjust the height and width.

Lesson 4: Wrapping Text Around an Image

Word places text above and below an image when you first insert it. Although some images look better with no text to the left or right sides, you might want to wrap text around the image. ***Wrapping style*** refers to how text wraps around an image.

You can have text appear on top of or behind an image, wrap tightly around the outer edges of the image itself, or wrap above or below the image.

In this lesson, you choose ***tight wrap*** to wrap text around the edge of the image itself instead of the square boundary of the image.

To Wrap Text Around an Image

1 **In the Company Newsletter file, click the image to select it.**

2 **Click the Text Wrapping button on the Picture toolbar to see a list of text-wrapping options, as shown in Figure 7.9.**

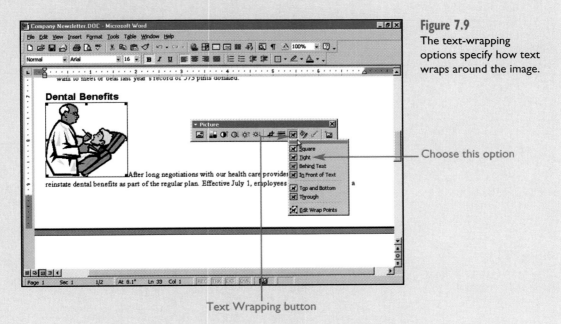

Figure 7.9
The text-wrapping options specify how text wraps around the image.

Choose this option

Text Wrapping button

3 **Choose <u>T</u>ight from the menu.**
Text now wraps around the image, not the square boundary of the image (see Figure 7.10).

 Seeing the Image
After selecting the wrap option, you might see the top of the page. Scroll back down to the bottom of the page to see your image and how text wraps around it.

continues ▶

To Wrap Text Around an Image   (continued)

Figure 7.10
Text tightly wraps around
the edge of the image.

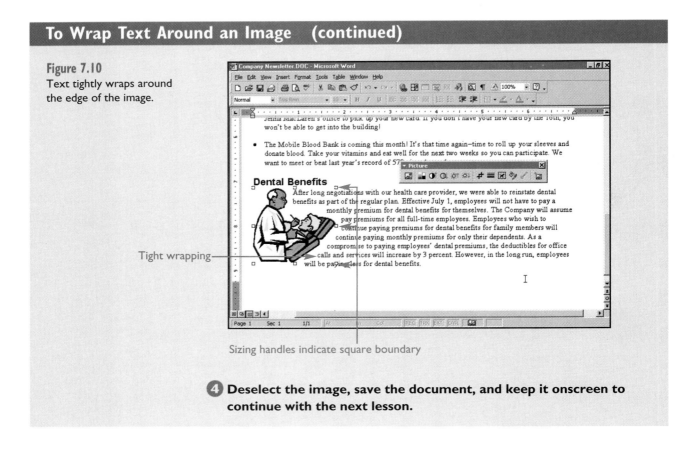

Tight wrapping

Sizing handles indicate square boundary

**④ Deselect the image, save the document, and keep it onscreen to
continue with the next lesson.**

 Selecting Wrap Style and Alignment
You can display the Format Picture dialog box and then click the Layout tab to
select a wrapping style (see Figure 7.11). In addition, you can choose the horizontal alignment of the image, such as centering it between the left and right
margins.

Figure 7.11
You can select a wrapping
style and horizontal
alignment.

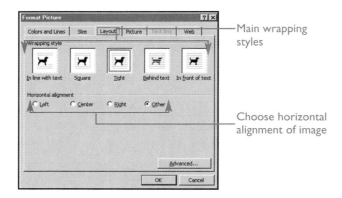

Main wrapping
styles

Choose horizontal
alignment of image

Lesson 5: Creating a Text Box

In addition to inserting clip art, you might want to create a text box. A text box is a
graphics object that contains text. You can place the text box within a paragraph, add a
border, and use other graphics options to customize how the text appears.

Text boxes are used to draw attention to text on the page. Magazines typically use text boxes to highlight a quote, special information, or exciting news. To make a text box stand out, you should select a different font and font size. In this lesson, you create a text box to make people more inclined to read information on the page.

To Create a Text Box

1 **In the Company Newsletter file, press** Ctrl+Home **to position the insertion point at the top of the document.**

2 **Choose Insert, Text Box.**
You must draw the box area where you want to place the text box.

3 **Click and drag to form a small box that looks like the one in Figure 7.12. To do this, start clicking below the word** job **on the third line of the first paragraph. Then drag down and to the right until the mouse pointer is at the end of the second line of the second paragraph.**

Text Box toolbar

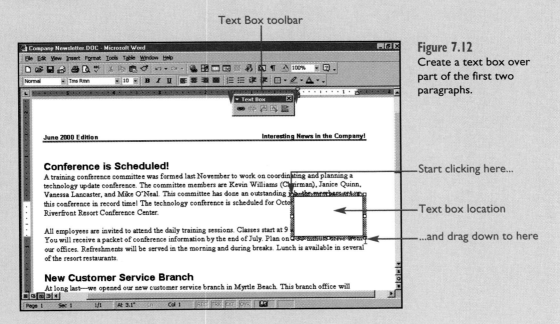

Figure 7.12
Create a text box over part of the first two paragraphs.

Start clicking here...

Text box location

...and drag down to here

4 **Click the drop-down arrow to the right of the Font option on the Formatting toolbar and choose Comic Sans MS.**
You want to choose a sans serif font to stand out from the serif font used in the paragraphs.

5 **Click the drop-down arrow to the right of the Font Size option and choose 12.**
You want to make the text bigger to draw the reader's eyes to the text box.

6 **Type** Update your computer skills at the conference! **in the text box.**

7 **Click and drag the middle-left sizing handle to the left to increase the size of the text box a little if you can't read the text you just typed.**

continues ▶

To Create a Text Box   (continued)

Your text box now contains text in a different font, as shown in Figure 7.13.

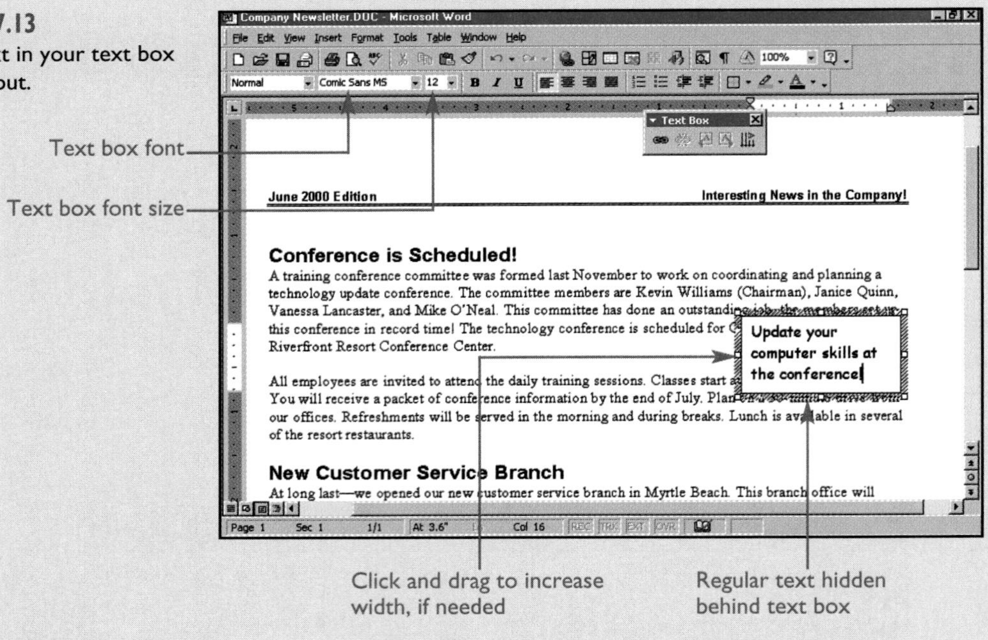

Figure 7.13
The text in your text box stands out.

Text box font—

Text box font size—

Click and drag to increase
width, if needed

Regular text hidden
behind text box

Now you need to adjust the wrap option so the text box does not cover up regular text in the paragraphs.

8 Position the mouse pointer along the outer border of the text box.

9 When you see a four-headed arrow, right-click the border of the text box and choose Format Text Box from the shortcut menu.
You see the Format Text Box dialog box. It looks similar to the Format Picture dialog box you used in previous lessons.

10 Click the Layout tab.

11 Click the Square option and click the Right option; then click OK.
The text box does not cover the paragraph text any more.

12 Deselect the text box, save the document, and keep it onscreen to continue with the next lesson.

Using Text Boxes
You can apply a fill to a text box. Click the Format Text Box button (looks identical to the Format Picture button) on the Picture toolbar. Then click the Colors and Lines tab and choose a fill color. You can also change the border line style and select different fonts and font sizes for the text in the text box.

Formatting a Text Box
Instead of right-clicking on the border of the text box and choosing Format Text Box, you can choose Format, Text Box from the menu bar.

Lesson 6: Using Fills and Borders

You can enhance text boxes and images by selecting fills and borders. ***Fill*** refers to a shading color that appears in the background of a text box or around the image within its square boundaries. A ***border*** is a line style that creates a frame around an object.

The text box currently has a single black line border. In this lesson, you will choose a pale blue fill and a dark blue border.

To Use a Fill and Border

1 **In the Company Newsletter file, position the mouse pointer on the text box border and click the right mouse button.**
You see the shortcut menu of options to adjust the text box settings.

2 **Choose Format Text B_ox_ and click the Colors and Lines tab.**
You see the options to specify a fill color and line color and style.

3 **Click the drop-down arrow to the right of the _C_olor option in the Fill section of the dialog box.**
You see a color palette from which to choose a fill color (see Figure 7.14).

Click to see fill
color palette

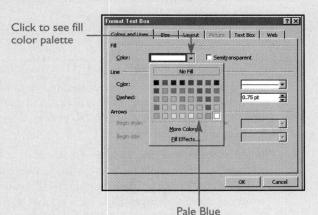

Pale Blue

Figure 7.14
Select the color you want to fill in the text box background.

4 **Click the Pale Blue color.**

5 **Click the drop-down arrow to the right of the Line Color option.**
You see the same colors for the line color.

 Choosing Fill and Border Colors
Choose complementary fill and border colors. For example, choose a light blue fill and a dark blue border color.

6 **Click the Blue color.**

7 **Click OK.**
Your text box looks much better with a touch of color (see Figure 7.15).

continues ▶

To Use a Fill and Border   (continued)

Figure 7.15
Fill and border colors
improve the appearance
of text boxes.

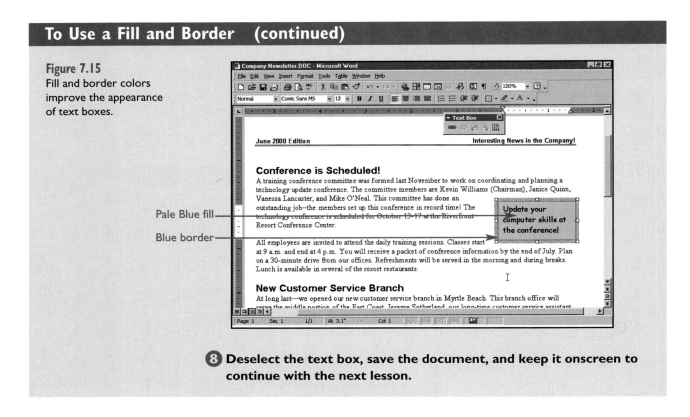

Pale Blue fill

Blue border

8 **Deselect the text box, save the document, and keep it onscreen to continue with the next lesson.**

Customizing the Fill Color
You can choose additional colors besides those shown on the Fill color palette. Click the More Colors option on the palette and click the Custom tab in the Colors dialog box. You can click any part of the color pad to choose any color you see on the color palette.

In addition, you can select special fill effects by choosing Fill Effects from the Fill color palette. For example, you can blend two colors (such as light blue and dark blue) to form a *gradient* appearance. In addition, you can choose from a variety of texture backgrounds, such as marble.

Lesson 7: Creating WordArt

Another exciting graphic feature is WordArt. WordArt shapes text into designs for you. You can use WordArt to create unique banners and titles for flyers, brochures, and other advertising documents. Because WordArt is a graphic object, you can use similar options to those you used to customize your clip art.

In this lesson, you create a WordArt object for the title of your newsletter.

To Create WordArt

1 **In the Company Newsletter file, position the insertion point at the top of the document.**

② **Choose Insert, Picture, WordArt.**
The WordArt Gallery dialog box appears (see Figure 7.16). The first step is to select a style or shape for your text.

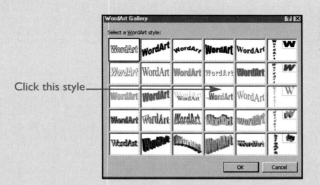

Click this style

Figure 7.16
Select a style or shape for your text.

③ **Click the fourth style on the third row.**

④ **Click OK.**
The Edit WordArt Text dialog box appears, as shown in Figure 7.17. This is where you type the text and select the font and font size you want.

Click to see list of fonts

Type your text here

Figure 7.17
Type and format your WordArt text.

Click to select a font size

⑤ **Type The Millennium Group in the text area and click OK.**
You need to choose a smaller font for your title.

⑥ **Click the drop-down arrow to the right of the Size option and choose 28.**
Although the insertion point was at the beginning of the document, the WordArt object appears in a different position (see Figure 7.18).

⑦ **Position the mouse pointer inside the WordArt area. Click and drag the WordArt to the top of the page.**

⑧ **Click the Format WordArt button on the WordArt toolbar.**
You see the Format WordArt dialog box, which is similar to the Format Picture dialog box.

⑨ **Click the Layout tab, click the Center button, and click OK.**
Your WordArt object is now positioned at the top of the page and is centered between the left and right margins (see Figure 7.19).

continues ▶

To Create WordArt   (continued)

Figure 7.18
You need to move the WordArt object to the top of the page.

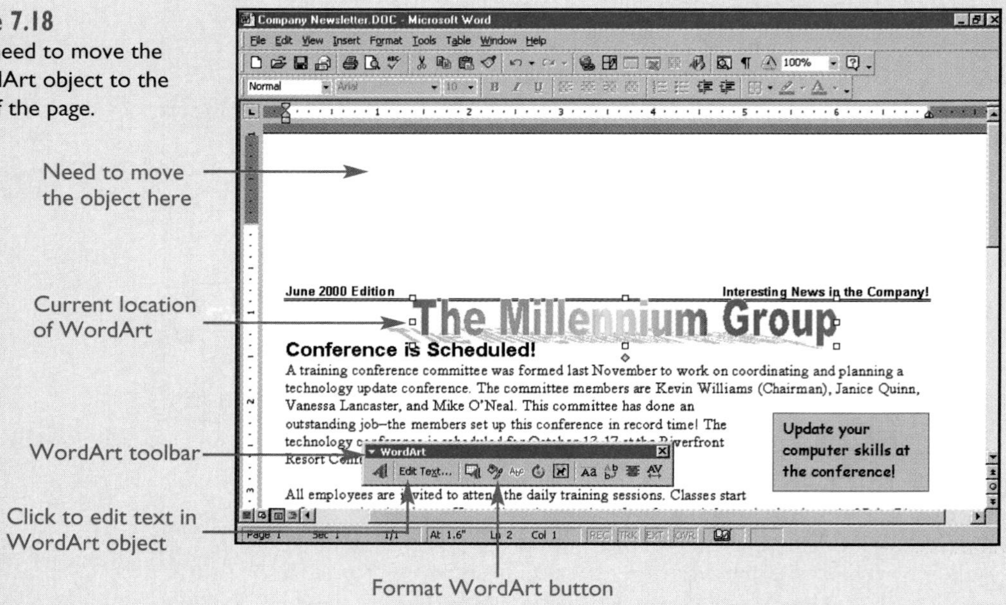

Need to move the object here →

Current location of WordArt —

WordArt toolbar —

Click to edit text in WordArt object —

Format WordArt button

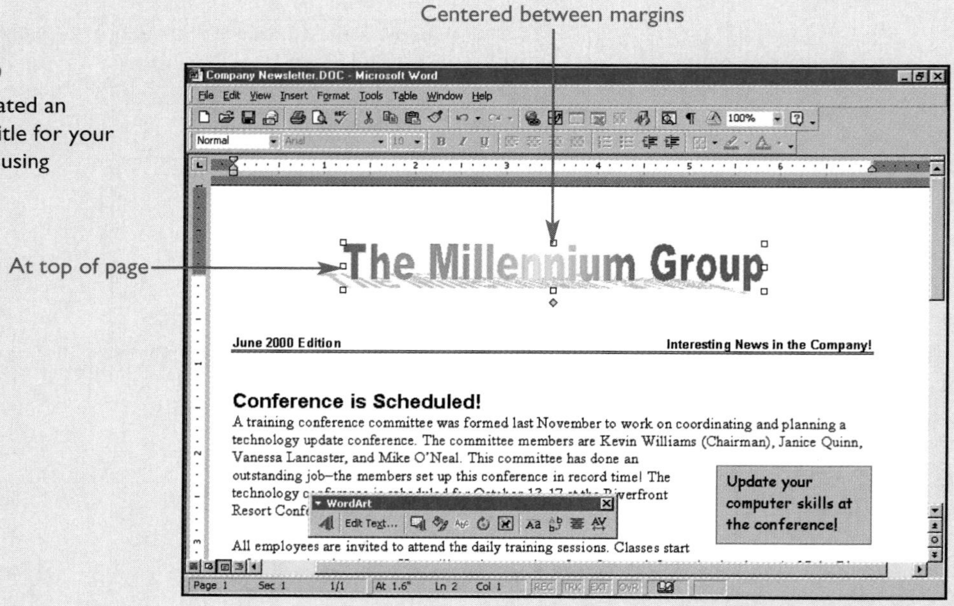

Centered between margins

Figure 7.19
You've created an attractive title for your newsletter using WordArt.

At top of page—

⓾ **Deselect the WordArt object, save the document, print it, and then close the document.**

Customizing WordArt

If you need to edit your WordArt object later, double-click the WordArt object to change the text, font, or font size.

If you want to customize the WordArt object, click it to see the WordArt toolbar. Then you can select options from the toolbar to enhance the appearance of the object. For example, you can rotate the object, select a different style from the gallery, or choose a different shape.

Summary

You should be able to create exciting graphics in your documents now. You can insert pictures, change the sizes and location, and adjust the text wrap style. In addition, you can create attention-getting text boxes with pleasing fill and border colors. Finally, you learned how to design exciting WordArt objects to make headings and banners.

Although much information about graphics is included here, Word provides many more choices for customizing pictures, text boxes, and WordArt. You can learn a lot by simply exploring the different options on the toolbars and by using onscreen Help.

Checking Concepts and Terms

True/False

For each of the following, check *T* or *F* to indicate whether the statement is true or false.

__T __F **1.** When you access the Insert ClipArt dialog box, the first step is to choose a category. [L1]

__T __F **2.** When you right-click an image and choose Insert, Word inserts the image at the beginning of the document. [L1]

__T __F **3.** If you click and drag the middle-right sizing handle to the left, you decrease the width of an image. [L3]

__T __F **4.** Clicking and dragging the sizing handles gives you more specific measurements than setting the size in the Format Picture dialog box. [L3]

__T __F **5.** Square wrap enables text to wrap on both sides of the image but maintains a box around the image. [L4]

__T __F **6.** To create a line that forms a frame around an image, you need to create a border for the image. [L6]

__T __F **7.** The text box is a special graphic object that creates interesting shapes for the text you type. [L7]

__T __F **8.** After creating a WordArt object, you can use some of the same formatting techniques you use for a picture. [L7]

__T __F **9.** A fast way to edit the text in WordArt is to double-click the object. [L7]

__T __F **10.** If you want to move an object to a location you can't see onscreen, you should click and drag the image there. [L2]

Multiple Choice

Circle the letter of the correct answer for each of the following.

1. You must install a special filter to insert which type of graphic image? [L1]
   a. .jpg
   b. .gif
   c. .wpg
   d. .bmp

2. You can do all of the following to an image that has sizing handles around it except _____. [L2–4]
   a. adjust the image's width
   b. move the image to a different location
   c. increase the height of the image
   d. adjust the text wrapping around the image

3. Which wrap option allows text to wrap around the specific image itself, not the graphics area? [L4]
   a. Square
   b. Tight
   c. Top to Bottom
   d. Through

4. What option is efficient for moving an image to another location you can see onscreen? [L2]
   a. clicking and dragging the image to the new location
   b. clicking the Copy button, moving the insertion point, and clicking the Paste button
   c. clicking and dragging the upper-right sizing handle
   d. all of the above

5. Which of the following increases the width of an image? [L3]
   a. clicking and dragging the upper-middle sizing handle upward
   b. clicking and dragging the middle-left sizing handle to the right
   c. clicking and dragging the bottom-middle sizing handle upward
   d. clicking and dragging the middle-right sizing handle to the right

6. To adjust how text appears around the left and right sides of the image, what option should you adjust? [L4]
   a. the size
   b. text wrapping
   c. cropping marks
   d. colors and lines

7. All of the following are ways to insert a picture from the Clip Gallery except _____. [L1]
   a. double-clicking the image
   b. right-clicking the image and choosing Insert
   c. clicking the image, clicking the Copy button in the dialog box, and clicking the Paste button on the Standard toolbar
   d. clicking the image and clicking the Insert Clip button that appears

8. Which of the following formatting techniques does not highlight the information in a text box? [L5]
   a. 8-point size
   b. light fill color
   c. using a different font, such as Arial
   d. interesting text

9. What option lets you select a color background within a text box? [L6]
   a. highlight
   b. border
   c. fill
   d. wrapping

10. When creating a WordArt object, what is typically the first step? [L7]
    a. typing the text
    b. selecting the WordArt style
    c. choosing a font and font size
    d. choosing a rotation option

Screen ID

Label each element of the Word screen shown in Figure 7.20.

Figure 7.20

A. Clip art image

B. Fill

C. Format Picture (Object) button

D. Picture toolbar

E. Sizing handles

F. Text box

G. Text Wrapping button

H. WordArt

I. WordArt toolbar

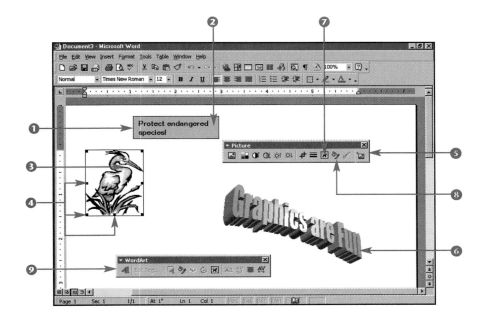

1. _____ 4. _____ 7. _____

2. _____ 5. _____ 8. _____

3. _____ 6. _____ 9. _____

Discussion Questions

1. Explain how clip art images enhance documents. Make a list of documents that would be appropriate for including clip art images. Also identify at least two types of documents where you should not use clip art images.

2. Describe the text wrapping feature.

3. What is the purpose of a text box in a publication, such as a magazine? Look through current issues of different magazines. Discuss what makes some boxes effective. Make a list of suggestions for ineffective text boxes.

4. What is the purpose of WordArt? Identify examples of when WordArt is appropriate.

Skill Drill

Skill Drill exercises reinforce project skills. Each skill reinforced is the same, or nearly the same, as a skill presented in the project. Detailed instructions are provided in a step-by-step format.

1. Inserting an Image in a School Newsletter

The local Parent Educator Association (PEA) has asked you to create this month's newsletter for parents about school activities. You have been given the basic text, but you decide clip art and quotes will enhance the newsletter's appearance and encourage parents to read it. [L1]

1. Open **WD1-0702** and save it as **PEA Newsletter**.

2. Position the insertion point at the end of the first sentence after the heading **Book Fair**.

3. Choose Insert, Picture, Clip Art.

4. Scroll through the picture categories and click **Academic**.

5. Right-click the image of the three books and choose Insert.

6. Click the Close button in the upper-right corner of the dialog box.

7. Save the newsletter and leave the document onscreen to continue with Exercise 2.

2. Sizing an Image in the Newsletter

When you insert the image of three books in the newsletter, it appears in a predetermined size. You need to adjust the image's size so it fits better within the newsletter. [L3]

1. With the PEA Newsletter displayed, click the image to select it.

2. Click the Format Picture button on the Picture toolbar.

3. Click the Size tab.

4. Click and drag across the value in the Height box.

5. Type **1.71**.

6. Press Tab to make the Width box active. The width should automatically change to 1.95".

7. Click OK.

8. Save the document and keep it onscreen to continue with Exercise 3.

3. Moving an Image in the Newsletter

After inserting the image in the newsletter, you want to move it around on the page until you are satisfied with its location. [L2]

1. In the PEA Newsletter, click the image to select it.

2. Position the mouse pointer on the image and hold down the mouse button.

3. Drag the image to the right margin. Release the mouse button when the image is in position.

4. Save the document and keep it onscreen to continue with Exercise 4.

4. Wrapping Text Around an Image

After moving the image, the spacing of the lines is uneven; you need to adjust the text wrapping. You decide to wrap text around the edge of the image itself, instead of the square boundary of the image. [L4]

1. In the PEA Newsletter file, click the image to select it.

2. Click the Text Wrapping button on the Picture toolbar.

3. Choose Tight from the menu. If the image shifts in position, drag it back into place.

4. Deselect the image, save the document, and keep it onscreen to continue with Exercise 5.

5. Inserting a Text Box

You decide to create a text box to emphasize information about the upcoming PEA Halloween Party for the children of the school. [L5]

1. With the PEA Newsletter onscreen, choose Insert, Text Box.

2. Click and drag to form a small box approximately 2" wide and .75" high below the last paragraph.

3. Click the drop-down arrow to the right of the Font Size option and choose 14. Click the drop-down arrow to the right of the Font option and choose Arial.

4. Type the following lines:

Friday, October 29

6:30-8:00 p.m.

Halloween Party

5. Click and drag the sizing handles to increase the text box a little if you can't read the text you just typed.

6. Right-click the text box and choose Format Text Box from the shortcut menu that appears.

7. Click the Layout tab.

8. Click the Square option and click the Center option; then click OK.

9. Deselect the text box, save the document, and keep it onscreen to continue with Exercise 6.

6. Enhancing a Text Box

Because the text box is advertising the PEA Halloween Party, you want to add an orange fill and heavy black border to the text box. [L6]

1. In the PEA Newsletter file, position the mouse pointer on the text box border and click the right mouse button.

2. Choose Format Text Box and click the Colors and Lines tab.

3. Click the drop-down arrow to the right of the Color option in the Fill section.

4. Click the Light Orange option.

5. Click the drop-down arrow to the right of the Style option and select the 6-point option.

6. Click OK.

7. Deselect the text box, save the document, and keep it onscreen to continue with Exercise 7.

7. Creating a Banner for the Newsletter

The PEA newsletter looks good, but you need to identify the school next to the PEA logo. You decide to use WordArt to create an attractive banner. [L7]

1. In the PEA Newsletter file, position the insertion point at the top of the document.

2. Choose Insert, Picture, WordArt.

3. Click the third style on the third row.

4. Click OK.

5. Click the drop-down arrow to the right of the Font Size option and choose 40.

6. Type Maple Elementary in the Text area and click OK.

7. Position the mouse pointer inside the WordArt area; click and drag the WordArt to the top of the page and right of the PEA Logo.

8. Deselect the WordArt object, save the document, and print it.

Challenge

Challenge exercises expand on or are somewhat related to skills presented in the lessons. Each exercise provides a brief narrative introduction followed by instructions in a numbered step format that are not as detailed as those in the Skill Drill section.

1. Editing a Fourth of July Invitation

You are in charge of the annual Family Fourth of July celebration. You decide to create an eye-catching invitation for your extended family members using WordArt, clip art and a text box.

1. Open WD1-0703 and save it as Family Invitation.

2. Apply the Fireworks Art border to the page. It is the 28th border option in the Art border drop-down list.

3. Position your insertion point immediately before the **Special Guests** line. From the Home and Family clip art category, locate the Seniors clip art image. Use the Copy and Paste commands to insert the image in your document.

4. Use the Format Picture dialog box to set the Seniors image size to 3" high and 3.67" wide.

5. Position your insertion point at the bottom of the document. From the Special Occasions clip art category, locate the Fourth of July fireworks clip art image. Use the Copy and Paste commands to insert the image in your document.

6. Using the sizing handles, change the Fourth of July fireworks clip art image to approximately 1" high.

7. Position your insertion point between the lines **Grandpa is bringing his fiddle** and **Don't miss the fiddling and fireworks!** Create a text box approximately 2" wide and enter the following information:

   Where: Anderson Memorial Park

   When: July 4, 3 p.m.

8. Change the text box fill color to tan and the text box line border to blue.

9. Use WordArt to insert a heading at the top of your invitation. The heading should read **Family 4th of July Picnic**. Use the WordArt style of your choice and adjust the position as needed.

10. Save the document and print it.

2. Enhancing a Field Trip Permission Slip

You need a permission slip for parents to sign allowing their children to attend a concert of the local high school orchestra. You decide to reuse a permission slip you have already created but with added enhancements.

1. Open WD1-0704 and save it as **Field Trip Slip**.

2. Using the WordArt feature, insert the school name in the permission slip. Use the fifth style on the fifth row. Use 32-point Arial Black. The school name is **Canyon Ridge Elementary School**.

3. Position your WordArt at the top of the page and center align it between the left and right margins.

4. Position your cursor below the last line of the letter text, but before the return slip. Insert the clip art image **Musicians** from the Entertainment category.

5. From the Format Picture dialog box, click the size tab and set a 1.5" height and 2.67" width.

6. Save the document and print it.

3. Creating a Notepad with WordArt

You enjoy using the WordArt feature to twist text into interesting shapes; so you decide to create your own personal notepad.

1. Open WD1-0705 and save it as **Personal Notepad**.

2. Set 0.5" top and bottom margins. Set 0.75" left and right margins.

3. Change the heading font to 36-point Bremen Bd BT (or another designer font).

4. Choose the WordArt Option. Select the sixth style on the fourth row. This will vertically align each letter of your name. Choose 36-point Bremen Bd (or a sans serif font), and click the bold and italic buttons. Type your name in the text area.

5. Drag your WordArt object to the top of your page. Using the Format WordArt dialog box, set the horizontal alignment to <u>R</u>ight.

6. Print a copy of your notepad page.

7. Customize the WordArt object by clicking it and bringing up the WordArt toolbar. Select options from the toolbar to enhance the appearance of the object. For example, you can rotate the object, select a different style from the gallery, or choose a different shape.

8. Save and print a copy of your revised notepad page.

4. Creating a Letterhead

You decide to create a personal letterhead as a gift for your eight-year-old sister. You use clip art and a text box.

1. In a new blank document, set a 0.5" top margin.

2. Save the document as **Letterhead**.

3. Using the copy and paste method, insert the clip art image Rose from the Plants category. Use the sizing handles to make the image approximately 1" tall. Check the size in the Format Picture dialog box and adjust it if necessary.

4. Use WordArt for your sister's name **Michelle**. Select the second style in the first row. Select the font as Monotype Corsiva (or a script font, such as Snell) and set the font size to 24 points. Position it next to the rose.

5. Drag the vertical scrollbar until you see the bottom of the page. Drag to create a text box approximately 4" wide. Type your address within the text box. Separate the street address from the city, state, and zip code by inserting a flower symbol from the Monotype Sorts symbol set. Select the address and change the font to 14-point Monotype Corsiva. If part of the text is not visible, use the sizing handles to enlarge the box. Set the text box layout to Horizontal alignment: <u>C</u>enter.

6. Change the fill in the text box to a texture. In the Format Text Box dialog box, select the Color and Lines tab. Click the down arrow next to the <u>C</u>olor option. Click <u>F</u>ill Effects. Select the Texture tab and choose Pink tissue paper.

7. Save the document and print it.

5. Enhancing a Report

Your Internet report needs a text box calling attention to a key point. In addition, you decide to add a WordArt title and a clip art image.

1. Open **WD1-0706** and save it as **Class Report**.

2. Format the left and right margins to 1". Set paragraph spacing to 6 points before. Set page numbering to Top of Page, Right alignment. Do not number the first page of the report.

3. Create the title **Internet Addressing** using the WordArt feature. Use the fourth style on the second row. Set the font size to 16 points. Format the WordArt so it is horizontally aligned at <u>C</u>enter.

4. Create a text box approximately 2.5" wide on the right side of the Internet Protocol section. Choose Arial as the font for the text box. Type `Each connected com-puter receives a unique IP address!` in the text box. Use the sizing handles to adjust the width of the box if needed.

5. Use the Layout tab of the Format Text Box dialog box and adjust the wrap option of the text box to Square. Set the horizontal alignment to <u>R</u>ight.

6. Use a White marble texture for the fill of the text box.

7. Position the insertion point at the beginning of the second paragraph under domain names. Insert the Directions clip art image located in the Metaphors category. Change the size of the clip art image to 0.75" high and 0.86" wide.

8. Change the text wrapping option of the image to <u>T</u>ight.

9. Save the document and print it.

6. Enhancing a Health Club Letter

You decide to add two action clip art images to your letter requesting membership renewal in your health club. You use two tennis images to call attention to your new tennis courts.

1. Open `WD1-0707` and save it as `Renewal Request`.

2. Create a letterhead using the company name. Using WordArt, select the fourth style of the fourth row in the WordArt Gallery. Drag the WordArt to the top of the letter and set horizontal alignment to <u>C</u>enter.

3. Insert the image of a woman playing tennis from the clip art category of Sports and Leisure. Format the size to 1" high and 0.95" wide. Drag the image to the third paragraph. Set the layout to <u>T</u>ight and the horizontal alignment to <u>L</u>eft.

4. Insert the image of a man playing tennis from the clip art category of Sports and Leisure. Format the size to 1" high and 1.18" wide. Drag the image to the third paragraph. Set the layout to <u>T</u>ight and the horizontal alignment to <u>R</u>ight.

5. Insert a hard space in the appropriate location, if needed.

6. Save the document and print it.

Discovery Zone

Discovery Zone exercises require advanced knowledge of topics presented in *Essentials* lessons, application of skills from multiple lessons, or self-directed learning of new skills.

[?] 1. Using Clip Art to Create a Watermark

You decide a large clip art image of a computer would make the Computer Training Concepts course description document more interesting. Open `WD1-0708` and save it as `Computer Courses`.

Before inserting the computer image in the document, you need to research the following topics in Help:

- Add a watermark to a printed document.
- Format a watermark.

In a header, insert the Computers clip art image located in the Science and Technology category. Set the wrapping behind text. Drag the image so it is centered vertically and horizontally over the body of the text. Save the document and print.

2. Inserting Clip Art in a Table

You need to create a flyer advertising your cat. To help you create the layout, you use the table feature. Before inserting the cat's image in the document, you need to research the following topics in Help:

- Using tables to create page layout.
- Ways to position text and graphics.

Create a new blank document and save it as `Cat Flyer`. Insert the `Cat photo.jpg` located on the student CD. Use Figure 7.21 to create the advertisement. Apply the formats as indicated. Save the flyer and print it.

Figure 7.21
Create the cat-adoption flyer.

[?] 3. Inserting Scanned Images in a Flyer

You have been assigned to create a flyer for a Hawaiian Touring Agency. The company has sent you three scanned photographs from the island of Kauai for you to include in the flyer.

Open WD1-0709 and save it as Hawaii Flyer. Before positioning the scanned images in the flyer, you need to research the following topic in Help: Position a drawing object in relation to page, text, or other anchor.

Use Figure 7.22 to create the flyer. Apply the formats as indicated. Insert Hawaii1.jpg, Hawaii2.jpg, and Hawaii3.jpg from the CD that accompanies this textbook. Use text boxes to create the captions for the photos. Save the flyer and print it.

Figure 7.22
Create the Hawaii flyer.

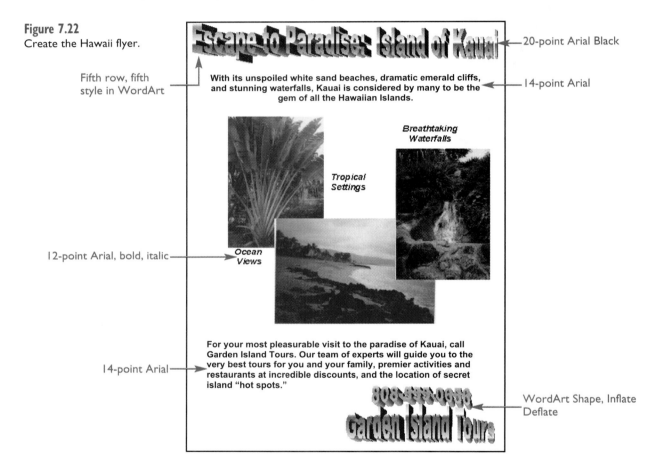

20-point Arial Black

14-point Arial

Fifth row, fifth style in WordArt

12-point Arial, bold, italic

14-point Arial

WordArt Shape, Inflate Deflate

Project 8

Project 8

Integrating Information and Using Specialized Features

Objectives

In this project, you learn how to

➤ **Insert an image from the Internet**

➤ **Insert a File within the Current Document**

➤ **Insert an Excel Worksheet**

➤ **Insert an Excel Chart**

➤ **Create an Organization Chart**

➤ **Apply a Background Texture**

➤ **Save a word Document as a Web Page**

➤ **View the Document in a browser**

Key terms in this project include

- associated keywords
- background
- browser
- Excel
- gradient
- hypertext links
- link

- MS Organization Chart 2.0
- placeholders
- Tile Windows Vertically option
- worksheet

Why Would I Do This?

As you work on a document in Word, you might need to include additional information or objects that are available in other sources. For example, you can download clip art from the Internet, insert data created in a spreadsheet (worksheet) program, and create an organization chart. You can use different programs and applications in Office 2000 to create powerful Word documents.

Visual Summary

Figure 8.1 shows a photo downloaded from the Internet, an entire Word document inserted within the current document, and an Excel worksheet imported as a table.

Figure 8.1
Special objects and text are inserted from various sources to complete your document.

Entire Word document inserted within current document

Excel worksheet imported into Word

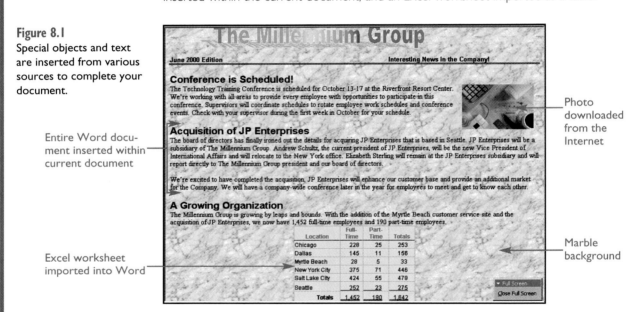

Photo downloaded from the Internet

Marble background

Figure 8.2 shows an organization chart created with MS Organization Chart 2.0 and a column chart imported from Excel. Both Figures 8.1 and 8.2 contain a marble background image to enhance the document when saved as a Web page.

Figure 8.2
You can insert objects created with other applications.

Organization chart

Excel chart inserted

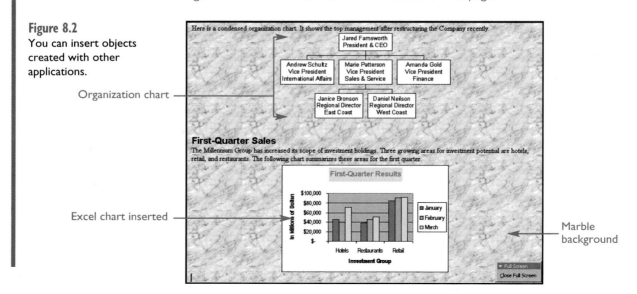

Marble background

Lesson 1: Inserting an Image from the Internet

The Internet contains a vast number of clip art images. You can use a search engine, such as Excite, to search for Web sites that contain clip art images that you can purchase or download free. For example, registered users of Microsoft Word can download additional clip art free.

Using Downloaded Clip Art

When you find clip art on the Internet, you need to review that particular Web site's policy on acceptable use of its images. Many sites allow you to download a copy for your personal use only. Others might allow you to include their images in limited advertising, brochures, and company newsletters. You are typically restricted from making unlimited copies of the clip art for other people or selling the clip art for personal gain.

In this lesson, you open a company newsletter similar to the one you created in Project 7, "Using Graphic Elements." You decide to explore downloadable images on Microsoft's Web site.

To Insert an Image from the Internet

1 **Open** WD1-0801 **and save it as** Updated Newsletter.

2 **Click at the beginning of the first paragraph and choose Insert, Picture, Clip Art.**

The Insert ClipArt dialog box appears. Instead of choosing an image on your computer, you want to download a picture from Microsoft's Web site.

3 **Click Clips Online at the top of the dialog box.**

4 **Click OK when you see a dialog box telling you that the clips you select will be added to your Clip Gallery.**

Internet Explorer starts and displays the End-User License Agreement. Read through the agreement to learn about acceptable uses of the clips.

5 **Click Accept when you read and agree to accept the terms.**

The Microsoft Clip Gallery Live Web page appears. You see three color tabs that let you choose the pictures, sound, or motion category.

6 **Click the Pictures tab to see new pictures.**

7 **Click the Browse clips by category drop-down arrow and choose Office to display office-related clips, as shown in Figure 8.3.**

continues ▶

To Insert an Image from a Web Site   (continued)

Click to see previous images in this category

Figure 8.3
The gallery contains several categories of pictures from which to choose.

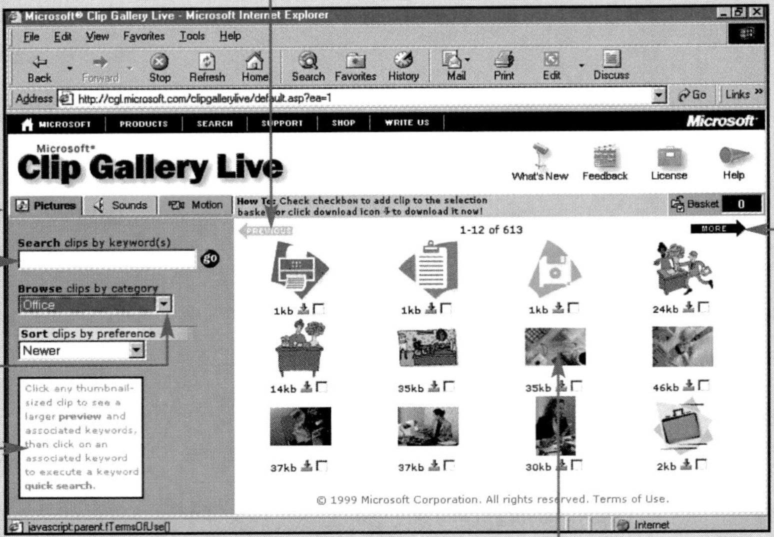

Click to see pictures →

Type words to search for particular types of pictures

Choose a specific category

Preview window —

Click to see preview of image   Click to see additional images in this category

⚠ **Different Web Options**
Web pages constantly change; therefore, you might see different objects and images in the Web page on your screen than those shown in this book. You should be able, however, to use the category and search options to locate the images specified in the steps.

8 **Click the picture of the keyboard, mouse, and coffee cup.**
You should see a preview of the image in the left frame of the Web page, as shown in Figure 8.4. You also see a list of associated keywords to the right of the image. **Associated keywords** are words that are associated with the clip. Microsoft uses keywords to help organize clips and help you find clips that contain the same keywords. The keywords are formatted as hypertext links. When you click a **hypertext link** you connect to another Web page.

9 **Click the preview image to download it.**
The picture is downloaded into the ClipArt Gallery.

❌ If you are using Netscape, the image is not automatically downloaded. You must choose to save the image to your network drive, hard drive, or data disk. The saved image is not included in the ClipArt Gallery. You must select it by choosing Insert, Picture, From File.

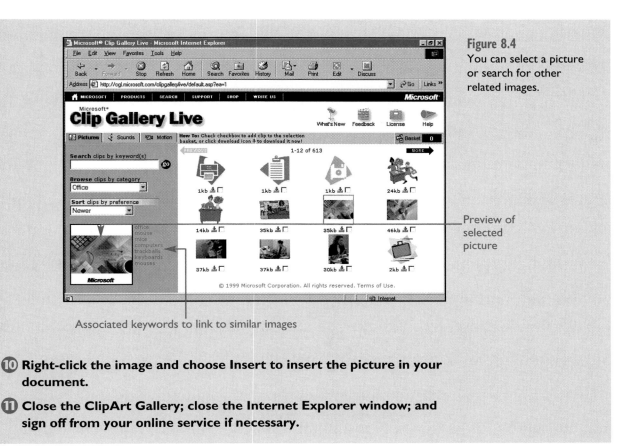

Figure 8.4
You can select a picture or search for other related images.

Preview of selected picture

Associated keywords to link to similar images

10 **Right-click the image and choose Insert to insert the picture in your document.**

11 **Close the ClipArt Gallery; close the Internet Explorer window; and sign off from your online service if necessary.**

Using the Downloaded Clip Again
When you initially download a clip, it automatically appears in the ClipArt Gallery window. You can use the downloaded clip again at any time. The next time you display the ClipArt Gallery dialog box, click the category that contains the clip you downloaded from Internet Explorer. The clip is typically downloaded into the same category in which you selected it from the Web site.

After you insert the image, you need to decrease the size of the picture and place it in the right margin.

To Adjust the Picture

1 **Right-click the picture and choose Format Picture from the shortcut menu.**

2 **Click the Size tab and type 1 in the Height box.**

3 **Click the Layout tab and click the Square wrapping style.**

4 **Click the Right horizontal alignment. Then click OK.**
The picture is now positioned on the right side of the paragraph, as shown in Figure 8.5.

continues ▶

To Adjust the Picture (continued)

Figure 8.5
The image downloaded from the Internet is now formatted in your document.

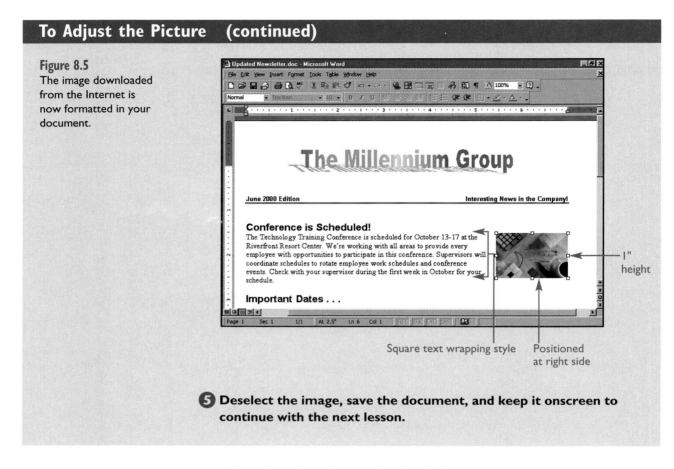

Square text wrapping style

Positioned at right side

1" height

⑤ **Deselect the image, save the document, and keep it onscreen to continue with the next lesson.**

 Saving Other Images from the Internet
When you want to save a graphic image from another Web site, right-click the image and choose Save Picture As. You can typically save images in jpeg, bmp, or gif format. Then choose Insert, Picture, From File to insert the image you downloaded from the Internet.

Lesson 2: Inserting a File within the Current Document

At some time you might need text that you saved as another file, or you might want to insert text that someone sends to you as an email attachment. You can use the Insert File dialog box to insert an entire document within the current document. Inserting an existing document can save you from having to type the same information again.

In this lesson, you insert a short file that someone else in your organization has created for you.

To Insert a File within the Current Document

1 **In the Updated Newsletter file, position the insertion point on the blank line between the table of dates and the heading A Growing Organization.**
You want to insert a file between the table and the next heading.

2 **Choose Insert, File to display the Insert File dialog box.**

3 **Choose WD1-0802 and click Insert.**
Word inserts the WD1-0802 file at the insertion point location, as shown in Figure 8.6. Although the original document's font size is 12-point, the text is inserted at 10-point.

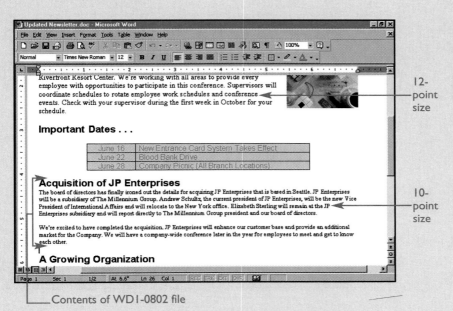

Contents of WD1-0802 file

Figure 8.6
The file is inserted within the current document.

4 **Select the two paragraphs in the Acquisition of JP Enterprises section.**

5 **Choose Times New Roman and 12-point from the Formatting toolbar; then deselect the text.**
The paragraphs are now formatted to match the existing paragraphs in your document (see Figure 8.7).

continues ▶

To Insert a File within the Current Document (continued)

Figure 8.7
The inserted text is in the same format as the existing text.

12-point size for original text

12-point size for inserted text

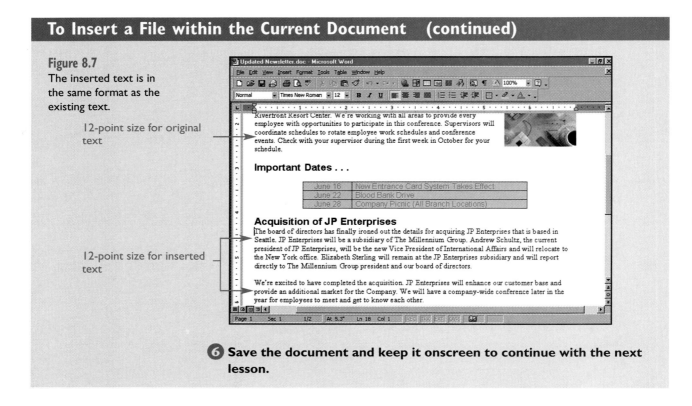

6 Save the document and keep it onscreen to continue with the next lesson.

 Copying and Pasting between Two Word Documents
You might want to use only a portion of a document in another Word document. Instead of inserting the entire file, open both documents. Select and copy the text you want to use in another document. Then maximize the other document window and paste text there. Refer to Help for more information about copying and pasting between open document windows.

Lesson 3: Inserting an Excel Worksheet

Each application in Office 2000 is designed to create and use different documents for specific purposes. For example, you use Word to create and format letters, memos, and reports. **Excel** is a spreadsheet application in which you format numerical data and perform calculations. Although you should use the appropriate application for what you're doing, you might need the same data in another application.

In this lesson, you use the copy and paste commands to copy part of a **worksheet** (Excel's term for spreadsheets) into your Word document.

 Using the Clipboard Between Applications
With the Office 2000 Clipboard, you can store up to 12 pieces of data from various applications, such as Word and Excel, and then use Paste to paste the Clipboard contents in one location.

Application Windows
While completing this lesson, make sure you are not running other applications, such as Internet Explorer or PowerPoint. The more applications you open, the greater the chance that your computer will lock up.

To Insert an Excel Worksheet

1 **In the Updated Newsletter file, position the insertion point on the blank line between the two paragraphs in the A Growing Organization section.**

You should position the insertion point where you want to insert the worksheet data. Now you need to start Excel and open the worksheet that contains the data you want.

2 **Click Start on the taskbar, choose _P_rograms, and choose Microsoft Excel.**

Excel appears and covers the Word window. If you can still see part of the Word window, click Excel's maximize button.

3 **Click the Open button on the Excel Standard toolbar and open WD1-0803.xls.**

You see the worksheet in the Excel window, as shown in Figure 8.8.

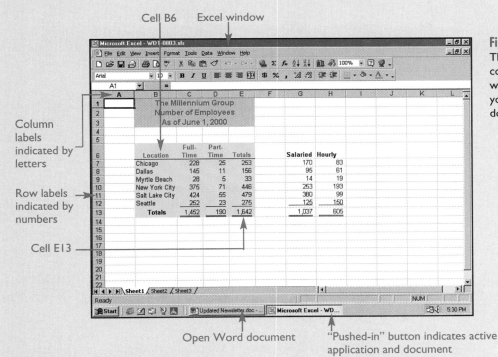

Cell B6   Excel window

Column labels indicated by letters

Row labels indicated by numbers

Cell E13

Open Word document

"Pushed-in" button indicates active application and document

Figure 8.8
This worksheet contains data you want to use in your Word document

You see alphabetic labels at the top of the worksheet and numbered labels on the left side. These labels help you identify columns and rows, respectively, within the worksheet. For example, the cell containing Location is cell B6.

continues ▶

To Insert an Excel Worksheet (continued)

4 **Position the mouse pointer in cell B6, which contains Location. When the mouse pointer resembles a big plus sign, drag down and over to cell E13, which contains 1,642, as shown in Figure 8.9.**

Click to copy selected cells to Clipboard

Figure 8.9
Select the data you want to copy to your document.

Click here...

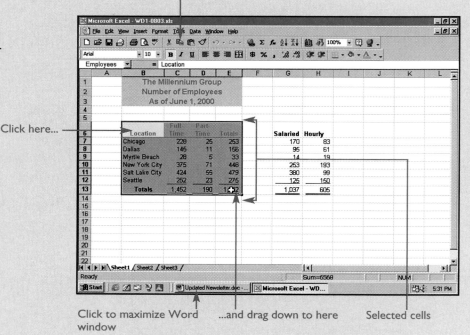

Click to maximize Word window   ...and drag down to here   Selected cells

5 **Click the Copy button on Excel's Standard toolbar.**
The selected worksheet data is copied to the Clipboard. Once data is in the Clipboard, you can paste it into most Windows-based programs.

6 **Click the Word button on the taskbar to maximize Word.**
You know Excel is still open because you see the Excel worksheet button on the taskbar.

7 **Click the Paste button on the Standard toolbar.**
The worksheet data is pasted into the Word document as a table, as shown in Figure 8.10.

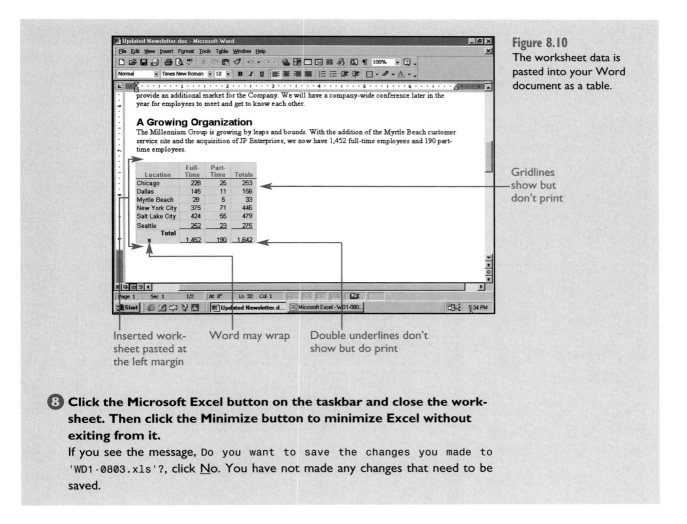

Figure 8.10
The worksheet data is
pasted into your Word
document as a table.

Gridlines
show but
don't print

Inserted work-
sheet pasted at
the left margin

Word may wrap

Double underlines don't
show but do print

8 **Click the Microsoft Excel button on the taskbar and close the worksheet. Then click the Minimize button to minimize Excel without
exiting from it.**

If you see the message, Do you want to save the changes you made to
'WD1-0803.xls'?, click <u>N</u>o. You have not made any changes that need to be
saved.

When you paste worksheet data into Word, the formulas convert to numbers. Therefore,
the results do not recalculate if you change numbers.

 Other Methods of Inserting a Worksheet

You have other options for inserting an Excel worksheet into your document,
depending on the desired outcome.

You can use the copy command in Excel to copy the data to the Clipboard.
Then, in Word, choose <u>E</u>dit, Paste <u>S</u>pecial to insert the worksheet as an object.
When you choose this option, the formulas are copied. You can double-click the
object and edit the values from within Word. The results are automatically
recalculated.

If you think you might change the original data in the Excel worksheet, you
might want to ***link*** the Word document to the worksheet. Then when you
update the worksheet, the changes are reflected in the data you linked to the
Word document.

You need to format the table after inserting the worksheet data. For this, you'll use some
of the format techniques you learned in Project 6, "Using Tables."

To Format the Inserted Worksheet Table

1 **Right-click the worksheet table within Word and choose Table Properties.**

2 **Choose Center alignment and click OK.**
The worksheet table is centered between the left and right margins. The inserted worksheet table looks better after formatting it (see Figure 8.11).

3 **Double-click the gridline between the first and second columns to widen the first column.**

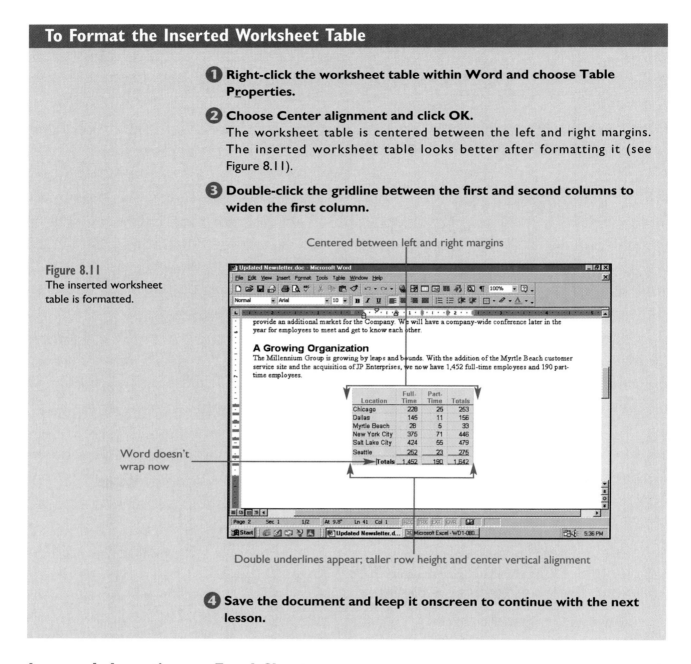

Centered between left and right margins

Figure 8.11
The inserted worksheet table is formatted.

Word doesn't wrap now

Double underlines appear; taller row height and center vertical alignment

4 **Save the document and keep it onscreen to continue with the next lesson.**

Lesson 4: Inserting an Excel Chart

Although you can create charts from within Word, you might want to use an existing chart created with Excel. Inserting an Excel chart is similar to inserting an Excel worksheet. You can simply copy and paste the chart from Excel into Word. After you paste the chart into Word, you format the chart the same way you formatted images in Project 7.

In this lesson, you insert a chart into your document. Check the taskbar to make sure you have Excel running. If not, start the program as you did in Lesson 3.

To Insert an Excel Chart into a Word Document

1 In the Updated Newsletter file, position the insertion point on the blank line above the heading Dental Benefits on the second page.

2 Click the Microsoft Excel button on the taskbar to maximize the Excel window.

Now you need to open the worksheet that contains the chart you want.

3 Open WD1-0804.xls in Excel.

You need to select the chart; then you'll copy and paste it into the Word document.

4 Click the chart area to select the chart.

Sizing handles appear around the chart, as they do when you select a graphic image (see Figure 8.12).

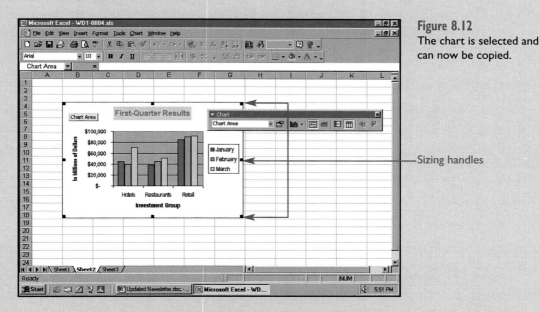

Figure 8.12
The chart is selected and can now be copied.

Sizing handles

5 Click the Copy button on Excel's Standard toolbar to copy the chart to the Clipboard.

6 Click the Word button on the taskbar to maximize the Word window containing Updated Newsletter.

7 Click the Paste button to paste the chart at the insertion point location (see Figure 8.13).

continues ▶

To Insert an Excel Chart into a Word Document (continued)

Figure 8.13
The Excel chart is inserted in your Word document.

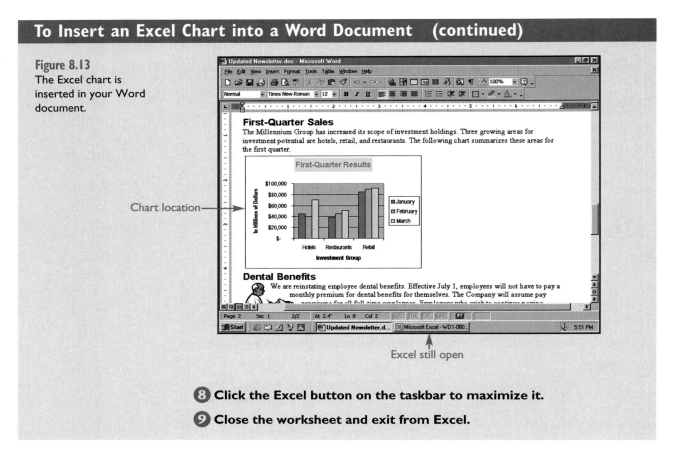

Chart location

Excel still open

8 **Click the Excel button on the taskbar to maximize it.**

9 **Close the worksheet and exit from Excel.**

You need to adjust the chart. You will use the same types of options you used to position clip art in Project 7.

To Adjust the Chart

1 **Right-click the chart and choose Show Picture Toolbar from the shortcut menu.**
You need to adjust how text wraps around the chart.

2 **Click the Text Wrapping button and choose Top and Bottom.**
This option doesn't let text wrap on either side of the chart. Also, you can now center the chart between the margins.

3 **Right-click the chart and choose Format Object.**
You see the Format Object dialog box. It contains the same types of options as the Format Picture dialog box.

4 **Click the Layout tab. Click Center horizontal alignment and click OK.**
The chart is now centered between the margins (see Figure 8.14).

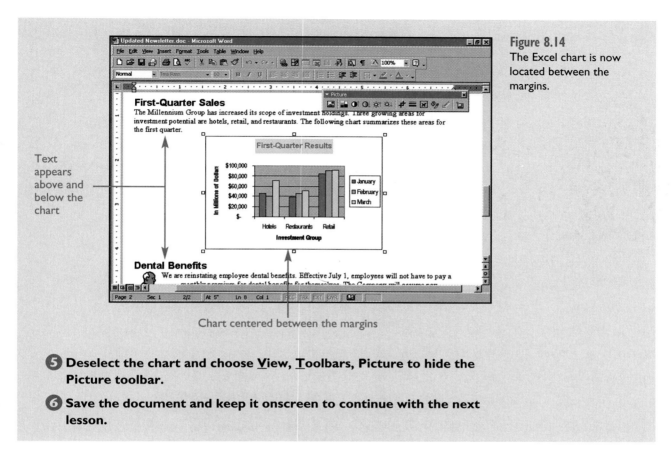

Figure 8.14
The Excel chart is now located between the margins.

Text appears above and below the chart

Chart centered between the margins

 5 **Deselect the chart and choose View, Toolbars, Picture to hide the Picture toolbar.**

6 **Save the document and keep it onscreen to continue with the next lesson.**

Dragging and Dropping a Chart

There's another easy way of copying and pasting a chart from Excel to Word. You can display both the Word and Excel windows side by side by using the *Tile Windows Vertically option*. To do this, right-click the gray space on the taskbar and choose Tile Windows Vertically.

After you select the chart, hold down Ctrl and drag the chart to where you want to copy it in the Word window. Release the mouse and Ctrl. A copy of the chart appears in Word. If you don't press and hold Ctrl during the entire drag and drop process, you move the chart instead of copying it.

Lesson 5: Creating an Organization Chart

An organization chart shows the hierarchy of positions within an organization. The chart shows who reports to whom and the different positions within a department or division.

To create an organization chart in Word, you access an application called **MS Organization Chart 2.0**. This application contains the tools you need to create, edit, and customize an organization chart. You use MS Organization Chart 2.0 in this lesson.

To Create an Organization Chart

① **In the Updated Newsletter file, position the insertion point on the blank line above the heading** First-Quarter Sales **at the top of page 2.**
This is where you want the organization chart to appear.

② **Choose Insert, Object to open the Object dialog box.**

③ **Scroll through the list until you see MS Organization Chart 2.0 (see Figure 8.15).**

Figure 8.15
The Object dialog box contains different tools for creating objects to insert into Word.

Option to create an organization chart

④ **Choose MS Organization Chart 2.0 and click OK.**
The Microsoft Organization Chart window appears (see Figure 8.16). The title bar indicates that the object will be embedded in your Word document. The chart contains *placeholders*, text and space reserved for entering data.

Click to maximize window

Figure 8.16
Create, edit, and format your organization chart.

Toolbar to add positions to chart

Type name of top executive

Placeholders

Press ⏎Enter to type title

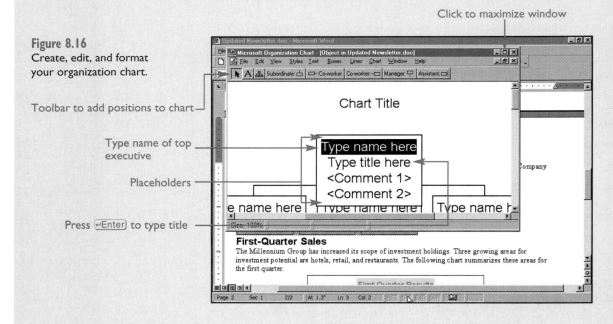

⑤ **Click the Maximize button to maximize the Microsoft Organization Chart window and see more of the organization chart as you create and edit it.**

6 Type `Jared Farnsworth` over the `Type name here` placeholder.

7 Press <kbd>↵Enter</kbd> and type `President & CEO` over the `Type title here` placeholder.

You don't have to replace the `Comment` placeholders. If you don't type text over them, they disappear when you go to another position.

8 Press <kbd>Ctrl</kbd>+<kbd>↓</kbd> to move to the first position on the next level.

9 Type the following data in the three remaining positions, pressing <kbd>↵Enter</kbd> to move to the next placeholder for the current position. Press <kbd>Ctrl</kbd>+<kbd>→</kbd> to go across the chart.

`Andrew Schultz`	`Marie Patterson`	`Amanda Gold`
`Vice President`	`Vice President`	`Vice President`
`International Affairs`	`Sales & Services`	`Finance`

Your organization chart now contains names and titles, as shown in Figure 8.17. After typing `Finance`, the insertion point is in that field. You still see the `<Comment 2>` field. The comment placeholder, however, will not print.

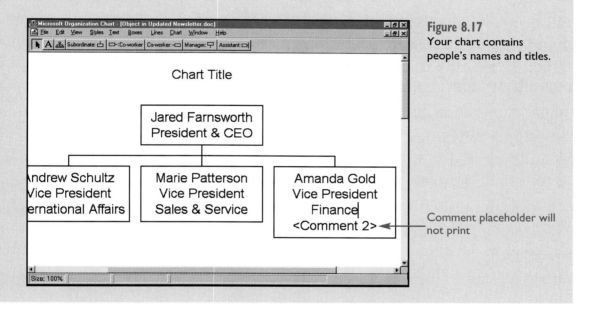

Figure 8.17
Your chart contains people's names and titles.

Comment placeholder will not print

The default organization chart provides the main position and three subordinate positions. You can, however, add subordinates, co-workers, managers, and assistants. Let's add two subordinates for Marie Patterson.

To Add Positions

1 Click the Subordinate button on the toolbar.
The mouse pointer displays as the icon you see on the Subordinate button.

2 Click inside Marie Patterson's box.
A subordinate position appears below Marie's box (see Figure 8.18).

continues ▶

To Add Positions (continued)

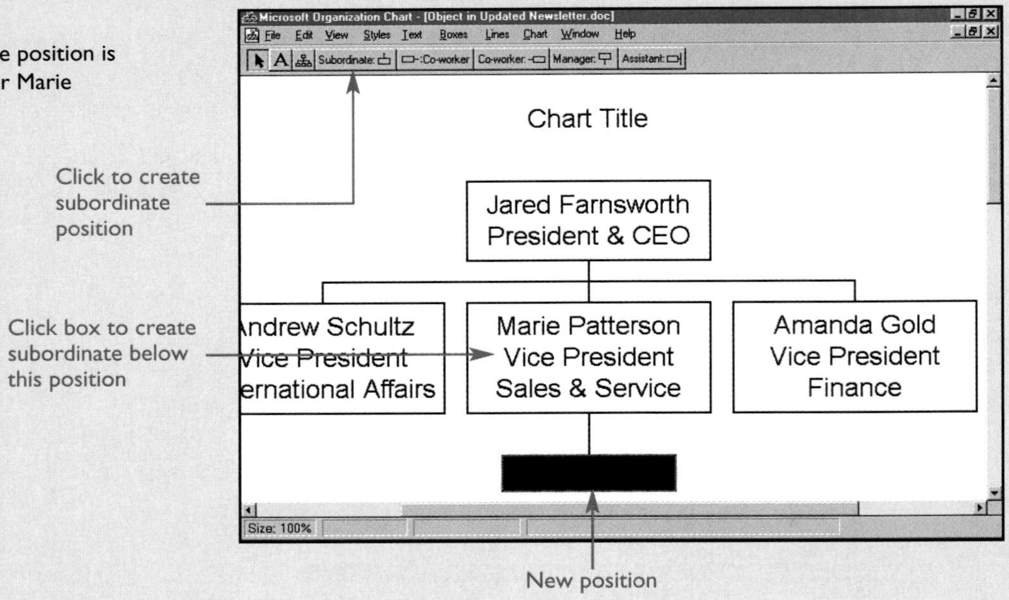

Figure 8.18
A subordinate position is created under Marie Patterson.

Click to create subordinate position

Click box to create subordinate below this position

New position

```
Microsoft Organization Chart - [Object in Updated Newsletter.doc]
File  Edit  View  Styles  Text  Boxes  Lines  Chart  Window  Help
```

Chart Title

Jared Farnsworth
President & CEO

Andrew Schultz
Vice President
International Affairs

Marie Patterson
Vice President
Sales & Service

Amanda Gold
Vice President
Finance

Size: 100%

3 **Click in the new position box.**
Clicking in the new box displays the placeholders, so you can type text. You might need to scroll down to see the entire box.

4 **Type the following data, pressing** ↵Enter **to go from one placeholder to the next.**
`Janice Bronson`
`Regional Director`
`East Coast`
You need to add a co-worker position for Janice. You want to place the co-worker's data to the right of Janice's box. Notice you have two Co-worker buttons on the toolbar. The second Co-worker button is the one that places a box to the right of the current one.

5 **Click the Right Co-worker Button on the toolbar.**

6 **Click Janice's box to create a co-worker box to the right of that box.**

> **X** If you accidentally create the wrong position, press Del while the box is selected. That will delete the box, and you can try again.

7 **Click in the new box and type the following data, pressing** ↵Enter **to go from one placeholder to the next.**
`Daniel Neilson`
`Regional Director`
`West Coast`
You are now ready to insert the organization chart into your document.

8 **Click the Close button in the top right corner of the window and click Yes when you see the prompt** `The object has been changed. Do you want to Update Object in A:\Updated Newsletter.doc before proceeding?`

The organization chart appears in your document (see Figure 8.19).

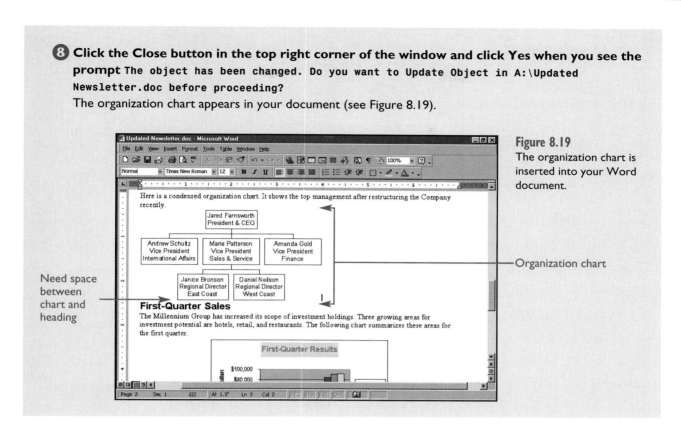

Need space between chart and heading

Organization chart

Figure 8.19
The organization chart is inserted into your Word document.

The chart will look better if you center it. Furthermore, you need to insert a hard return to separate the chart and the heading `First-Quarter Sales`.

To Adjust the Chart

1 **Press** `⏎Enter` **to insert a blank line below the chart.**

2 **Right-click the organization chart and choose Show Picture Toolbar.**

3 **Click the Text Wrapping button on the Picture toolbar and choose Top and Bottom.**

4 **Right-click the organization chart and choose Format Object.**

5 **Click the Layout tab, choose Center horizontal alignment, and click OK.**

The organization chart is better positioned on the page (see Figure 8.20).

continues ▶

To Adjust the Chart (continued)

Figure 8.20
The organization chart is
now properly positioned.

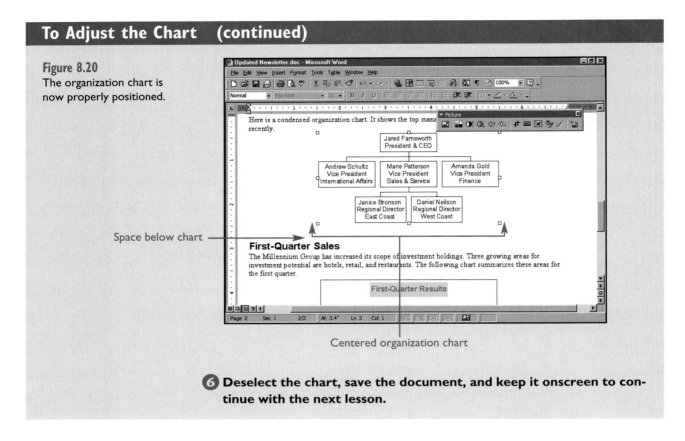

Space below chart ———

Centered organization chart

6 **Deselect the chart, save the document, and keep it onscreen to continue with the next lesson.**

 Editing Organization Charts
After inserting an organization chart into Word, double-click it to display MS
Organization Chart 2.0; then modify the chart.

If you do not want a position box, select it and press Del.

Furthermore, you can customize an organization chart by changing the lines, colors, and fill colors. Refer to Help within MS Organization Chart 2.0 for more
information.

Lesson 6: Applying a Background Texture

You can apply a background to enhance printed documents. A **background** is a shading
color, texture, or pattern that appears behind the printed text. Backgrounds are also helpful when you want to enhance a document you plan to upload to a Web site.

In this lesson, you apply a marble background to your newsletter.

To Apply a Background

1 **In the Updated Newsletter file, choose Format, Background.**

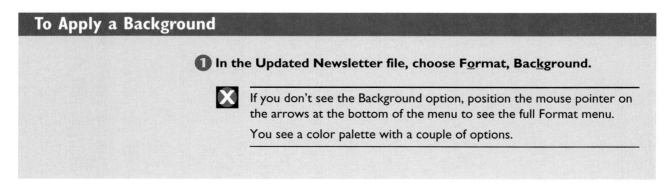
If you don't see the Background option, position the mouse pointer on
the arrows at the bottom of the menu to see the full Format menu.

You see a color palette with a couple of options.

2 **Choose Fill Effects.**

The Fill Effects dialog box appears, as shown in Figure 8.21. The **gradient** options let you blend from one color to another.

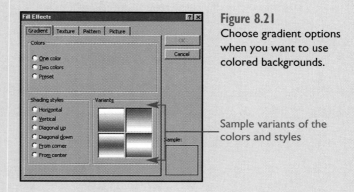

Figure 8.21
Choose gradient options when you want to use colored backgrounds.

Sample variants of the colors and styles

3 **Click the Texture tab to display the texture options (see Figure 8.22).**

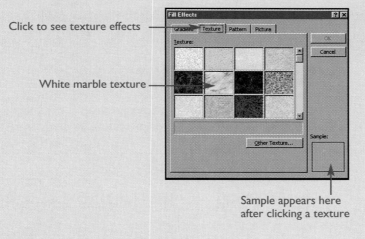

Click to see texture effects

White marble texture

Figure 8.22
Choose a texture for your background.

Sample appears here after clicking a texture

4 **Click the white marble texture; then click OK.**

The white marble texture background appears throughout your document (see Figure 8.23). Notice the view automatically changes to Web Layout view.

continues ▶

To Apply a Background   (continued)

Figure 8.23
Your document has a white marble background.

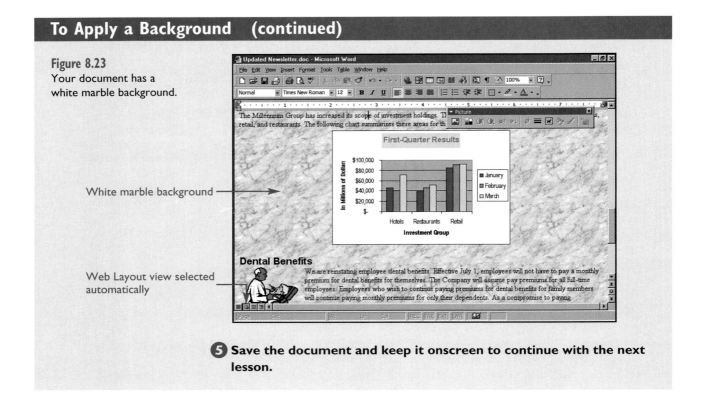

White marble background ——→

Web Layout view selected automatically ——

 Save the document and keep it onscreen to continue with the next lesson.

Choosing a Background
When you're choosing a background, keep in mind that the text must be easy to read on the background color or texture. Some textures create beautiful colors, but they also make it more difficult for the reader to read your document text.

Lesson 7: Saving a Word Document as a Web Page

More and more people are creating their own personal and business Web pages. If you want to create several linked Web pages or use enhanced Web formats, you need to use the Web Wizard or a special program. With Microsoft Front Page, for instance, you can create sophisticated Web pages; however, you can take an existing Word document and save it in a Web page format.

In this lesson, you will save your newsletter as a Web page.

To Save a Word Document as a Web Page

1 **In the Updated Newsletter file, choose File, Save as Web Page.**
The Save As dialog box appears, as shown in Figure 8.24. The original filename appears in the File name box; however, it contains the .htm extension. The Save as type option displays Web Page (*.htm; *.html).

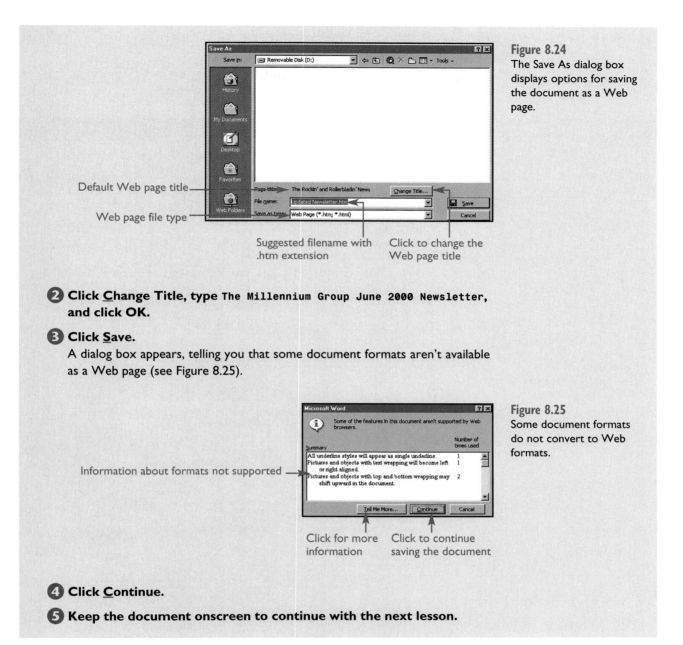

Default Web page title

Web page file type

Suggested filename with .htm extension

Click to change the Web page title

Figure 8.24
The Save As dialog box displays options for saving the document as a Web page.

2 **Click Change Title, type The Millennium Group June 2000 Newsletter, and click OK.**

3 **Click Save.**

A dialog box appears, telling you that some document formats aren't available as a Web page (see Figure 8.25).

Information about formats not supported

Click for more information

Click to continue saving the document

Figure 8.25
Some document formats do not convert to Web formats.

4 **Click Continue.**

5 **Keep the document onscreen to continue with the next lesson.**

Formatting Changes
Some formatting is lost when you save a document as a Web page. For example, the text wrap options, such as Tight wrap, are not supported in Web documents. Word makes necessary changes as it saves the document in html format. You might need to adjust some formatting yourself after you see how the document looks.

Lesson 8: Viewing the Document in a Browser

Although the Web Layout view shows basically what the document will look like, you should launch a browser to get a better indication of how the document will look on the

Internet. A ***browser*** is a software program, such as Internet Explorerthat lets you display Web pages.

In this lesson, you display the document in Internet Explorer, make a change to the html document, save the change, and view it again in Internet Explorer.

To View the Web Document

1 **Click the Internet Explorer button on the taskbar.**

> **X** If you don't see an Internet Explorer button on the taskbar, choose Start, <u>P</u>rograms, Internet Explorer.

2 **Type Updated Newsletter.htm in the A<u>d</u>dress text box.**
You must include the full path and filename, such as C:\Updated Newsletter.htm.

3 **Click the Go button.**
You see the document as it will appear on the Web (see Figure 8.26).

Figure 8.26
Your document appears in the Internet Explorer browser.

Document name ——

WordArt not
completely visible

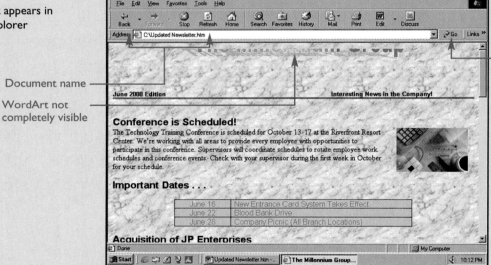

Click after typing document name in Address box

4 **Scroll through the Web page.**
The double underlines and gridlines do not appear in the worksheet table when you save the document as a Web page. The tight word wrap around the keyboard, mouse, and coffee cup image changes to square wrap.

5 **Click the Word button on the taskbar to maximize Word.**
You need to move the WordArt object down a little.

6 **Click and drag the WordArt object down and make sure it's centered between the left and right margins.**

7 **Save the document.**

8 **Click the Internet Explorer button on the taskbar.**

9 **Click the Refresh button on the Internet Explorer toolbar.**

The WordArt object is now completely visible, as shown in Figure 8.27.

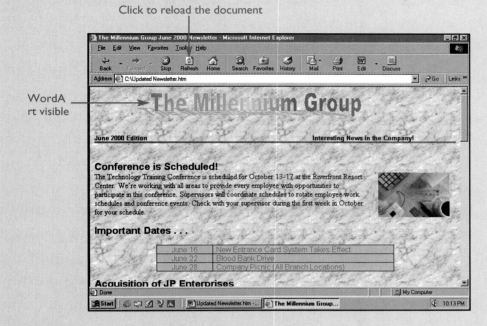

Click to reload the document

WordArt visible

Figure 8.27
You can see the WordArt object at the top of the Web page.

10 **Close Internet Explorer and close any open documents in the Word window.**

Summary

Congratulations! You just finished the last project of this book! With your newfound knowledge and skills, you can locate clip art on the Internet and download it for personal use, insert worksheets and charts into Word, create organization charts, and save documents as Web pages. In addition, you know how to combine two documents onscreen using the Insert File dialog box.

The next step is to complete the exercises on the following pages. You'll learn more about these features, use Help for additional information, and download additional clips from the Internet.

Checking Concepts and Terms ✓

True/False

For each of the following, check *T* or *F* to indicate whether the statement is true or false.

__T __F   **1.** All clip art found on the Internet is free to use in any way you want. [L1]

__T __F   **2.** Microsoft's Web site contains download-able pictures that store in your Clip Gallery. [L1]

__T __F   **3.** You can search for particular clips on Microsoft's Web site by typing associated keywords in the Search box. [L1]

__T __F   **4.** The best way to combine two documents on the screen is to open both documents and then copy and paste an entire document from one window to the next. [L2]

__T __F   **5.** When you copy and paste an Excel worksheet into Word, Word places the data as an object, similar to a graphic image. [L3]

__T __F   **6.** If you want worksheet data in Word to change when you change the original Excel file, you should link the worksheet instead of copying and pasting it. [L3]

__T __F   **7.** After pasting an Excel chart in a Word document, you can use the same types of format options that you use to format a picture. [L4]

__T __F   **8.** If you decide not to use an organization chart placeholder, such as `Comment1`, you must delete it. [L5]

__T __F   **9.** When you apply a background to a document, Word displays the document in the Web Layout view. [L6]

__T __F **10.** You can edit your Web document through Internet Explorer. [L8]

Multiple Choice

Circle the letter of the correct answer for each of the following.

  1. You can download all of the following from the Microsoft Clip Gallery Live, except _____. [L1]

   a. clip art

   b. pictures

   c. sounds

   d. organization charts

  2. To find particular types of clip art in Microsoft Clip Gallery Live, what can you do? [L1]

   a. Type a word that describes what you're looking for in the Search box.

   b. Click the Browse drop-down arrow and select a category.

   c. If you have a preview image, click one of its associated words to look for similar images.

   d. all of the above

  3. When you use the Insert File dialog box, what happens to the file you select? [L2]

   a. The file's contents are inserted at the insertion point location within the current document.

   b. The document opens into a separate document window.

   c. The document is inserted at the beginning of the current document.

   d. The document is inserted at the end of the current document.

  4. What happens to an Excel worksheet when you paste it into Word? [L3]

   a. The formulas are still active, so when you change a number in Word, the results are updated.

   b. When you change the original worksheet in Excel, the changes are automatically updated in the Word file.

   c. The pasted worksheet is treated as a table, so you can use table options to format it.

   d. The table is centered between the margins by default.

  5. All of the following downloads or imports are treated as objects, except _____. [L1, 3–4]

   a. pictures

   b. copied/pasted worksheets

   c. Excel charts

   d. copied/pasted special worksheets

6. To see both the Excel and Word windows side by side, what should you do? [L3]

    a. Right-click the taskbar and choose Tile Vertically.

    b. Right-click the taskbar and choose Tile Horizontally.

    c. Open the Excel worksheet into a Word window.

    d. Maximize both windows.

7. If you want to add a person who has the same rank as another person, which button do you click on the MS Organization Chart 2.0 toolbar? [L5]

    a. Assistant

    b. Manager

    c. Subordinate

    d. Co-Worker

8. When you apply a texture background to a document, Word automatically displays the document in which view? [L6]

    a. Normal view

    b. Web Layout view

    c. Print Layout view

    d. Outline view

9. When you save a document as a Web page, what extension is assigned to the document name? [L7]

    a. .doc

    b. .web

    c. .htm

    d. .www

10. What type of program should you use to see how a Web document will look on the Internet? [L8]

    a. word processing

    b. browser

    c. worksheet

    d. all of the above

Screen ID

Label each element of the Word screen shown in Figure 8.28.

Figure 8.28

A. Background

B. Chart

C. Excel button on taskbar

D. Excel window

E. Internet Explorer icon

F. Organization chart

G. Subordinate position

H. Word button on taskbar

I. Word window

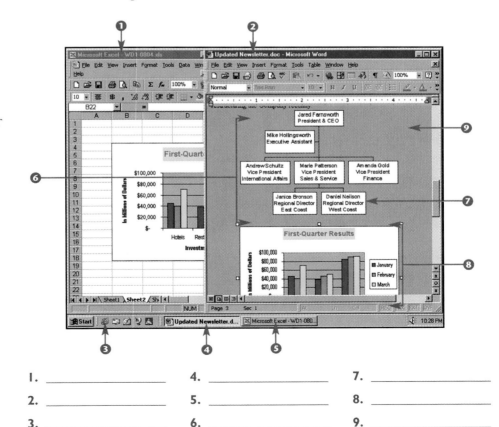

1. _____   4. _____   7. _____

2. _____   5. _____   8. _____

3. _____   6. _____   9. _____

Discussion Questions

1. What are some common policies about download-ing images from the Internet? Provide examples of how you might use downloaded images in confor-mity with standard guidelines.

2. Explain the difference in using the Open and Insert File dialog boxes. Also discuss when to use Insert File and when you might want to display two Word documents and copy and paste between them.

3. Explain the results of each of the following ways of bringing a worksheet into Word:
   - copy and paste
   - copy and paste special
   - link

4. Explain why you should view a Web document in Internet Explorer that you created in Word.

Skill Drill

Skill Drill exercises reinforce project skills. Each skill reinforced is the same, or nearly the same, as a skill presented in the project. Detailed instructions are provided in a step-by-step format.

1. Inserting a Document within the Current Document

You are writing an update to tell your family about your semester. You just finished the letter, but you want to include a document you always insert into your letters, a plea to get your family to help pay for your spring-break ski trip! [L2]

1. Open **WD1-0805** and save it as **Personal Letter**.

2. Position the insertion point on the blank line above **Family Tree**.

3. Choose Insert, File.

4. Choose **WD1-0806** and click Insert.

5. If needed, delete an extra blank line below the para-graph and insert a blank line above **Spring Break is Around the Corner**.

6. Select the heading **Spring Break is Around the Corner** and the paragraph below it.

7. Choose 14-point Technical font from the Formatting toolbar.

8. Deselect the text.

9. Save the document and leave the document onscreen to continue with the next exercise.

2. Inserting a Picture from the Internet

You want to insert a picture from the Internet to correspond with your ski trip paragraph. [L1]

1. With Personal Letter displayed, position the inser-tion point at the beginning of the paragraph dis-cussing your ski trip plans.

2. Choose Insert, Picture, Clip Art.

3. Click the Clips Online button. Click OK when you see a prompt. Click Accept after reading about appropriate uses of the clips.

4. Click the Pictures tab.

5. Click in the Search box, type **downhill skiers**, and click Go.

6. Click the third or fourth image to preview it.

7. Click the preview image to download the picture.

8. Right-click the image in the Insert ClipArt window and choose Insert.

9. Close the Insert ClipArt window and close Internet Explorer.

10. Right-click the picture. Choose Format Picture. Click the Size tab, and type **1** for the height.

11. Click the Layout tab. Choose Square. Click Right, and click OK.

12. Click and drag the picture down to align it with the top of the spring break paragraph.

13. Save the document and keep it onscreen to con-tinue with the next exercise.

3. Inserting a Worksheet

You created a simple budget in Excel and want to copy it into your Word document. [L3]

1. With Personal Letter onscreen, position the insertion point between the two paragraphs in the `Update on Expenses` section.
2. Choose Start, Programs, Microsoft Excel.
3. Open `WD1-0807.xls` from within Excel.
4. Click in Cell A1 and drag down to Cell B10 to select the area containing the budget data.
5. Click the Copy button in Excel.
6. Click the Word title bar and click the Paste button.
7. Right-click the worksheet and choose Table Properties.
8. Click Center alignment and click OK.
9. Click in the second row of the table and choose Table, Delete, Rows to delete the blank row.
10. Position the insertion point to the immediate left of the dollar sign in the first row and press `Backspace`. Do the same on the last row.
11. Position the insertion point to the immediate left of **75** and press `Backspace` three times to line up the numbers. Repeat this process for the other expenses.
12. Position the insertion point at the end of the paragraph above the table and press `Enter` to insert a blank line above the table.
13. Save the document and keep it on the screen to continue to the next exercise. Keep Excel and the worksheet open also.

4. Inserting an Excel Chart into Word

Your worksheet file also contains a pie chart that shows each expense's proportion of your total budget. You want to include it in your personal letter. [L4]

1. With Personal Letter onscreen, position the insertion point on the blank line above `Spring Break is Around the Corner`.
2. Click the Excel button on the taskbar.
3. Click the chart to select it and click the Copy button in Excel.
4. Click the Word button on the taskbar and click the Paste button.
5. Right-click the chart in Word and choose Show Picture toolbar.
6. Click the Text Wrapping button and choose Top and Bottom.
7. Click the Format Object button on the Picture toolbar. Click the Layout tab. Click the Center horizontal alignment, and click OK.
8. Click the Excel button on the taskbar; click the Close button to close the program.
9. Save the Word document and keep it onscreen to continue with the next exercise.

5. Creating an Organization Chart

You want to create an organization chart that shows your family tree. [L5]

1. With Personal Letter onscreen, position the insertion point on the blank line before the last paragraph.
2. Choose Insert, Object. Choose MS Organization Chart 2.0, and click OK.
3. Click the Maximize button to maximize the window.
4. Type `Me`, press `Enter`, and type your name.
5. Press `Ctrl`+`↓`, type `Mom`; press `Enter`, and type your mother's name.
6. Press `Ctrl`+`→`, type `Dad`; press `Enter`, and type your father's name.
7. Click the third box to select it and press `Del`.
8. Click the Subordinate button and click your mother's box. Repeat this step to add another position below your mother's box.
9. Repeat Step 8 for your father's box.
10. Double-click the first box below your mother's box, type `Grandma`; press `Enter`, and type your maternal grandmother's name.

11. Press Ctrl+→, type `Grandpa`; press ↵Enter), and type your maternal grandfather's name.

12. Press Ctrl+→, type `Grandma`; press ↵Enter), and type your paternal grandmother's name.

13. Press Ctrl+→, type `Grandpa`; press ↵Enter), and type your paternal grandfather's name.

14. Click the Close button. Click Yes to insert the family tree in the document.

15. Right-click the organization chart and choose Format Object.

16. Click the Size button, type **2** in the height box, and click OK.

17. Deselect the chart, save the document, and keep it onscreen to continue to the next exercise.

6. Applying a Background Color

You want to apply a background so the document will look nice when printed on a color printer. [L6]

1. With Personal Letter on the screen, choose Format, Background, Fill Effects.

2. In the Gradient tab, click the Two Colors option.

3. When the Color 1 option appears, click the Color 1 drop-down arrow and choose Lavender.

4. Click the Color 2 drop-down arrow and choose White.

5. Click the From Center option. Click the second variant and click OK.

6. Save the document, print it, and keep it onscreen to continue with the next exercise.

7. Saving the Document as a Web Page and Viewing It

You want to save the document as a Web page. Some schools or online service providers allow people to upload their documents to the Web. You want to save the document as a Web page so you can upload it if you have access to do so. [L7–8]

1. With Personal Letter on the screen, choose File, Save as Web Page.

2. Click the Change Title button. Type `John's College Update`, changing `John` to your name. Click OK.

3. Click Save, and then click Continue when you see a message about formats that don't save in html format.

4. Click Start. Choose Programs; then choose Internet Explorer.

5. Click in the Address box and type `Personal Letter.htm`. Be sure to include the drive where you stored the file.

6. Click Go to display the Web page.

7. Click the Print button within Internet Explorer.

8. Compare your Web printout with your regular document printout.

9. Close Internet Explorer and close the document within Word.

Challenge 💡

Challenge exercises expand on or are somewhat related to skills presented in the lessons. Each exercise provides a brief narrative introduction followed by instructions in a numbered step format that are not as detailed as those in the Skill Drill section.

I. Putting Together a List of Workshops

You are in charge of the monthly status to division managers. This month's report concerns the upcoming Information Technology Training Conference. You want to add a sampling of the scheduled computer workshops.

1. Open WD1-0808 and save it as `Conference Workshops`.

2. Position the insertion point at the end of the document. Insert the file WD1-0809. Check the spacing between paragraphs and correct if needed.

3. Format the inserted text to match the font used in the original document.

4. Each workshop has been assigned a number. Use the cut and paste commands to organize the workshops by number. Check the spacing between workshops and correct if needed.

5. Use the Keep with ne<u>x</u>t option, if needed, to make sure a heading isn't isolated from its paragraph between page breaks.

6. Save the document and print it.

2. Enhancing a Halloween Invitation

The Halloween invitation you created can be enhanced with Halloween clip art and WordArt.

1. Open WD1-0810 and save it as `Halloween Fun`.

2. Using the WordArt feature, insert `It's a Halloween Party!` at the top of the invitation. Use the second style on the fourth row. Use 44-point Comic Sans MS. Set horizontal alignment to <u>C</u>enter.

3. Create a text box at the bottom of the invitation text. Type `Don't forget your costume!` in 30-point Comic Sans MS, bold. Set horizontal alignment to <u>C</u>enter. Select the Light Orange fill for the text box and set a 3-point line border.

4. Position your cursor below the text box where you will insert a clip art image from Microsoft's Web site. Access Microsoft's Web site from the <u>C</u>lips Online option of the Insert Clipart dialog box. Search for Clips by Keyword `Halloween`. Select an appropriate image and insert it into your invitation.

5. Format the picture for 1.5" high, S<u>q</u>uare wrapping style, and <u>C</u>enter horizontal alignment.

6. Save the document and print it.

3. Creating Organization Charts

You need to create two organization charts showing the hierarchy of your school. The first chart should reflect the structure of your administration and the second should reflect your business department.

1. Research the structure of your school hierarchy. Use the school's course catalog or browse the school's Web page, if it has one. Refer to Figure 8.29 for sample organization charts. Sketch out the structure of your school before beginning this exercise. Refer to this sketch as you create your organization chart using MS Organization Chart 2.0.

2. Set 1" top, bottom, left, and right margins.

3. Create a heading using the title of your top administration. Center the heading and format it with 20-point Arial Black.

4. Create the organization chart and insert it into your document. Format it for S<u>q</u>uare wrapping and <u>C</u>enter horizontal alignment.

5. Create a heading using the title of your department. Center align the heading and format it as 20-point Arial Black.

6. Create the organization chart and insert it into your document. Format it for Square wrapping and Center horizontal alignment.

7. Adjust spacing as needed.

8. Save the document as **Organization** and print it.

Figure 8.29
Use these sample charts to create your charts.

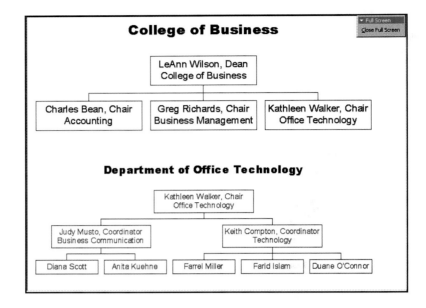

4. Inserting a Mortgage Worksheet into a Word Letter

A customer calls the loan officer at your mortgage company. The loan officer asks you to prepare a short letter that includes some calculations for the loan.

1. Open WD1-0811 and save it as **Loan Letter** in Word; open WD1-0812.xls in Excel.

2. Select and copy the worksheet data (cells A5 through B8). Then paste it between the first and second paragraphs in your Word document.

3. Center the table between the margins.

4. Make sure you have only one blank line before and after the table.

5. Press (Spacebar) as needed to align text within the cells in the second column.

6. Add the Pale Blue fill shading for all cells in the table.

7. Save the document and print it.

5. Creating an Airline Information Sheet

You work for a small airline service that provides transportation from Oklahoma City to special-attraction vacation spots, such as Las Vegas, Denver, and Salt Lake City. You want to design an attractive information sheet about safety instructions for the passengers.

1. Open WD1-0813 and save it as **Airline Information**.

2. After the last paragraph, insert the Word file WD1-0815. Insert the following bullet item between the second and third items.

```
Please turn off all portable, electronic devices (such as cell
phones) until the captain says that it is safe to turn them on
again.
```

3. Select the bullet list and adjust the tab to avoid having so much space between the symbol and the items. Also add a border with a light yellow shading color.

4. Position the insertion point at the beginning of the document and access the Microsoft Clip Gallery Live Web site.

5. Select the transportation category in the pictures section.

6. Preview the clip of the plane with the sun in the background; then download it.

7. Insert the clip in your document. Move it to the right side of the paragraph. Set a 2" height, <u>B</u>ehind Text wrapping style in the Layout section, and a 58% picture Brightness.

8. Start Excel and open `WD1-0814.xls`.

9. Select and copy the map. Then paste and position it between the two paragraphs in your Word document. Center it between the margins and set a 2.39" height. Close Excel.

10. Select Center vertical alignment in the Page Setup dialog box.

11. Save and print the document.

Discovery Zone

Discovery Zone exercises require advanced knowledge of topics presented in *Essentials* lessons, application of skills from multiple lessons, or self-directed learning of new skills.

1. Saving an Image from the Internet

A very interesting site containing beautiful computer-generated designs is `www.digitalblasphemy.com`, created and copyrighted by Ryan Bliss. Access the Internet and connect to this Web site. Explore the different images. When you see an image you really like, click it to see it full screen. Although you can download the image as wallpaper for your Windows desktop, you want to save the image to use in Word. Right-click the image and choose Save Picture As. Save the image.

In Word, use the option that inserts a graphic file. Adjust the format to size the image and place it on the page. Write a brief paragraph about the `www.digitalblasphemy.com` Web site. Create a footnote that cites the Web site. Refer to a reference manual for the correct format for creating this type of footnote entry.

Save the document as `Digital Image` and print it. Compare your printouts and descriptions with your classmates.

2. Enhancing an Organization Chart

You want to enhance the organization charts you created in Challenge exercise 3. Open `Organization` and save it as `Enhanced Organization Charts`. Edit the organization chart and explore the MS Organization Chart 2.0 Help menus in the Contents area to learn about the basics of an organization chart, including borders, box colors, and moving boxes.

Within the second organization chart, move one coordinator and his or her staff in front of another coordinator. For example, in Figure 8.29, you would move Judy Musto and her staff to the right of Keith Compton's staff. Choose blue box (fill) color for the coordinators and yellow for their employees. Create an assistant position and insert the name of the dean's secretary. Use a light green color for the box. Choose a different line style to connect the secretary to the dean's box. Save the document and print it. Compare it to your printouts for Challenge exercise 3.

[?] 3. Linking and Updating a Worksheet

You have a niece who has a Ty, Inc. Beanie Babies™ collection. Early in 1999, you created a worksheet that lists some of her special beanies and their prices. She needs your help in preparing a report for her fifth-grade class. Open `WD1-0816` in Word and open `WD1-0817.xls` in Excel.

You want to duplicate the worksheet data in your Word file, but you want to create a link so when you change the original worksheet, the changes are reflected in the Word document. Use the onscreen Help to learn about linking worksheets into Word by using the Copy and Paste Special commands. Then create a link to include the data into Word. Center the linked object within Word. Select a blue 2.5-point line border around the object.

Save the Word file as `Collection` and save the Excel file as `Inventory`. Print both documents.

Edit the worksheet in Excel by changing the current values in the `Current` column. Refer to a collectibles magazine or the Internet to find current market values. One good location is `www.pjcc.com`, a Web site for Paul and Judy's Coins & Cards Co., Inc. Save the Excel worksheet. Update the link, if needed, so the new current values are shown.

Insert a footnote at the end of the title that states that the term `beanies` is a trademark of Ty, Inc. Insert another footnote after `values` in the second paragraph that cites the source, such as a magazine or Web site, you used to obtain the current market values.

Save the updated worksheet and Word document. Print both documents.

4. Creating, Saving, and Viewing a Personal Web Page

Many colleges and universities let students upload Web pages to the college Web site, provided the content conforms to acceptable standards. Some Internet Service Providers (ISPs), such as America Online, allow members to upload documents for their own personal Web pages.

Create a document in Word that describes yourself, your hobbies, your major, and other interests. Use headings to separate each section. Create one table within the document.

If you have access to a scanner, scan a picture of yourself. If you want, scan one additional picture to include on your page. Insert these graphic files into your document. Choose an appropriate background color, making sure you can read the text through the background. Save the Web document as `My Web Page`. Type an appropriate title for it. View your document in Internet Explorer and print it.

If you have access to upload the document to your school Web site or to an online site, find out how to do so and upload your document. Then tell all your friends about it!

Task Guide

A book in the *Essentials* series is designed to be kept as a handy reference beside your computer even after you have completed all the projects and exercises. Any time you have difficulty recalling the sequence of steps or a shortcut needed to achieve a result, look up the general category in the alphabetized listing below, and then quickly home in on your task at hand. For your convenience, some tasks have been duplicated under more than one category. If you have difficulty performing a task, turn to the page number listed in the third column to locate the step-by-step exercise or other detailed description. For the greatest efficiency in using this Task Guide, take a few minutes to familiarize yourself with the main categories and keywords before you begin your search.

To Do This	Use This Command	Page Number
Application and File Management		
Close a document	Choose File, Close.	[pg. 19]
Exit from Word	Choose File, Exit.	[pg. 19]
Insert file within the current file	Position the insertion point. Choose Insert, File. Select a file, and click Insert.	[pg. 213]
Open a document	Choose File, Open.	Bonus
Print dialog box: display	Choose File, Print.	[pg. 14]
Print entire document	Click the Print button on the Standard toolbar.	[pg. 14]
Print Preview	Click the Print Preview button on the Standard toolbar.	[pg. 14]
Save document: first time	Choose File, Save or Save As. Select the Save in location and type the name of the file in the File name box; then click Save.	[pg. 11]
Save document: new name	Choose File, Save As. Select the Save in location and type the new name of the file in the File name box; then click Save.	[pg. 11]
Save document: same name	Click the Save button on the Standard toolbar.	[pg. 11]
Save document: Web page	Choose File, Save as Web Page. Click Change Title, type a new title, and click OK. Click Save; then click Continue.	[pg. 228]
Save images from Internet as graphics	Right-click an image and choose Save Picture As.	[pg. 209]
Start Excel	Click Start, choose Programs, and choose Microsoft Excel.	[pg. 215]

continues ▶

To Do This	Use This Command	Page Number
Application and File Management		
Start Internet Explorer	Click the Internet Explorer button on the taskbar, or choose Start, Programs, Internet Explorer.	[pg. 230]
Start Word	Click Start, Programs, Microsoft Word.	[pg. 3]
View Word Web document in Internet Explorer	Type path and filename in the Address box and click the Go button.	[pg. 230]
Display and View Options		
Formatting marks: display/hide	Click the Show/Hide ¶ button.	[pg. 31]
Go To dialog box	Press Ctrl+G.	Bonus
Headers and Footers	Choose View, Header and Footer.	[pg. 138]
Menu from menu bar	Click the menu name or press Alt+the underlined letter in the menu name.	[pg. 7]
Next page	Press Ctrl+PgDn or click the Next Page button.	[pg. 32]
Normal View	Choose View, Normal. Or, click the Normal view button	[pg. 41]
Office Assistant: display	Choose Help, Show the Office Assistant.	[pg. 15]
Office Assistant: turn off	Click Office Assistant, click Options, click the Options tab. Deselect the Use the Office Assistant check box, and click OK.	[pg. 15]
Previous page	Press Ctrl+PgUp or click the Previous Page button.	[pg. 32]
Print Layout View	Choose View, Print Layout. Or, click the Print Layout view button	[pg. 41]
Print Preview	Click the Print Preview button on the Standard toolbar.	[pg. 13]
ScreenTip about button's purpose	Position mouse pointer over button or icon.	[pg. 7]
Toolbar: Clipboard	Choose View, Toolbars, Clipboard.	[pg. 65]
Toolbar: Picture	Choose View, Toolbars, Picture.	[pg. 65]
Toolbar: Standard and Formatting on separate rows	Choose Tools, Customize. Click the Standard and Formatting toolbars share one row check box to deselect it, and click Close.	Bonus
	You can also simply place the cursor over the vertical bar on the left edge of one of the toolbars. The cursor will change into a four-headed anchor. Click and drag the toolbar to position it wherever you want on the screen.	
Toolbar: Tables and Borders	Choose View, Toolbars, Tables and Borders.	[pg. 165]
Word Web document in Internet Explorer	Type path and filename in the Address box and click the Go button.	[pg. 230]
Zoom dialog box	Choose View, Zoom.	[pg. 42]

To Do This	Use This Command	Page Number
Edit Text		
Clipboard toolbar: display	Choose <u>V</u>iew, <u>T</u>oolbars, Clipboard.	[pg. 65]
Copy text	Select text and click the Copy button or press Ctrl+C.	[pg. 65]
Cut text	Select text and click the Cut button or press Ctrl+X.	[pg. 65]
Delete character: left of insertion point	Press ←Backspace.	[pg. 10]
Delete character: right of insertion point	Press Del.	[pg. 10]
Delete word: left of insertion point	Press Ctrl+←Backspace.	[pg. 37]
Delete word: right of insertion point	Press Ctrl+Del.	[pg. 37]
Grammar-check	Right-click text with wavy green underlining and choose correct grammar.	[pg. 74]
Overtype mode: activate	Double-click OVR on the status bar. Or, press Insert.	[pg. 38]
Paste	Click the Paste button or press Ctrl+V.	[pg. 65]
Redo an Undo action	Click the Redo button.	[pg. 68]
Select a block of text	Click and drag the mouse.	[pg. 35]
Select entire document	Press Ctrl+A.	[pg. 36]
Select paragraph	Triple-click the paragraph.	[pg. 35]
Select sentence	Hold down Ctrl while clicking the sentence.	[pg. 35]
Select word	Double-click the word.	[pg. 35]
Spell-check	Right-click word with wavy red underlining and choose correct spelling.	[pg. 72]
Synonym: choose	Right-click word, choose Synonyms, and choose appropriate synonym from list.	[pg. 76]
Undo multiple actions	Click the drop-down arrow to the right of the Undo button. Then select the sequence of actions you want to undo.	[pg. 68]
Undo single action	Click the Undo button or press Ctrl+Z.	[pg. 68]
Format Characters		
Bold existing text	Select text and click the Bold button or press Ctrl+B.	[pg. 60]
Bold text as you type	Click the Bold button, type text, and then click the Bold button again.	[pg. 58]
Case of text: change	Select text, choose F<u>o</u>rmat, Change Cas<u>e</u>. Choose option, and click OK. Alternatively, select text and press ◆Shift+F3 until you see the case you want.	[pg. 64]

continues ▶

To Do This	Use This Command	Page Number
Format Characters		
Cells in a table	Select cells and choose formats, such as font, font size, bold, etc.	[pg. 165]
Font: select	Click the Font drop-down arrow on the Formatting toolbar and choose the desired font.	[pg. 99]
Font effects: select	Choose Format, Font. Click the check boxes for the effects you want and click OK.	[pg. 99]
Font size: set	Click the Font Size drop-down arrow on the Formatting toolbar and choose the desired font size.	[pg. 100]
Format Painter	Click inside formatted text, double-click the Format Painter button, and click and drag across other instances of text to copy the character formats. Then click the Format Painter button or simply press Esc to turn off the feature.	[pg. 61]
	To copy the format once only, click once instead of double-clicking the button. The feature will become inactive and the paintbrush image next to the insertion point will disappear as soon as you reapply the formatting the first time.	
Highlight text	Select text and click the Highlight button on the Formatting toolbar.	[pg. 106]
Italicize existing text	Select text and click the Italic button or press Ctrl+I.	[pg. 60]
Italicize text as you type	Click the Italic button, type text, and then click the Italic button again.	[pg. 58]
Underline existing text	Select text and click the Underline button or press Ctrl+U.	[pg. 60]
Underline text as you type	Click the Underline button, type text, and then click the Underline button again.	[pg. 60]
Format Paragraphs		
Align: center	Click the Center button on the Standard toolbar.	[pg. 94]
Align: justify	Click the Justify button on the Standard toolbar.	[pg. 94]
Align: left	Click the Align Left button on the Standard toolbar.	[pg. 94]
Align: right	Click the Align Right button on Standard toolbar.	[pg. 94]
Border and shading: select	Choose Format, Borders and Shading. Click a border setting, choose a color, select other options, and click OK.	[pg. 107]
Bulleted list: create	Click the Bullets button on the Formatting toolbar, type text, and press ↵Enter to continue list; press ←Backspace to delete extra bullet and end list when done.	[pg. 104]

To Do This	Use This Command	Page Number

Format Paragraphs

Cells in a Table	Select cells and choose formats, such as font, font size, bold, etc.	[pg. 165]
Format Painter	Select an entire paragraph and double-click the Format Painter button; then select other paragraphs to which you want to reapply the formatting of the original paragraph. Click the Format Painter button or simply press Esc to turn off the feature when you are done.	[pg. 61]
	To copy the formats only once, click once instead of double-clicking the button. The feature will become inactive and the paintbrush image next to the insertion point will disappear as soon as you reapply the formatting the first time.	
Hanging indent: create	Click in the paragraph, choose Format, Paragraph. Click the Indents and Spacing tab, click the Special drop-down arrow and choose Hanging; then click OK. Or, press Ctrl+T	[pg. 141]
Indent from both margins	Choose Format, Paragraph. Type a value in the Left and Right Indentation boxes, and click OK.	[pg. 96]
Indent from left margin	Choose Format, Paragraph. Type a value in the Left Indentation box, and click OK.	[pg. 96]
Line spacing: change	Choose Format, Paragraph. Click the Line spacing drop-down arrow, choose the line spacing option, and click OK.	[pg. 92]
Line spacing: double	Press Ctrl+2.	[pg. 93]
Line spacing: one and one-half	Press Ctrl+5.	[pg. 93]
Line spacing: single	Press Ctrl+1.	[pg. 93]
Numbered list: create	Click the Numbering button on the Formatting toolbar, type text, and press ←Enter to continue list. Press ←Backspace to delete extra number and end list when done.	[pg. 104]
Same page as next paragraph: keeping on	Select text and choose Format, Paragraph. Click the Line and Page Breaks tab. Click the Keep with next option, and click OK.	[pg. 130]

Format Document

Background: apply	Choose Format, Background. Choose Fill Effects, click the Texture tab, choose a texture, and click OK.	[pg. 226]
Center text vertically	Choose File, Page Setup, click the Layout tab, click the Vertical alignment drop-down arrow, and choose Center. Select the Apply to option, and click OK.	[pg. 122]
Margins: set	Choose File, Page Setup. Type margin settings in the boxes, and click OK.	[pg. 90]
Page border: select	Choose Format, Borders and Shading. Click Page Border, choose options, and click OK.	[pg. 107]

continues ▶

To Do This	Use This Command	Page Number
Format Document		
Page break: insert	Choose Insert, Break, click the Page break option, and click OK. Or, press Ctrl+↵Enter	[pg. 129]
Page numbering: restart for section	Choose Insert, Page Numbers. Click Format, and then click the Start at option and type 1. Click OK; then click OK again.	[pg. 124]
Page numbers: insert	Choose Insert, Page Numbers. Choose the Position. Choose the Alignment. Select or deselect Show number on first page, and click OK.	[pg. 124]
Paragraphs: keeping together on same page	Select text; then choose Format, Paragraph. Click the Line and Page Breaks tab, click the Keep with next option, and click OK.	[pg. 130]
Section break: insert	Choose Insert, Break, click the Next page option, and click OK.	[pg. 128]
Graphics: Clip art and Objects		
Clip art image: insert	Choose Insert, Picture, Clip Art. Choose a category, right-click an image, and choose Insert.	[pg. 183]
Download image from Microsoft Web site	Choose Insert, Picture, Clip Art. Click Clips Online, click Accept; then click a category, such as Pictures. Click an image to preview it and then click the previewed image to download it.	[pg. 209]
Excel chart: insert	Click the chart in Excel and click the Copy button. Click the Word button on the taskbar and click Word's Paste button.	[pg. 219]
Fill and Border: select	Click the image, click the Format Picture button on the Picture toolbar, and click the Colors and Lines tab. Select fill and lines options and click OK.	[pg. 193]
Image: move to nonvisible area	Click image, click the Cut button, move insertion point to new location, and click the Paste button.	[pg. 186]
Image: move to visible area	Click image to see sizing handles; then click and drag to a new location within view onscreen.	[pg. 186]
Organization chart: add positions	Click position button on toolbar; then click existing position from which to create the new one.	[pg. 222]
Organization chart: create	Choose Insert, Object. Choose MS Organization Chart 2.0 and click OK. Maximize the window. Type data in the placeholders.	[pg. 219]
Picture: insert from file	Choose Insert, Picture, From File. Select path and filename and click Insert.	[pg. 183]
Save images from Internet as graphics	Right-click an image and choose Save Picture As.	[pg. 209]
Size image: "eyeball approach"	Click and drag a sizing handle to adjust the width and height.	[pg. 187]
Size image: specific setting	Click image, click Format Picture button on the Picture toolbar, and click the Size tab. Set the height and width and click OK.	[pg. 187]
Text box: create	Choose Insert, Text Box. Click and drag to create text box area. Type text in text box, adjust size, and choose other formats.	[pg. 191]

To Do This	Use This Command	Page Number
Graphics: Clip art and Objects		
WordArt object: create	Choose Insert, Picture, WordArt. Select a shape from the gallery, click OK, type text, select the font and font size, and click OK.	[pg. 195]
Wrap and align text around image	Click image, click the Format Picture button on the Picture toolbar, and click the Layout tab. Select the text wrapping option and alignment and click OK.	[pg. 189]
Help		
Get Help	Choose Help, Microsoft Word Help.	[pg. 15]
Help Index	With Office Assistant off, choose Help, Microsoft Word Help, and click the Index tab. Type what you are looking for in the Type keywords text box and click Search. Or, scroll through the keywords listed and click a topic in the Choose a topic list.	[pg. 15]
Office Assistant: change	Click Office Assistant, click Options, click the Gallery tab, click Back or Next to display other assistants. When you have found the one you want, click OK.	[pg. 15]
Office Assistant: display	Choose Help, Show the Office Assistant.	[pg. 15]
Office Assistant: get help	Click Office Assistant, type your question, and click Search.	[pg. 17]
Office Assistant: turn off	Click Office Assistant, click Options, click the Options tab, deselect Use the Office Assistant check box, and click OK.	[pg. 15]
Insert		
Clip art image	Choose Insert, Picture, Clip Art. Choose a category, right-click an image, and choose Insert.	[pg. 183]
Column in table: insert to left	Choose Table, Insert, Columns to the Left.	[pg. 158]
Column in table: insert to right	Choose Table, Insert, Columns to the Right.	[pg. 158]
Date and Time	Choose Insert, Date and Time. Choose format and click OK.	[pg. 38]
Endnote	Choose Insert, Footnote. Click the Endnote option button. Click Options and choose options if desired; then click OK.	[pg. 134]
Excel chart	Click the chart in Excel and click the Copy button. Click the Word button on the taskbar and click Word's Paste button.	[pg. 219]
File within current file	Position the insertion point. Choose Insert, File, select a file, and click Insert.	[pg. 213]
Footnote	Choose Insert, Footnote. Click the Footnote option button. Click Options and choose options if desired; then click OK.	[pg. 134]

continues ▶

To Do This	Use This Command	Page Number
Insert		
Headers and Footers	Choose View, Header and Footer. Type text for header for first section or leave blank. Click the Show Next button on the Header and Footer toolbar, and deselect the Same as Previous button. Type text for the header for second section.	[pg. 138]
Nonbreaking hyphen	Type the first word and press Ctrl+Shift+-.	[pg. 133]
Nonbreaking space	Type the first word, press Ctrl+Shift+Spacebar, and type the second word to keep together.	[pg. 133]
Organization chart	Choose Insert, Object. Choose MS Organization Chart 2.0 and click OK. Maximize the window. Type data in the placeholders.	[pg. 222]
Page break	Press Ctrl+Enter or choose Insert, Break. Click Page break, and click OK.	[pg. 129]
Page numbers	Choose Insert, Page Numbers, choose the Position, choose the Alignment. Select or deselect Show number on first page and click OK.	[pg. 124]
Picture	Choose Insert, Picture, From File. Select path and filename and click Insert.	[pg. 183]
Row in table: insert above	Choose Table, Insert, Rows Above.	[pg. 158]
Row in table: insert below	Choose Table, Insert, Rows Below.	[pg. 158]
Section break	Choose Insert, Break. Click Next page, and click OK.	[pg. 128]
Symbol	Choose Insert, Symbol.	[pg. 105]
Text box	Choose Insert, Text Box. Click and drag to create text box area. Type text in text box, adjust size, and choose other formats.	[pg. 191]
WordArt object	Choose Insert, Picture, and WordArt. Select a shape from the gallery, click OK, type text, select the font and font size, and click OK.	[pg. 195]
Integration		
Download image from Microsoft Web Site	Choose Insert, Picture, and Clip Art. Click Clips Online, click Accept, and then click a category, such as Pictures. Click an image to preview it; then click the previewed picture to download it.	[pg. 209]
Excel chart: insert	Click the chart in Excel and click the Copy button. Click the Word button on the taskbar and click Word's Paste button.	[pg. 219]
Excel spreadsheet: link	Select data in Excel and click the Copy button. Click the Word button on the taskbar and choose Edit, Paste Special. Click the Paste link option button, choose Microsoft Excel Worksheet Object, and click OK.	[pg. 215]

To Do This	Use This Command	Page Number
Integration		
Excel worksheet: insert	Select data in Excel and click the Copy button in Excel. Click the Word button on the taskbar and click the Paste button in Word.	[pg. 215]
Insert file within the current file	Position the insertion point. Choose Insert, File. Select a file and click Insert.	[pg. 213]
Open Internet Explorer	Click the Internet Explorer button on the taskbar or choose Start, Programs, Internet Explorer.	[pg. 230]
Save a document as a Web page	Choose File, Save as Web Page. Click Change Title. Type a new title and click OK. Click Save; then click Continue.	[pg. 228]
Save images from Internet as graphics	Right-click an image and choose Save Picture As.	[pg. 209]
View Word Web document in Internet Explorer	Type path and filename in the Address box and click the Go button.	[pg. 230]
Organization Chart		
Add positions	Click position button on toolbar; then click existing position under which you are creating the new one.	[pg. 222]
Create	Choose Insert, Object. Choose MS Organization Chart 2.0 and click OK. Maximize the window. Type data in the placeholders.	[pg. 222]
Move to next placeholder	Press ↵Enter.	[pg. 223]
Move to next position	Press Ctrl+→.	[pg. 223]
Move to subordinate position	Press Ctrl+↓.	[pg. 223]
Tables		
Cells: shade	Click the drop-down arrow to the right of the Shading Color button on the Tables and Borders toolbar; then click a color.	[pg. 167]
Column width: adjust automatically	Double-click the Move Table Column marker to adjust width of column based on text in column.	[pg. 162]
Column width: adjust manually	Click and drag the Move Table Column marker.	[pg. 162]
Create	Click the Insert Table button on the Standard toolbar and choose the number of rows and columns.	[pg. 155]
Delete current column	Choose Table, Delete, Columns.	[pg. 160]
Delete current row	Choose Table, Delete, Rows.	[pg. 160]
Delete text in table	Select cell(s) and press Del.	[pg. 161]

continues ▶

To Do This	Use This Command	Page Number
Tables		
Format cells in table	Select cells, and choose formats, such as font, font size, bold, etc.	[pg. 165]
Insert column to the left	Choose Table, Insert, Columns to the Left.	[pg. 158]
Insert column to the right	Choose Table, Insert, Columns to the Right.	[pg. 158]
Insert row above current row	Choose Table, Insert, Rows Above.	[pg. 158]
Insert row below current row	Choose Table, Insert, Rows Below.	[pg. 158]
Move	Click and drag the table marker to a new location.	[pg. 169]
Position horizontally	Choose Table, Table Properties, and choose an option in the Alignment section.	[pg. 169]
Row height: adjust	Click Adjust Table Row marker and click and drag to change the row height.	[pg. 162]
Tables and Borders toolbar: display	Choose View, Toolbars, Tables and Borders.	[pg. 165]
Tools		
AutoCorrect entry: create	Choose Tools, AutoCorrect. Type in the Replace box. Type in the With box. Click Add.	[pg. 69]
Envelope: create	Choose Tools, Envelopes and Labels.	[pg. 44]
Grammar-check	Right-click a text with wavy green underlining and choose correct grammar.	[pg. 74]
Spell-check	Right-click a word with wavy red underlining and choose correct spelling.	[pg. 72]
Synonym: replace word with	Right-click word, choose Synonyms, and choose appropriate synonym from list.	[pg. 73]

Glossary

All key terms appearing in this book (in bold italic) are listed alphabetically in this Glossary for easy reference. If you want to learn more about a feature or concept, turn to the page reference shown after its definition. You can also use the Index to find the term's other significant occurrences.

action   Any task or change you make in a document. [pg. 68]

alignment   Placement of text between the left and right margins. The default alignment is left, which perfectly aligns text at the left margin. [pg. 94]

associated keywords   Words associated with a clip on Microsoft's Web page. The keywords help you locate other clips that have some of the same characteristics. [pg. 210]

AutoComplete   A feature that helps you by completing text. For example, if you start typing today's date, you'll see a ScreenTip that displays the entire date. Press ⏎Enter to complete the date automatically. [pg. 40]

AutoCorrect   A feature that automatically corrects typos and some capitalization errors "on the fly." [pg. 69]

background   A shading color, texture, or pattern that appears behind printed text. When you select a background, Word automatically displays the document in Web Layout view. [pg. 226]

border   A line style that surrounds text, table cells, or an object. [pg. 107]

browser   A program, such as Internet Explorer, that displays Web pages. [pg. 230]

bullet   A special symbol to attract attention to text on a page. [pgg. 102]

bulleted list   An itemized list or enumeration that contains bullet symbols at the left side of each item. [pg. 102]

buttons   Small pictures that represent tasks. When you click a button, Word performs a task or provides menus for making specific selections. [pg. 8]

case   Capitalization style of text. [pg. 62]

cell   The intersection of a column and row in a table. [pg. 154]

clip art   Graphic images, pictures, or drawings. [pg. 182]

Clip Gallery   A collection of clip art images, photographs, sound clips, and movie clips that you can insert into your document. [pg. 183]

close   The process of removing a document from the screen. [pg. 19]

close button   A button that closes a window or dialog box. [pg. 5]

column   A group of table cells arranged vertically. [pg. 154]

column headings   Text that appears at the top of table columns to identify the contents of each column. [pg. 158]

column width   The setting or horizontal measurement of a column. [pg. 161]

Control menu box   Displays a menu that controls the application program. Double-click the box to exit (close) the application. [pg. 5]

copy   Makes a copy of the selected text or object and places the copy temporarily in the Office Clipboard. [pg. 64]

cut   Removes text or an object from its location and places it temporarily in the Office Clipboard. [pg. 64]

default   Refers to a standard setting determined by Microsoft that is used unless you change it. For example, the default top margin is one inch. [pg. 4]

document window   Displays text and formats for documents you create. [pg. 5]

double indent   Indenting text from both the left and the right margins. [pg. 95]

double-space   Text spacing that leaves one blank line between text lines. [pg. 92]

ellipsis   Three dots that appear to the right of some menu names on pull-down menus. Ellipsis indicate that a dialog box appears when you choose that option. [pg. 7]

endnote   Reference for information you obtained elsewhere or annotations to text. This reference appears at the end of the document. [pg. 133]

end-of-document marker   Small horizontal line that indicates the end of a document. [pg. 5]

Excel   A spreadsheet software package that comes with Office 2000. [pg. 214]

exit   The process of closing the Word application program. [pg. 19]

fill   The shading color used within a graphic object, drawing object, or text box. [pg. 193]

font   Style, weight, and typeface of a set of characters. The default font is Times New Roman. [pg. 98]

font size   The height of the characters, typically measured in points, where 72 points equal one vertical inch. [pg. 99]

footer   Information pertaining to a document, such as a filename or date, that appears at the bottom of the document's pages. [pg. 137]

footnote   A reference for information you obtained elsewhere or annotations to text. This information appears at the bottom of the page that contains the footnote reference mark. [pg. 133]

footnote reference mark   The number, letter, or symbol that appears in text to refer the reader to a footnote or endnote of the same number, letter, or symbol that contains citations or additional information. [pg. 135]

footnote text   The actual citation or supplemental text for a footnote. [pg. 135]

Format Painter   A feature that helps you copy existing text formats to other text. [pg. 60]

formatting marks   Nonprinting symbols and characters that indicate spaces, tabs, and hard returns. You display these symbols by clicking the Show/Hide ¶ button on the Standard toolbar. These symbols are useful when selecting text. [pg. 30]

Formatting toolbar   The toolbar that contains a row of buttons that help you format text. For example, this toolbar helps you select a font, boldface text, and select text alignment. [pg. 5]

full menu   A pull-down menu that lists all the commands available from that menu. You display the full menu by pointing to the arrows at the bottom of the short menu. (see also **short menu**) [pg. 6]

Full Screen view   A document view that displays the document on the entire screen. You do not see the title bar, toolbars, or other screen elements. [pg. 42]

gradient   A fill that blends two or more colors. [pg. 194]

gridlines   Horizontal and vertical lines that separate cells within a table. [pg. 155]

hanging indent   A paragraph format that keeps the first line of a paragraph at the left margin and indents the remaining lines from the left margin. [pg. 98]

hard page break   A break you insert to immediately start text at the top of the next page. [pg. 128]

hard return   Defines the end of a line where you press ⏎Enter. [pg. 30]

header   Information pertaining to a document, such as a filename or date, that appears at the top of the document's pages. [pg. 137]

heading   Text between paragraphs or sections that helps identify the content of that section. [pg. 61]

Help   Onscreen assistance or reference manual. It provides information about features, step-by-step instructions, and other assistance. [pg. 15]

Help Topic Pane   The right side of the Help window. It contains information about the topic you select from the Navigation Pane. This window provides information, links to other topics, and step-by-step instructions for performing tasks. [pg. 15]

highlight   Places a color behind text, similar to a highlighting marker, to draw attention to text. [pg. 105]

horizontal scrollbar   Adjusts horizontal view of text going left to right. [pg. 5]

hypertext links   Underlined words or phrases that appear in a different color. In Help, clicking a hypertext link displays another topic. On the Web, clicking a hypertext link displays a different Web page. [pg. 210]

indent   Sets a temporary left margin to indent the left side of a paragraph, making it stand out. [pg. 98]

Insert mode   When you type within existing text, Word inserts the new text and keeps the other text; it does not replace text to the right of the insertion point. [pg. 38]

insertion point   Blinking vertical line that shows the current location in the document. [pg. 5]

inside address   The address of the person who will receive your letter. [pg. 38]

line spacing   Amount of vertical space from the bottom of one text line to the top of the next text line. The default line spacing is single. [pg. 91]

links   A connection within a document to another document. For example, you can link a spreadsheet to a Word document. When you change the spreadsheet, the data in Word also changes. [pg. 217]

margins   Amount of white space around the top, left, right, and bottom of text on a page. [pg. 89]

maximize button   Clicking this button, located in the top right corner of a window, displays the window in its full size. You will see either the maximize button or the restore button, depending on the current view of the application or document. [pg. 5]

menu bar   A row of menu names displayed below the title bar. Tasks are categorized by nine different menus. [pg. 6]

minimize button   Clicking this button, located in the top right corner of a window, reduces the current document to an icon on the taskbar. [pg. 5]

Navigation Pane   The left side of the Help window. It contains Contents, Answer Wizard, and Index tabs. These tabs provide different methods for accessing onscreen Help. [pg. 16]

nonbreaking hyphen   A special type of hyphen that prevents hyphenated words from being separated by the word-wrap feature. For example, you can insert nonbreaking hyphens to keep 555-1234 from wrapping. [pg. 133]

nonbreaking space   A special type of space that prevents words from separating by the word-wrap feature. For example, pressing Ctrl+⬆Shift+Spacebar keeps October 16 from word-wrapping. [pg. 132]

Normal view   A document view that shows text without displaying space for margins, page numbers, headers, or other supplemental text. [pg. 41]

object   A non-text item, such as a clip art image. [pg. 64]

Office Assistant   An animated image that provides onscreen assistance and help. You can click it and ask it a question to learn how to do something in Word. [pg. 15]

Office Clipboard   An area of memory designed to store items that you cut or copy from a document. The Office Clipboard holds up to 12 different pieces of data, which you can paste within the same application or other applications. [pg. 64]

opening   The process of retrieving a document from storage, such as from a data disk, and displaying it onscreen. [pg. 29]

organization chart   A chart showing the hierarchy of positions within an organization. [pg. 221]

orphan   The first line of a paragraph that appears by itself at the bottom of a page. [pg. 129]

Overtype mode   When you type in this mode, the text you type replaces existing text at the insertion point. [pg. 37]

paste   Inserting the contents of the Office Clipboard in the insertion point's location. [pg. 64]

placeholders   Temporary text or fields in which you type your own text, such as in an organization chart. [pg. 222]

Print Layout view   A document view that shows you what the document will look like when it's printed. You see margins, page numbers, headers, and so on. [pg. 41]

redo   Reverses an undo action. [pg. 67]

restore button   Clicking this button, located in the top right corner of a window, restores the window to its previous size. [pg. 5]

row   A group of table cells arranged horizontally. [pg. 154]

row height   The vertical space from the top to the bottom of a row. [pg. 161]

ruler   Shows the location of tabs, indents, and left and right margins. [pg. 5]

salutation   The greeting in a letter, for example, Dear Ms. Sullivan. [pg. 38]

sans serif font   A font that does not have serifs. This type of font is useful for headings, making them stand out from body text. [pg. 101]

save   The process of storing a document for future use. [pg. 12]

ScreenTip   A little yellow box that displays the name of a button when you position the mouse on the button. [pg. 8]

scroll buttons   Help you to move quickly through a document. You can scroll up or down a page at a time or scroll to a particular object within the document. [pg. 5]

scrolling   The process of moving the insertion point through your document. [pg. 32]

section break   A page break that marks the end of a section in a document. Section breaks allow you to use different formats, such as page numbering. [pg. 122]

selecting The process of defining a section of text. After you select text, you can delete, format, cut, or copy it. [pg. 35]

serif font A font that displays tiny little lines or extensions at the tops and bottoms of most characters in the font. The serifs guide the reader's eyes across the text. [pg. 101]

shading A background color, similar to highlight, behind text in a paragraph, table cells, or a graphic image. [pgs. 109, 167]

short menu Also known as adaptive menu. This is a pull-down menu from the menu bar. When you first select from the menu bar, you see a short menu of the most commonly used tasks. The short menu adapts based on your use of the features. (see also **full menu**) [pg. 6]

shortcut A fast keyboard method for performing a task. For example, the keyboard shortcut for bolding text is Ctrl + B. [pg. 7]

single-space Text spacing in which lines are close together, one immediately above the next. [pg. 91]

sizing handles Little black boxes that appear at intervals around a selected object. They allow you to change the size or move the object. [pg. 185]

soft page break Page breaks inserted by Word when you fill an entire page. These breaks adjust automatically when you add and delete text. [pg. 129]

spinners The up and down arrows that increase or decrease a numeric setting in a dialog box. [pg. 90]

Standard toolbar The toolbar that contains a row of buttons that perform common tasks, such as save and print. [pg. 5]

status bar Displays the current page number and location of the insertion point. [pg. 5]

submenu A menu that appears to the side of a main pull-down menu. It provides more specific options and features. For example, choosing View, Toolbars displays the Toolbars submenu that lists specific toolbars. [pg. 7]

suppress To hide or remove something. For example, suppressing the page number prevents the number from displaying onscreen and printing on a page. [pg. 125]

synonym A word with the same or similar meaning as another word. Word contains a feature that helps you select appropriate synonyms for words. [pg. 71]

table A series of rows and columns that organize data effectively. [pg. 154]

table alignment The horizontal position of a table between the left and right margins. [pg. 169]

text box A graphic box that contains text. It's treated as an object so you can size and place it on a page. [182]

text enhancements Formats such as bold and font color that enhance the appearance of text. [pg. 57]

tight wrap A wrapping style that lets text contour or wrap tightly around the outer edges of the image itself instead of the square border area that surrounds an image. [pg. 189]

title bar Window feature that displays the name of the file you are currently working on, as well as the name of the application. Dialog boxes also have title bars that show the name of the dialog box. [pg. 5]

undo Reverses actions that you perform in the document. Actions are undone in reverse sequential order; so the last action performed is the first reversed. [pg. 67]

vertical alignment Positions text between the top and bottom edges on a page. [pg. 122]

vertical scrollbar Moves up and down in a document. [pg. 5]

view buttons Buttons that enable you to switch between different view modes, such as Normal view and Print Layout view. [pg. 5]

widow The last line of a paragraph that appears by itself at the top of a page. [pg. 129]

WordArt Feature that creates interesting shapes and designs for text. Useful for creating banners and titles on flyers and advertisements. [pg. 182]

word-wrap feature Continues text on the next line if it can't fit at the end of the current line. [pg. 9]

worksheet An electronic document that displays data, text, and values, in columns and rows. Used to perform simple and complex calculations and for organizing financial data. [pg. 214]

wrapping style Specifies how text wraps around an object, such as a clip art image. [pg. 189]

WYSIWYG Stands for What You See Is What You Get. This means that your printout will look like what you are seeing onscreen. [pg. 30]

Zoom The magnification percentage of how your document appears onscreen, compared to the actual size of the document on the printed page. [pg. 41]

Index